Rock & Roll Reference Series

TOM SCHULTHEISS, Series Editor

1. **ALL TOGETHER NOW**
   The First Complete
   Beatles Discography, 1961-1975
   by Harry Castleman & Walter J. Podrazik

2. **THE BEATLES AGAIN**
   [Sequel to *All Together Now*]
   by Harry Castleman & Walter J. Podrazik

3. **A DAY IN THE LIFE**
   The Beatles Day-By-Day, 1960-1970
   by Tom Schultheiss

4. **THINGS WE SAID TODAY**
   The Complete Lyrics and a Concordance
   to The Beatles' Songs, 1962-1970
   by Colin Campbell & Allan Murphy

5. **YOU CAN'T DO THAT!**
   Beatles Bootlegs
   & Novelty Records, 1963-1980
   by Charles Reinhart

6. **SURF'S UP!**
   The Beach Boys On Record, 1961-1981
   by Brad Elliott

7. **COLLECTING THE BEATLES**
   An Introduction & Price Guide
   to Fab Four Collectibles, Records
   & Memorabilia
   by Barbara Fenick

8. **JAILHOUSE ROCK**
   The Bootleg Records
   of Elvis Presley, 1970-1983
   by Lee Cotten & Howard A. De Witt

9. **THE LITERARY LENNON**
   A Comedy of Letters
   *The First Study of All the Major
   and Minor Writings of John Lennon*
   by Dr. James Sauceda

10. **THE END OF THE BEATLES?**
    Sequel to *The Beatles Again*
    and *All Together Now*
    by Harry Castleman & Walter J. Podrazik

11. **HERE, THERE & EVERYWHERE**
    The First International
    Beatles Bibliography, 1962-1982
    by Carol D. Terry

12. **CHUCK BERRY**
    Rock 'N' Roll Music
    Second Edition, Revised
    by Howard A. De Witt

13. **ALL SHOOK UP**
    Elvis Day-By-Day, 1954-1977
    by Lee Cotten

14. **WHO'S NEW WAVE IN MUSIC**
    An Illustrated Encyclopedia, 1976-1982
    by David Bianco

15. **THE ILLUSTRATED DISCOGRAPHY OF SURF MUSIC, 1961-1965**
    Second Edition, Revised
    by John Blair

16. **COLLECTING THE BEATLES, VOL. 2**
    An Introduction & Price Guide
    to Fab Four Collectibles, Records
    & Memorabilia
    by Barbara Fenick

17. **HEART OF STONE**
    The Definitive Rolling Stones
    Discography, 1962-1983
    by Felix Aeppli

18. **BEATLEFAN**
    The Authoritative
    Publication of Record
    For Fans of the Beatles, Vols. 1 & 2
    Reprint Edition, With Additions

19. **YESTERDAY'S PAPERS**
    The Rolling Stones In Print, 1963-1984
    by Jessica MacPhail

20. **EVERY LITTLE THING**
    The Definitive Guide To Beatles
    Recording Variations, Rare Mixes &
    Other Musical Oddities, 1958-1984
    by William McCoy & Mitchell McGeary

21. **STRANGE DAYS**
    The Music of John, Paul, George & Ringo
    Twenty Years On
    by Walter J. Podrazik

22. **SEQUINS & SHADES**
    The Michael Jackson Reference Guide
    by Carol D. Terry

23. **WILD & INNOCENT**
    The Recordings of Bruce Springsteen,
    1972-1985
    by Brad Elliott

24 TIME IS ON MY SIDE
The Rolling Stones Day-By-Day, 1962-1986
by Alan Stewart & Cathy Sanford

25 HEAT WAVE
The Motown Fact Book
by David Bianco

26 BEATLEFAN
The Authoritative Publication of Record For Fans of the Beatles, Vols. 3 & 4
Reprint Edition, With Additions

27 RECONSIDER BABY
The Definitive Elvis Sessionography, 1954-1977
Reprint Edition, With Additions
by Ernst Jorgensen, Erik Rasmussen & Johnny Mikkelsen

28 THE MONKEES
A Manufactured Image
The Ultimate Reference Guide To Monkee Memories & Memorabilia
by Ed Reilly, Maggie McManus and Bill Chadwick

29 RETURN TO SENDER
The First Complete Discography Of Elvis Tribute & Novelty Records, 1956-1986
by Howard Banney

30 THE CHILDREN OF NUGGETS
The Definitive Guide To "Psychedelic Sixties" Punk Rock On Compilation Albums
by David Walters

ROCK&ROLL Remembrances Series

TOM SCHULTHEISS, Series Editor

1 AS I WRITE THIS LETTER
An American Generation Remembers The Beatles
by Marc A. Catone

2 THE LONGEST COCKTAIL PARTY
An Insider's Diary of The Beatles
Reprint Edition, With Additions
by Richard DiLello

3 AS TIME GOES BY
Living In The Sixties
Reprint Edition, With Additions
by Derek Taylor

4 A CELLARFUL OF NOISE
Reprint Edition, With Additions
by Brian Epstein

5 THE BEATLES AT THE BEEB
The Story of Their Radio Career, 1962-65
Reprint Edition, With Additions
by Kevin Howlett

6 THE BEATLES READER
A Selection of Contemporary Views, News & Reviews of The Beatles In Their Heyday
by Charles P. Neises

7 THE BEATLES DOWN UNDER
The 1964 Australia & New Zealand Tour
Reprint Edition, With Additions
by Glenn A. Baker

8 LONG LONELY HIGHWAY
A 1950's Elvis Scrapbook
Reprint Edition, With Additions
by Ger Rijff

9 IKE'S BOYS
The Story Of The Everly Brothers
by Phyllis Karpp

A Manufactured Image

The Ultimate Reference Guide to Monkee Memories & Memorabilia

by

Edward Reilly, Maggie McManus
and William Chadwick

Pierian Press
1987

Copyright © 1987 by
Edward Reilly, Maggie McManus and William Chadwick.
All Rights Reserved.

No part of this data may be reproduced, stored in a retrieval system, or transmitted in any form or by any means, electronic, mechanical, photocopying, recording, or otherwise, without prior written permission of the copyright proprietor thereof.

All photographs are the property of their respective proprietors as credited herein. All Rights Reserved. Used by Permission.

Front cover and page iv photographs reproduced courtesy of Personality Photos Inc., P.O. Box 50, Midwood Station, Brooklyn, NY 11230.

Back cover photograph reproduced courtesy of Stan Brick, P.O. Box 9483, Trenton, NJ 08650.

Nielsen rankings are reproduced courtesy of A.C. Nielsen Company. All Rights Reserved. Used by Permission.

The U.S. singles and U.S. album chart data used in this work is copyright © 1966-1986 by Billboard Publications Inc. Compiled by the Billboard Research Department and reprinted with permission.

The continuing source for Monkees news and information is "Monkee Business Fanzine," published since 1977, available at a subscription of $8 per year: Monkee Business Fanzine, Maggie McManus, editor, 2770 S. Broad St., Trenton, NJ 08610.

Book design and layout by Diane Bareis and Tom Schultheiss.
Cover design and layout by Diane Bareis and Carol Jennet.
Text preparation by Tonya L. White.
Computer programming by Alex Przebienda.
Cover art is copyright © 1987 by The Pierian Press Inc.
All Rights Reserved.

ISBN 0-87650-236-2
LC 87-61976

Published by The Pierian Press Inc., P.O. Box 1808, Ann Arbor, Michigan 48106.

Contents

Preface	xi
Acknowledgements	xii
Then & Now: A Monkees Memoir, by Bill Chadwick	xiii

PART ONE: The Monkees Day-By-Day, 1965-1986
   The Chronology   3

1965............3		1969............75	
1966............9		The 70's........83	
1967............27		The 80's......101	
1968............61			

   The Monkees In Concert: A Complete Tour List   120

PART TWO: The Monkees On Film

TV: The Series and The Special	131
Head	159
The Nielsen Ratings	161

PART THREE: The Monkees On Record

The Songs: A Complete Session List	177
The Monkees' U.S. Singles	184
The "Billboard" Singles Charts, 1966-1986	187
The Monkees' U.S. Albums	191
The "Billboard" Album Charts, 1966-1986	199
Foreign Record Releases	216
The International Singles Charts, 1966-1968	227
Monkee Solo Recordings	243

PART FOUR: Monkee Memorabilia

Photo Inventory	257

PART FIVE: Indexes

Song & Album Title Index	279
Index To People, Places & Things	285
Record Number Index	301
Date Index	303

This work is lovingly dedicated to Barbara and to our son Robert
for their continued support, understanding and patience
during my persistence on this project.
Ed Reilly

To Ed and Bill, for permitting me to be a part of this project,
and to The Cousins and Michael Adam Hartman,
who showed me the way.
Maggie McManus

To the memory of my brother John,
consummate romantic, my mentor and confidant.
Bill Chadwick

Preface

The seeds for this work were planted back in 1978 when I became frustrated at the fact that there were no books available on The Monkees or, at the time, any plans for one. It seemed that every time I'd visit a bookstore I would see books on The Beatles popping up like dandelions, but still nothing on the Monkees. So, with the encouragement and support of my wife, I set out to write the kind of book on The Monkees that I'd always wanted to purchase myself. Ironically, it was actually a Beatles book that inspired the form which such a Monkees book should take.

After contemplating things for quite awhile, in 1979 I mentioned my plan to Maggie McManus, editor of a then small publication known as *Monkee Business Fanzine*. Maggie not only encouraged me, but even announced my intentions in a small blurb in her December 1980 issue.

Naturally, with my procrastinating ways, things didn't start to move along until late 1982. It was around that time I met Bill Chadwick and told him of my desire to put together some sort of book on the group. I advised him that I had an enormous collection of Monkee memorabilia that I wanted to share with others. Ironically, Bill had also wanted to put something together himself, but wasn't sure exactly what. We decided to fuse our ideas together for what we hoped would be one mammoth project.

For months, Bill and I threw ideas back and forth, and the project moved along ever so slowly. Months became years and it looked like things had no place to go except towards a slow death.

By late 1985, with the book only about twenty-five percent completed, I decided to shelve it. It appeared to be going around in circles with no particular direction. As I mentioned previously, Maggie had encouraged me to continue the project, and had kept repeating that I should let her know if there was anything she could do to help. At that point, she proposed that if we could pull our resources together and complete it within a couple of months, she would give the book her top priority, providing I would assist her in producing a Monkees convention in 1986 to celebrate the group's twenty-year anniversary. I thought, "How difficult is it *really* to produce a convention?" And so I agreed.

We worked diligently for almost three months, stopping only to eat, sleep, and occasionally put in eight hours on our daily jobs. The rest of the time was spent in nonstop searching through files upon files upon files of clippings, notes, microfilms, interviews, and photos. We spent endless hours in libraries, and late nights typing, photographing, editing, rewriting, etc., until what seemed to be never ending was finally completed in February 1986. Meanwhile, we had prepared a masterpiece of a presentation and sent it out to various publishers, emphasizing that 1986 was going to be the *big* year for Monkeemania. Mind you, this presentation was being sent out at the end of 1985, months before MTV launched its Monkees revival. Almost all of the publishers denied interest in the project, saying that there was simply no market for such a book! I guess these were the same people who thought Nehru jackets and Quadraphonic sound were the wave of the future!

In the early part of 1986, a friend of ours recommended Pierian Press, which specializes in rock-and-roll reference books. After talking to Tom Schultheiss at Pierian about our project, I finally got the impression there was actually someone out there listening who understood the need for such a book. And so our manuscript was sent to Tom, who took a liking to it, and the rest, as they say, is history!

Oh, yes, between all of this enormous pressure and work on the book, I did finally keep my end of the bargain to Maggie and co-produced this so-called "quiet" convention in Philadelphia in August 1986. After all, I thought, maybe a few people from the Philadelphia area might have some free time to stop on by, and I could mention our upcoming book to them. I do believe a few people showed . . . over 1,000 from all over the world!

Ed Reilly

It wasn't easy for us to write about days, months, and years during which we weren't actually present. We didn't witness who said what to whom, or who felt what, or who did whatever. Only David, Peter, Micky and Mike themselves know what it was like to be a Monkee, and only they can attempt to tell the true inside story of their manic Monkee days, colored as those days may now be by the benefit of hindsight or the pitfall of faded memories. Since we weren't there in person, we've taken more of a facts and figures approach to the story of The Monkees, one gleaned from all of the information we've compiled over the years. Upon sorting it into chronological order, we were suddenly able to see the progression of events that led the guys to label themselves "manufactured" in the film "Head," and the phrase "A Manufactured Image" began to emerge as our only possible title. Although at first impression the phrase may denote negativity, we view it as having a more positive connotation. After twenty years, the record chart histories, the TV ratings, the record sales, the collectibles and other merchandise now stand on their own as a true "image" or sign that The Monkees "manufactured" a piece of history that stands as a milestone in the music and film industry today. These items, along with contemporaneous media accounts, have helped us to compile this reference guide to The Monkees.

Maggie McManus

ACKNOWLEDGEMENTS

Those contributing to the memorabilia section were: Joanne Caravello; George Massina; Maggie McManus; Flo Newrock; Ed Reilly; Joe Russo; Fred Velez and Shari Weinick.

The memorabilia section was photographed entirely by Gary Marshall.

Record sleeve, jacket and label reproductions by Bill Chadwick and Gary Marshall.

Our thanks go to:
Library of Congress	Bill Inglot
Barbara Handyside	Rhino Records
Anne Hastings	Peter Tork
Henry Diltz	Michael Nesmith
Howard Frank of Personality Photos Inc.	Peg McManus
	Barbara Reilly
	Steven Kent
Eric Lefcowitz	Art Fullan
Ken Sharp	Stan Brick
Lester Sill	George Massina
Bobby Hart	Fred Velez
Janelle Scott	

And finally our special thanks go to the guys who made it all possible:
Peter Tork	David Jones
Micky Dolenz	Michael Nesmith

Then and Now:
A Monkees Memoir

Growing up on the west side of Los Angeles gave me many of the opportunities that most young musicians' dreams are made of: access to the entire television, motion picture, and recording industries, a wealth of great clubs in which to see the hottest emerging talents, and, most importantly, the chance to be seen and heard.

In 1964, I met Mike Nesmith at the Troubadour. He was new in town and I recognized him as a fellow musician by the guitar case slung casually across his shoulder. It was but a few minutes 'til we had made our way up the narrow back stairway to the dressing rooms, where instruments were hurriedly uncased and the music began. We traded songs and styles late into the night. When at last we parted company, we were fast friends.

At that time I had just been assigned the task of forming a new group for Randy Sparks, founder of The New Christy Minstrels and The Back Porch Majority. Since Mike was exceptionally talented, new in town, and looking for work, he seemed like a natural choice for this project. Another natural for the group, called The Survivors, was Mike's long-time friend and traveling companion, bassist John Keanie, better known as John London. At the time, John would play the "Gomer Pyle" straight man against Mike's "Andy Griffith," the smart country boy role. Off stage, John was no dummy, and he was big enough and strong enough to deter anyone from treating him as such.

And so it was that we became The Survivors: Mike Nesmith, John London, Carol Strong, Nyles Brown, Owen Castleman, Mike Murphy, Del Ramos, and myself. We played our hearts out in two-bit clubs from California to Colorado, doing folk music, along with light comedy and heavy drama, but all the time dreaming of rock-and-roll.

It was a busy time for all of us. For a while I was playing in three bands in the same road show. Between quick costume changes, I would open the show with The Survivors, next appear with The Elementary School Band, and finally play backup for April Stevens and Nino Tempo.

When we were not out on the road or under psychiatric care for symptoms resembling battle fatigue, those of us in Randy's "stable" would gather each morning in groups of five or six and sequester ourselves in any one of the free offices about the complex. There we would spend countless hours honing our skills as songwriters, working on either assigned themes or our own ideas. This would usually go on until around three o'clock in the afternoon. The remainder of the day was set aside to rehearse the material to be performed that evening. The building would be deserted by 7:00 p.m., everyone having gone their separate ways - a quick shower, a change of clothes, and a bite to eat - only to meet again at 8:30 p.m. at Randy's West Los Angeles night club, Ledbetter's. The first show began at 9:00 p.m. and, depending on the size of the crowd, there might be a second, third, and sometimes even a fourth show scheduled.

After a while, the pressure and a mysterious fire that almost totally destroyed our home club, Ledbetter's (turning our instruments into steaming piles of ash and clumps of twisted metal), forced us all to make some soul-searching decisions. Owen Castleman and Michael Murphy left Sparks to form The Texas Twosome, which later became The Lewis

From the collection of Ed Reilly.

and Clarke Expedition. I continued playing rock-and-roll with The Elementary School Band, which was then under contract to Almo Records, a division of A&M Records, but every Monday night it was Mike, John, and I on stage in the Monday night "hoot" at Doug Weston's Troubadour, where we had first met, playing folk music.

The Monday night "hoot" at the Troubadour featured the best of the striving young artists from all over the country, gathered together to trade songs, show off, and otherwise try to impress the many record company "A&R" men who were always perched in the balcony, patiently waiting to swoop down on naive talents like birds of prey.

Each act was allowed to perform three songs or fifteen minutes, whichever was less. From 9:00 p.m. until 2:00 a.m. closing, you had better believe, it rocked, or folked, or whatever you were into, to the beat of: The Byrds, Buffalo Springfield, Hoyt Axton, The Dillards, Tim Buckley, Mary McCaslin, The Men (later to become The Association), The Nitty Gritty Dirt Band, Linda Ronstadt, The Stone Poneys, The Smothers Brothers, and, as they say, the list goes on. Every young pop musician who hit L.A. sooner or later found his way to the Troubadour.

The "Troub" had become the hottest spot in town to "present your product" (as the record company people called it), but it wasn't the only place. Every hole-in-the-wall beer bar in a twenty-mile radius that was big enough to accommodate a four-by-eight-foot platform and still leave room for a few paying customers became a showcase. Pueblo de Los Angeles, the City of the Angels, was hungry for something - *anything* - new, and it didn't even have to be good, just new.

The entire music industry was blasting off, and rock-and-roll was leading the way. Sales records were being set only to be broken, profits were soaring, and record companies were fighting tooth and nail to sign new artists. The competition was fierce between the major labels; monumental advances were being offered to entice previously unknown groups to sign exclusive contracts; rumors of $100,000 to even $250,000 advances abounded, these purportedly given on the strength of nothing more than a demo tape recorded in a garage.

Though we were primarily involved in our own projects, Mike, John, and I still remained in close touch with the Sparks organization. It was during this period that Barry Friedman, a former record distributor, joined the Sparks group. Barry was a born promoter of the P. T. Barnum school and added just the touch of circus that was badly needed. We were never quite sure of his loyalties, but we knew him to be extremely imaginative and hyper-aware of how the entertainment business worked and, more importantly, how to make it work to his (and therefore our) greatest advantage.

Barry kept an attentive eye on the "trades" - *Variety, Billboard, Cash Box,* and *The Hollywood Reporter* - and each morning he would post a list of the "cattle calls" (open auditions scheduled about town). More often than not, an appearance at one of these auditions was a total waste of time, but Barry kept right on posting his lists and we kept on going to the interviews. One of many such occasions was the result of a now famous ad in *Variety*.

```
MADNESS!!
AUDITIONS
Folk & Roll Musicians Singers
for acting roles in new TV series.
Running parts for 4 insane boys, age 17-21
Want spirited Ben Frank's-types.
Have courage to work.
Must come down for interview.
CALL: HO. 6-5188
```

"Madness" ad, *Variety*, Thursday, September 9, 1965

The initial interviews were held in a small office above an electronics supply store, just off Cahuenga, smack dab in the center of Hollywood. I was interviewed by Lester Sill. We talked about my goals and interests, and he listened attentively to my audition tapes, occasionally jotting down hurried notes in a yellow legal-size pad. After about three quarters of an hour, a young, dark-haired fellow arrived who Lester introduced to me as David Jones. Davy, he told me, had been under contract for some time and was seriously being considered for the project. It was easy to see why.

Another name that kept popping up was that of Micky Dolenz. Micky was still tied to Screen Gems from his "Circus Boy" days and was obviously a front-runner. It seemed clear from the very beginning that only two additional bodies, not four, were needed.

I made it through the first interview and was scheduled for a second, this time with the producers, Bob Rafelson and Bert Schneider. The weeks that followed were a succession of calls and callbacks, auditions and screen tests, adulations and rejections. For those of us who got a second look, it was a real education in the ways that the omnipotent of the television and record consortiums wielded the awesome power which rested in their hands.

I was one of the lucky ones. Although I was not chosen as one of the four Monkees, I was still permitted to participate in the project: as The Monkees' tour manager, their photographer, an extra on the series, and studio musician. It was time well spent and an experience I will never forget.

Bill Chadwick

RAYBERT PRODUCTIONS, INC.
1438 NORTH GOWER
HOLLYWOOD 28, CALIFORNIA

12 November 1965

Mr. Bill Chadwick
1427 So. Saltair Avenue
Los Angeles, California

Dear Bill:

Production of "THE MONKEES" begins tomorrow. It is really strange that I couldn't write this letter until this date -- but narrowing our selections was an agonizing process. I wish there could have been twelve Monkees, but perhaps when the series goes into production there'll be an opportunity for us to work together again.

In the meantime, thank you for your interest and the fun, and every best wish for your career.

Sincerely,

Bob

ROBERT RAFELSON
RR:jg

From the collection of Bill Chadwick.

Part one
The Monkees Day-By-Day, 1965-1986

Bert Schneider and Bob Rafelson on the set of the pilot episode. In the background, Larry Tucker confers with Mike Nesmith.
Photo courtesy Edmag Archives.

1965

SEPTEMBER 1965

September 9   "Madness" ad appears in *Hollywood Reporter*.
September 10   "Madness" ad appears in *Daily Variety*.

Two young television producers, Bob Rafelson and Bert Schneider of Screen Gems-Columbia Pictures, had come up with the concept for a TV comedy based on the adventures and misadventures of a struggling rock-and-roll group. They rejected the idea of using an already established group or professional actors, deciding to take the TV experiment one step further by working with amateur actors. It was a fresh approach to a fresh concept for television.

On two fateful days in the fall of 1965, Rafelson and Schneider placed ads in the major Hollywood trade publications to begin their massive talent search. Over 400 young men appeared in answer to the advertisement, including such notables as Danny Hutton (later a member of Three Dog Night), Keith Allison (later a member of Paul Revere & The Raiders), Stephen Stills, Paul Williams, Jerry Yester (a member of the Lovin' Spoonful), Tim Rooney (actor Mickey Rooney's son), Don Scardino (later a successful soap opera actor), and Paul Petersen (actor known for his work on "The Donna Reed Show"). Also among the applicants were people like Bill Chadwick and John London, who had worked with Michael Nesmith previously and eventually ended up on the Monkees' "team."

Not content to simply weed through the mob of applicants from the ads, the producers alerted the Screen Gems studio guards to send in any likely looking lads from the street. From this batch came one confused young man carrying a sack of laundry to the laundromat.

> ". . . . This guy came in for an audition with a wool hat on and a pack on his back. He said, 'I hope this ain't gonna take too much time, cause I'm in a hurry.' That was Mike Nesmith."
>
> Davy Jones

The interviews were as unconventional as everything else about the project. The boys were not quizzed; instead they found themselves in the middle of impossible situations, arguments, games,

1965

Paul Mazursky and Larry Tucker (r) on the set waiting for their cameo appearance in the Monkees pilot episode, which they co-scripted.
Photo courtesy Edmag Archives.

"Playbill" is the registered trademark of American Theatre Press, Inc., New York, NY. Used by permission.

etc., as a test of their ability to react and adlib. In this way the producers were better able to glimpse the personalities that were so important to the final casting. After all, they wanted to hire four guys who could play themselves.

David Jones was the first choice for the show. He had made his show biz splash two years earlier as the Artful Dodger in "Oliver!" on Broadway, where he was seen by then-Screen Gems Treasurer, Ward Sylvester. Sylvester spotted David's potential immediately and left his $100,000-a-year job to become his manager. He advised David to join the touring company of "Pickwick" and, when the company reached Los Angeles, Screen Gems executives came to view David's performance. They immediately placed him under contract and kept him on salary while searching for the perfect starring vehicle for him for TV. Larry Tucker, who later scripted the Monkees' pilot episode, had even proposed a show for David in which he'd play two parts- lookalike cousins. The show was later done by Patty Duke instead. When this new project came up, David was a natural choice and his British accent was seen as a distinct advantage in the days of "The British Invasion."

Director Mike Elliot demonstrating a scene to David.
Photo courtesy Edmag Archives.

OCTOBER 1965

October 9   Peter Tork signs contract to do "The Monkees."

Peter Tork, Micky Dolenz, and Michael Nesmith were among the group of applicants who were called back repeatedly for more questions, screen tests, and actual run-throughs of scenes.

> "Nyles Brown and I had to do a scene together for the cameras and we did it right the first time through. I think that counted heavily in our favor, that we were quick studies."
>
> Peter Tork

When the producers had narrowed the field to eight finalists, they took the eight screen tests to Audience Studies Inc., an audience research division of Screen Gems. Audiences between the ages of six and eighteen rated the finalists, and ASI's recommendations confirmed what Bert Schneider and Bob Rafelson had already decided.

The time had come to finally decide on a name for the new group. Among the titles considered were The Turtles, The Inevitables, and The Creeps. All were rejected. Schneider finally suggested "Monkees," following the then popular trend of rock groups with "misspelled" titles, The Byrds, The Beatles, and The Cyrkle.

Screen Gems official Jackie Cooper, once a famous child actor, allocated $225,000 to Rafelson and Schneider for the filming of the pilot episode, despite the fact that the show did not even have a written outline.

Fifties jigsaw puzzle of Micky as TV's "Circus Boy."

1965

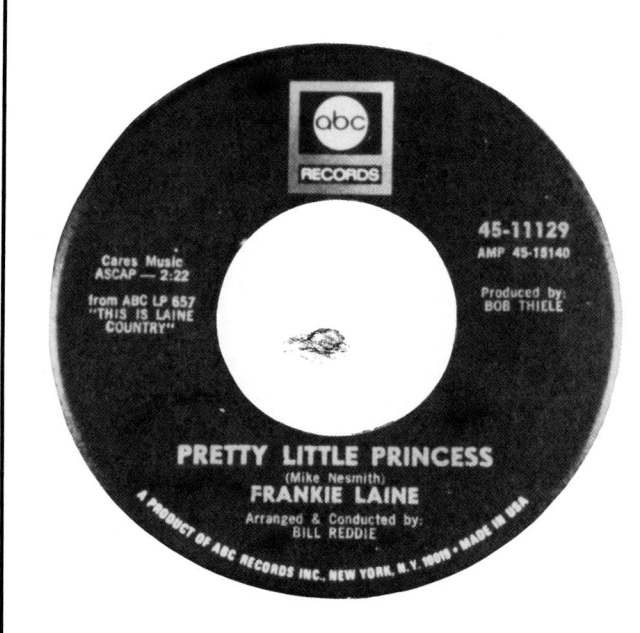

An early boost to Mike's career came when Frankie Laine recorded Nesmith's composition "Pretty Little Princess" on his Omnibus label. This gave Mike the opportunity to record and release his first single, "How Can You Kiss Me," by Mike, John and Bill, on Omnibus. Laine released "Pretty Little Princess" on the ABC label in 1968.

Photo courtesy Edmag Archives.

NOVEMBER 1965

November 13   Production began on "The Monkees" TV series with the filming of the pilot episode. The Monkees later had a reputation for being "quick professionals" and, true to form from the beginning, they knocked off the first show in an efficient five days. Afterwards they were told to go home and wait for the show to be sold.

"Micky phoned me and said he was up for a new TV series. I asked what the plot was and he said, 'No plot'."
                    Janelle Dolenz Scott

DECEMBER 1965

December 25   Micky Dolenz left Los Angeles to spend the Christmas holidays with his family at their home in Los Gatos. He invited David to join him, as David could not afford the air fare home to England. They told Micky's family about the pilot they had done and said they really did not expect anything to come of it.

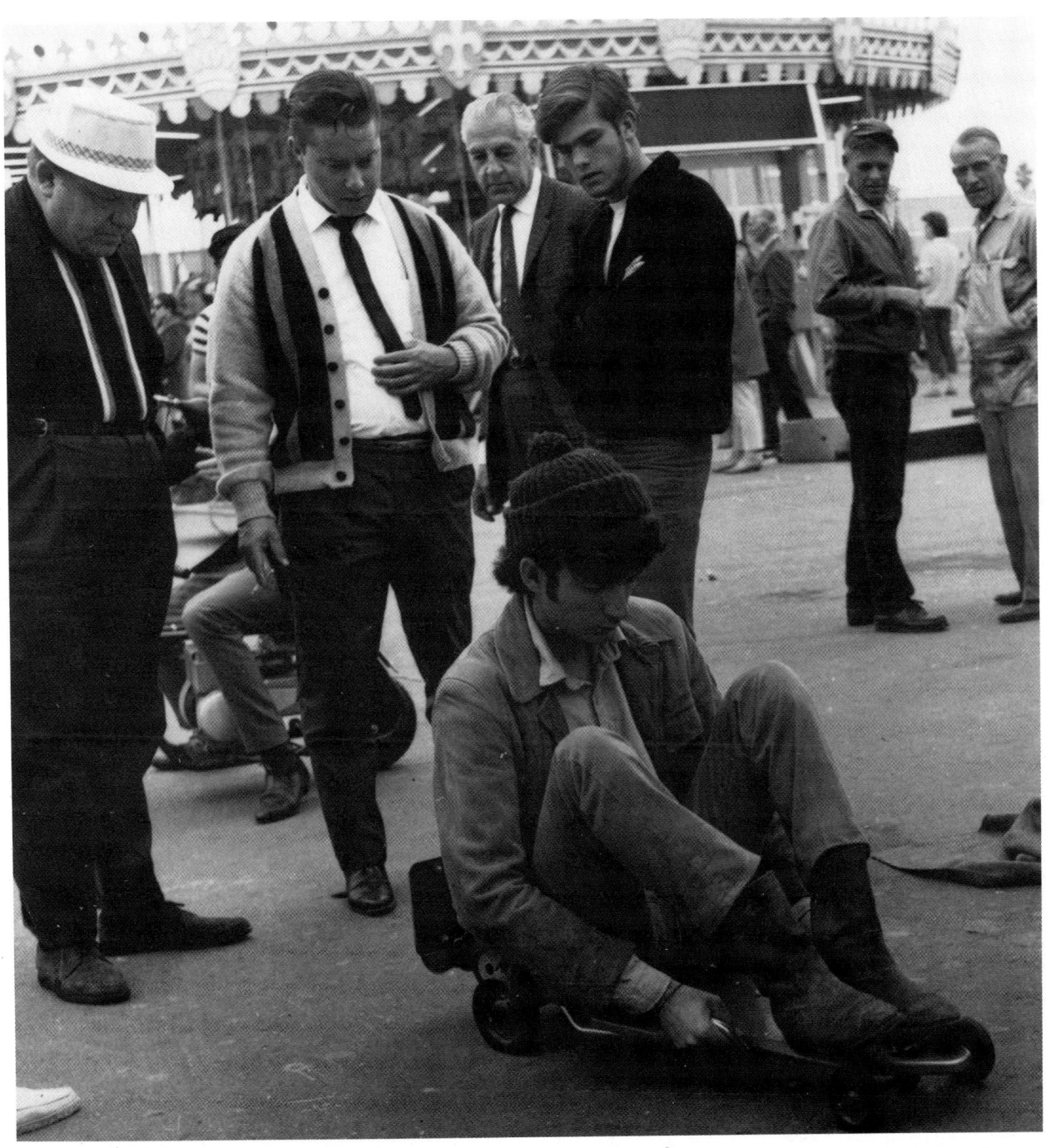
Mike on a motorized skateboard.
Photo courtesy Edmag Archives.

Photo courtesy Edmag Archives.

1966

JANUARY 1966

January 17   NBC-TV buys "The Monkees" series.

Bob Rafelson and Bert Schneider completed editing the pilot episode, including film speed-ups, slow motion, upside down frames, and totally non-sequitur segments. It was innovative and like nothing ever seen on television before. They sent the finished product to Audience Studies Inc., but the unconventional tricks confused the audience. The pilot received a disastrously low rating and Screen Gems all but abandoned the show.

The producers frantically tried to save their project and worked all night to edit out the items that had thrown the audience. They screened the second version for ASI and this time passed with flying colors. Twenty-four hours later NBC bought the series and sold it to two sponsors, Yardley and Kellogg's, within seventy-two hours.

FEBRUARY 1966

Rafelson and Schneider approached their task with determination. Now they needed to attend to the details of production. They appropriated a twenty-by-forty-foot cubicle inside the new Stage 3 on the Screen Gems lot. There the four Monkees were reassembled for the first time in over three months.

The boys came to work, got to know each other, and tried to work out their musical differences. Each represented a different style of sound and came from a different musical background. Davy came from musical theatre and did not play an instrument. Mike Nesmith was self-taught on guitar but could not read sheet music; his background was in folk/protest music. Peter Tork was an accomplished musician who had been classically trained on several instruments; he had worked steadily as a folk singer in Greenwich Village before relocating to California. Micky Dolenz played guitar and had been the lead singer in a rock-and-roll group called "The Missing Links"; when the instrumental chores for The Monkees were handed out, Micky was elected drummer and was sent to drum lessons daily.

Mike Nesmith with an early Mr. Schneider prototype.
Photo courtesy Edmag Archives.

1966

Director Jim Frawley giving the guys some pointers.
Photo courtesy Edmag Archives.

MARCH 1966

The Monkees began an intensive session on Stage 3 with James Frawley, an underground film director and comic actor who had been hired to make The Monkees into improvisational comedians. They worked together throughout March and April, becoming a cohesive acting and comedic unit.

"At first they were embarrassed, they were stiff and they were a little raw. All that had to be worked out. We started playing games with imaginary objects. 'Here's a screwdriver, do something with it. Here, I'll throw you a ball. Imagine you're inside a car. Here's a rifle, a bow and arrow. Now do everything in slow motion. Swim in slow motion.' We would roll over on the floor, sometimes, and do animals. 'You're a crab. Talk the way a giraffe would talk. Deal with an elephant. Now, talk the way a teapot would talk.' It was like a training period to free them physically, to start to use their bodies in a new way."

James Frawley from
Saturday Evening Post,
January 28, 1967

Photo courtesy Edmag Archives.

APRIL 1966

After five weeks of constant rehearsals, The Monkees were ready to audition their sound for record companies. Three major companies were approached, Columbia, Capitol, and RCA. Not only did RCA make the best manufacturing and distribution offer, they were also the parent company of the television network which had purchased the show, NBC. With this signing, The Monkees were assured good cooperation between their TV and record bosses. A new record label was established by RCA for the Monkees called "Colgems," short for Columbia-Screen Gems.

> "So, we went in to the studio and we recorded as a band a song called 'The Girl I Knew Somewhere,' which was a song that I wrote. That was the first time The Monkees actually had made music with me on lead guitar, Peter on bass and overdubbed keyboards, and Micky on drums. And I took it back to the producer and I said, 'Let's make this the next record, okay?' and he says, 'Okay, I'll go for it,' and the word came down from New York, 'Uh-Uh, no sir, now we've established Don Kirshner as the musical head of the show and Kirshner doesn't want that!"
> Michael Nesmith

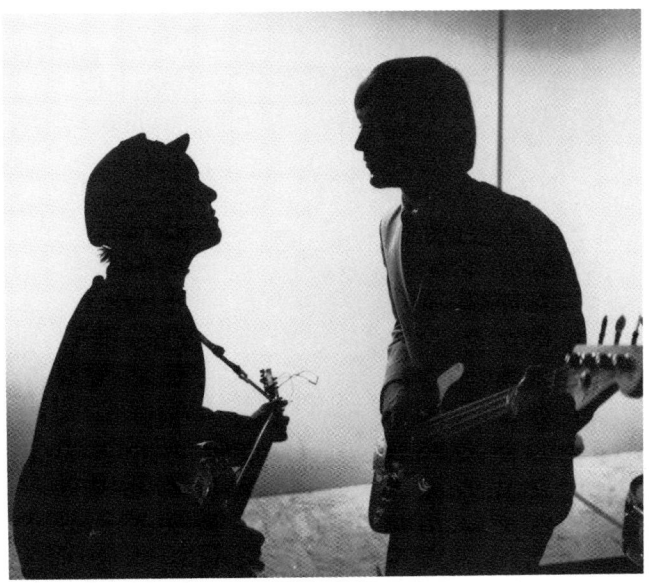

Silhouette of Davy and Peter.
Photo courtesy Edmag Archives.

1966

Photo courtesy Edmag Archives.

MAY 1966

The producers thought that the boys were alternately great and lousy musically. The group was gradually finding its own sound, but it was not coming together quickly enough for the producers' timetable. Rafelson and Schneider went looking for help in the form of Don Kirshner, a young record producer with a track record of mega-successes.

"Donnie Kirshner flew out from New York first time he got involved in it. Then they needed a head producer, so he hired Mickie Most, who was Donovan's producer. Then they sent back the tapes. Terrible stuff. Then he hired Snuffy Garrett and got the tapes back in. They were all cutting the theme song. So, it came back sounding like a Gary Lewis track. Scrap that. They flew out Gerry (Goffin) and Carole King. Carole went home in tears in the middle of the night, as she couldn't deal with the kids. Finally, we were getting down to the deadline, the show was coming on the air, so Tommy (Boyce) and I were tugging at Donnie's coattails and we said, 'We know what to do, man,' so I convinced him I'd take my group that were working clubs every night into a cheap rehearsal studio and we worked it out the way we heard it, and just come down to listen. It only cost ten dollars an hour. If he liked it, let us go in and do it, and that's what happened, that's how we got back into producing."

Bobby Hart

Bobby Hart's band was the Candy Store Prophets: Gerry McGee, guitar; Larry Taylor, bass; Billy Lewis, drums; and Bobby on keyboards. They went into the studio and created prototype records for The Monkees to re-create - vocally only. The instrumentals on the first recordings were done by the Candy Store Prophets with additional guitar work by Louis Shelton - who created the memorable guitar licks on "Last Train To Clarksville" and "Valleri" - and Wayne Irwin.

May 31 "The Monkees" TV series begins filming.

David, Michael and director Mike Elliot.
Photo courtesy Edmag Archives.

Filming a "romp" for the pilot.
Photo courtesy Edmag Archives.

1966

Photo courtesy Edmag Archives.

JUNE 1966

The first "official" Monkees recording sessions were held between June 10 and 25.

The recording of the first album took place at the same time as the filming of the first season of the TV series. Their daily schedules began on the set around 6:00 a.m. and ended in the recording studio at midnight or later.

> "At the end of the day, about 7:00 p.m., they threw the boys into a car and drove them over to the recording studios. It was one of the few times I visited the set, because I didn't want to be known as a stage mother. But they hadn't had a break all day and had nothing to eat, and now were expected to record all night. One of the things that was wrong with that setup was that they had no one looking out for *their* interests like the Beatles had Brian Epstein."
> Janelle Dolenz Scott

By the time the first few episodes were completed, the "Monkees look" had jelled, carefully choreographed in every aspect by the top artists in Hollywood to capture the attention of the young audience. The Monkees' long hair and specially designed mod wardrobe became an important trademark, so important, in fact, that the hairstylist on the set was reportedly paid more per week than The Monkees themselves.

> "On the set at Columbia we were hated-they didn't like the long hair. They thought it was rebel. They (the bosses) wanted it to be a whole different thing, and it certainly was on the set. Hollywood may be bizarre and strange, everyone thinks so, but our hair really threw them."
> Davy Jones

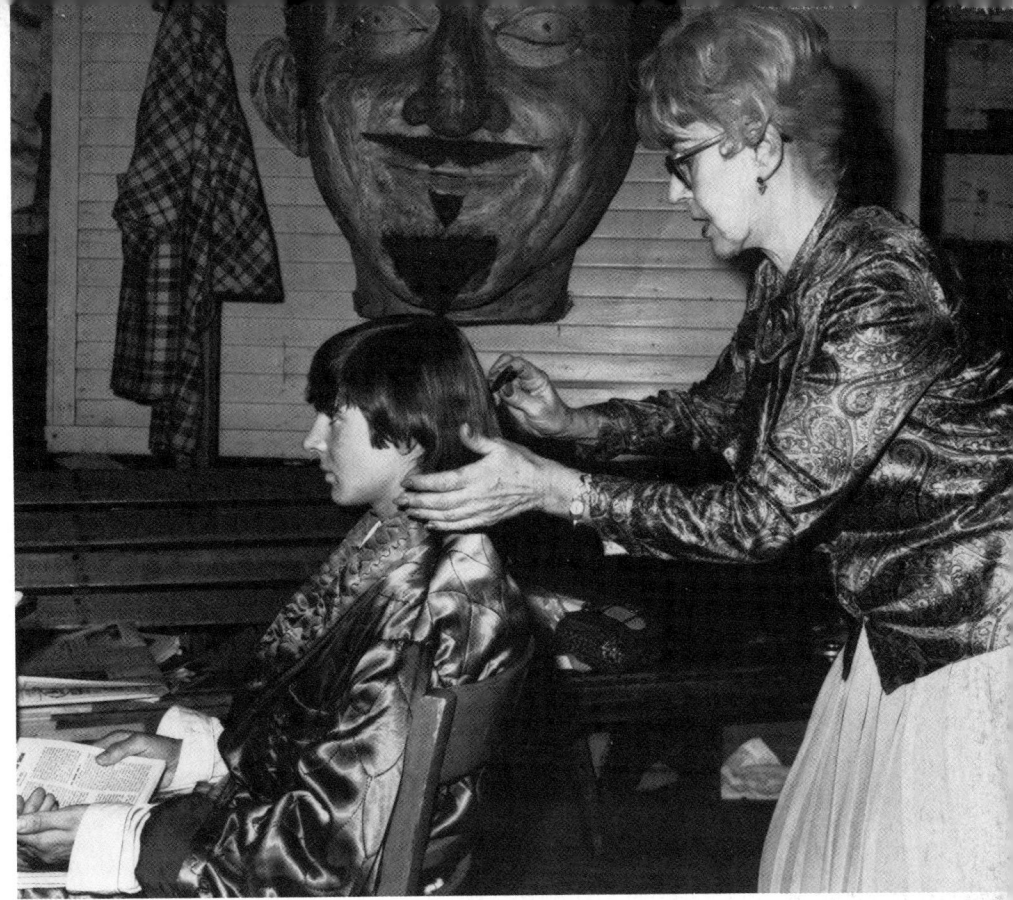

Photo courtesy Edmag Archives.

JULY 1966

The Monkees continued to film episodes of their television show, recording throughout the month as well.

> "They needed the theme right away for the TV show, so we went in and took all four guys into the room and put them all in front of the microphones. So we said, 'Take One.' We'd already done the track, of course, and all they had to do was sing. They all were going to sing together, I guess; we had no concept of what was going on. And we looked out there, and there they were all on the floor in this dogpile - wrestling! So, we tried to straighten them in the end. 'Take One' and they would not get serious. They were total pandemonium. I guess they were getting to know each other and they were all trying to outdo each other with zaniness. So, after a half hour, we dismissed the session and it was good, it set the pace, because after that we never again brought in more than one Monkee."
>
> Bobby Hart

From the advance media blitz for the Monkees.

1966

From "Billboard" magazine, September 10, 1966.

David reading a letter from home between takes.
Photo courtesy Edmag Archives.

AUGUST 1966

RCA began its massive promotional campaign for The Monkees' first single. The company sank $100,000 into the effort, sending a team of seventy-six promoters across the United States to tell the country that The Monkees were coming. Advance copies of the single went to six thousand disc jockeys. Promotional bumperstickers proclaiming "Everyone Is Going Ape For The Monkees" and "The Monkees Are The Greatest" were distributed. Ads to the same effect appeared in trade papers and teen magazines, all designed to make The Monkees a household name, over a month before their TV show hit the airwaves.

Screen Gems' merchandising department was also busy setting up licensing deals for over fifty Monkees products - dolls, toys, clothes, etc.- basically anything and everything that could be labeled with The Monkees' name or associated in any way with the band's hip image.

August 16 "Last Train To Clarksville" was released, selling 500,000 copies within weeks.

August 28 The Monkees were taken to the Beatles' concert at Dodger Stadium in Los Angeles to prepare them for the eventuality of doing live shows.

Actor Andre Phillippe poses next to the infamous Monkeemobile.
Photo courtesy Edmag Archives.

SEPTEMBER 1966

September 1 At a press party at Screen Gems in Los Angeles, The Monkees kicked off a ten-day promotional tour of personal appearances across the United States to herald the debut of their TV show.

September 3 The promoters rented out the Broadway Theatre in New York City for a Saturday afternoon and gave away free tickets through a local radio station. Two thousand frenzied teenagers showed up to watch the boys clown around and crack jokes. The boys experienced their first frightening mob scene with over-enthusiastic autograph seekers, all this before the show had even aired. The tour went on to other major cities, including Chicago and Boston.

September 11 The promotion closed with the biggest publicity stunt of all. The small California town of Del Mar became "Clarksville" for a day, and a train carrying 450 teenagers was sent to "Clarksville" to meet the group. For the return journey, The Monkees rode in a boxcar, playing their music all the way home.

September 12 "The Monkees" TV series debuted on NBC-TV at 7:30 p.m. Eastern Standard Time. This was in spite of a $6,850,000 lawsuit pending in the New York courts by David Bordon of United Artists and David Yarnell of RKO, who claimed Screen Gems had copied the idea for The Monkee's series from them. They tried unsuccessfully to have the series barred from airing until the lawsuit was settled.

The group had traded in the "woody" station wagon from the pilot episode for the George Barris custom-designed Monkeemobile, a modified, souped-up, fire-engine-red Pontiac GTO. In a promotional move, Pontiac had given each Monkee a GTO for his personal use; Peter and Micky received red ones, Mike's was white, and Davy's was blue with a black top. The Monkeemobile was used in the series during filming, and in the off-season it earned $3,000 an appearance on the car-show circuit.

1966

Nesmith using a Vox amplifier and Gretsch guitar.
Photo courtesy Edmag Archives.

Also part of the image were the musical instruments, the top of the line for the time, donated by manufacturers who leapt at the chance to have their products displayed on TV each week. About $10,000 worth of equipment was handed to the boys, including Gretsch guitars, Gretsch drums, and Voxx amplifiers.

OCTOBER 1966

October 10   The Monkees first LP was released.

October 14   The RIAA awarded Gold Records to "The Monkees" LP and "Last Train To Clarksville."

The Monkees first album was as much a mix of musical styles as the four Monkees themselves. "Papa Gene's Blues," a Nesmith composition, stood out as decidedly country in flavor and used the dobro, which no one had ever heard in rock-and-roll before. Despite the fact that the Monkees were limited to vocals on the first album, Michael Nesmith insisted that Peter Tork play on "Papa Gene's Blues." Peter was permitted to add an acoustic guitar track, but in the finished product it was barely audible.

October 24   *Newsweek* magazine reported that The Monkees were expected to earn $100,000 each before the end of the year from record sales, TV show and personal appearances.

Meanwhile, the boys' frantic pace had not lessened. They were still filming the television show's first season and were recording the tracks for the second album.

"Micky was quite insecure, but great as he sounded, he was quite insecure in the studio. Usually this would be the story: he would come in and we'd sing him the song. He'd kind of learn it. He'd go out there and sing a little bit. 'I can't sing this song.' He'd then get kind of depressed and then usually Tommy would take him next door to RCA Studios into the coffee shop there and they'd have a cup of soup or something. Then give him a little pep talk and come out, and go in and do it in one take and sing it great."

Bobby Hart

Five variations of the "Last Train To Clarksville" picture sleeve were released. The top row were color, the bottom were black and white.

The first pressing of "The Monkees" LP contained a misspelling of "Papa Gene's Blues." Later pressings include the correct spelling.

Despite the good reviews for the debut episode, the Nielsen numbers were disappointing. One of the problems the show faced was that it was not aired in every market in the country. Many affiliates, particularly in the more conservative areas, refused to air it, fearing the long hair would offend viewers.

"Last Train To Clarksville" zoomed up the charts as soon as the show went on the air. With the single an assured success, the time had come to release the remaining tracks from the first sessions as an album. Album tracks other than "Clarksville" would be familiar to the record-buying public from the television show. Every Monday night's segment served as a half-hour commercial for the record.

Photo courtesy Personality Photos Inc., P.O. Box 50, Midwood Station, New York, NY 11230.

Photo courtesy Edmag Archives.

"They were so busy filming the show and everything, that we had finished the first album and we had no cover. Nobody'd even thought to shoot an album cover. So, Tommy and I hired a photographer with Lester's help and brought him to the set and said, 'Look, we gotta have you guys for a cover.' And they said, 'No, no, we're too busy.' We said, 'Look, can you give us ten minutes?' So, Michael said, 'We'll give you five!' They were serious. They came out just in the alley there and if you look in the corner you can see he's [Michael] counting it off, the final ten seconds, his hand is counting off."

Bobby Hart

Around this time, The Monkees became so adept at their newfound television careers that they began filming entire episodes in only three days.

"Teen" magazine ad, 1966.

21

1966

Photo courtesy Edmag Archives.

Ad from a teen magazine.

NOVEMBER 1966

Except for a handful of tracks recorded late in the month, The Monkees put aside recording and replaced it in their busy schedules with evening and weekend rehearsals for their live stage shows. Choreographer David Winters was given the task of transforming the boys into a viable concert act. The stage show was cleverly designed to incorporate the swift pace and highly visual qualities of the TV series. Film clips and stills flashed onto a huge screen above the stage while the Monkees played and clowned below. Several costume changes were also added, and each Monkee had his moment to shine alone onstage with a solo number. The schedule did not allow a dull moment onstage -after all, audiences were accustomed to a half hour of non-stop, high-energy hijinks every Monday night and would expect no less of a Monkees concert.

November 11 *Time* magazine reported that the "flood of Monkee merchandise from guitars to comic books and Monkee pants, of which J. C. Penney alone has ordered $670,000 worth, will gross $20 million this year."

November 12 "I'm A Believer" was released as The Monkees' second single. An astounding 1,051,280 copies were ordered *before* the release date.

Mike converses with Army Archerd from "Variety."
Photo courtesy Edmag Archives.

DECEMBER 1966

December 3 The Monkees played their first live concert before a sellout crowd of 8,364 at Honolulu's International Center Arena in Hawaii. The show grossed $36,000 and earned high praise from the critics. As a result of this encouraging reception, the decision was made to book several more dates.

December 9 *Variety* reported that the Monkees were already making plans for their first feature film, due to start production "next March." Micky stated, "We want it to be as different a movie as the series was to TV."

December 10 The RIAA awarded a Gold Record to "I'm A Believer." *Billboard* reported that "for RCA this represented the warmest distribution reception ever gained with the exception of certain Elvis Presley records."

December 24 "Last Train To Clarksville" ranked fourth on *Billboard's* Top Records of 1966.

1966

"Parade" magazine.

December 25-31   The Monkees embarked on their first concert tour, which was run by Dick Clark Productions. The opening act was Bobby Hart's band, The Candy Store Prophets, who had played on the records. Prior to the start of the tour, Davy Jones flew home to England for a few days and put in a guest appearance on "The Top of the Pops" TV show.

By the close of 1966, The Monkees had completed twenty-five episodes of their TV series, had been awarded three Gold Records, the first album alone selling over three million copies, and had played concerts in seven cities. They began to realize their popularity after the first few concerts and were suddenly acknowledging that the media's comparisons between The Monkees and The Beatles were not so far afield:

> "I think we had it tougher than The Beatles. We had to be a hit in three media at one time, television, records, and personals, and we had no experience together in any."
>
> Michael Nesmith
> *Variety*, December 9, 1966

▶ The fifth Monkee - Mr. Schneider, the real dummy - on the set.
Photo by Henry Diltz.

Photo courtesy Edmag Archives.

1967

JANUARY 1967

January 1 That England was the home of The Beatles mattered not when The Monkees' television series debuted on the BBC in England at the start of 1967. The Monkees took Britain by storm, and the debut of the series sparked an overwhelming demand for their records. "I'm A Believer" was number one in the charts and sold 400,000 copies, an unheard of figure in Britain at the time, in its first week of U.K. release. The Monkees' phenomenal success captured the attention of everyone, even Mick Jagger:

"They've had a fantastic promotion in the States, but I think people will get tired of them. I'd give the Monkees until July in America, perhaps a little longer."
Mick Jagger
Fab 208, January 7, 1967

January 10 The Monkees' second LP, "More of The Monkees," was released. Five days later it earned a Gold Record from the RIAA. In England, it emerged to advance orders of 1.5 million and went on to sell four million copies.

Don Kirshner penned the album's liner notes and credited every producer and writer involved, barely squeezing in The Monkees' contributions in the last sentence. His words only added fuel to the already burning issue of The Monkees' musical validity.

Every major newspaper and magazine story on The Monkees since the debut of the show had alluded to the fact that the boys sang but did not play on their records. These same articles had in all fairness emphasized that the boys were indeed musicians with the ability, if not the time, to record their own instrumentals.

Unfortunately, jealous colleagues who resented the big hype RCA had given The Monkees' records began to use this situation to discredit the group. The boys were confronted with it most strongly when they set out to do live shows. Rumors abounded that they only went through the motions onstage while another band hidden backstage cranked out the music. The Monkees even tried to set the story straight in an interview segment at the end of one of the TV episodes.

1967

First appearance on the cover of "TV Guide." Reprinted with permission from "TV Guide®" magazine. Copyright © 1967 by Triangle Publications, Inc., Radnor, Pennsylvania.

Although the "She Hangs Out" single was pulled in the U.S., Canadian pressings did get as far as the consumer level.

"I was standing in a place where we were playing. We were backstage and it's like two minutes before we're supposed to go on, and this guy walks up. He's a little reporter, you know, and I'm standing with my guitar over my back. He walks up and he says, 'Is it true you don't play your own instruments?' I said, 'Wait a minute! I'm fixing to walk out there in front of 15,000 people, man. If I don't play my own instruments, I'm in a lot of trouble.' Why even talk about it? It's ridiculous. No, it's *not* true."

Michael Nesmith
from the episode
"Monkees at The Movies"

Nesmith was even more vocal in an interview with *Saturday Evening Post*:

"Tell the world we're synthetic, because, damn it, we are. . . . The music had nothing to do with us. It was totally dishonest."

Michael Nesmith
Saturday Evening Post, January 28, 1967

Meanwhile, The Monkees made the cover of *TV Guide* and filmed their concert in Phoenix for an upcoming episode of the television series, but the tension among them over the recording issue continued to grow. It was then that Don Kirshner made his power play:

"Kirshner released 'She Hangs Out' without the approval of Rafelson and Schneider, and over the objections of the powers-that-be at Columbia. The Monkees didn't like the record. The Monkees felt they wanted something else out and they just wanted some creative voice in it. Don Kirshner decided 'no.' He wanted that record out. He then released it and went to Florida, where you could not reach him. I felt it didn't make any difference, you could have put out *crap* at that point in time because they were so strong. They were called into a meeting at the Beverly Hills Hotel with the Monkees, Kirshner, Herb Moeblis, and myself. Nesmith got so angry about what was coming down because he said, 'Don't we have anything to say about it?' and Moeblis, who was an attorney actually, said, 'No, you don't, you're signed to us and we'll tell you what to record.' And Mike got so angry, he put his fist through the wall of the room, and David started to cry because at that point in time he knew that this thing was beginning to get shaky and either Kirshner had to go or one of the others. He [Kirshner] was fired as head of the (Colgems) record company."

Lester Sill

Photo courtesy Edmag Archives.

FEBRUARY 1967

For the first time in over a year of non-stop hard work, The Monkees were turned loose on an unsuspecting world for a three-week vacation. Also for the first time, they were able to enjoy the benefits of their new-found stardom, suddenly being able to afford to travel anywhere in the world and being invited to party with their heroes, The Beatles, The Rolling Stones, and other top names in the music business. Three of The Monkees headed for England, center of the pop world, while Peter quietly returned to New York to visit friends.

February 7 Micky met Paul McCartney at Paul's St. John's Wood home. Mike spent time with John Lennon and sat in on a 'Sgt. Pepper's' recording session.

February 9 Mike and Micky appeared on "The Top of The Pops" show in England to receive a silver disc for "I'm A Believer."

February 11 British magazine *Fabulous 208* reported that "I'm A Believer" had sold nearly 750,000 copies, and also that The Monkees first LP had sold 56,000 on the day of its release and over 88,000 by the fifth day.

Billboard magazine called the Monkees "The Top Banana" globally, setting sales records in the U.S., England, Holland, Sweden, Belgium, Norway, Germany, Canada, Japan, Australia, and the Philippines.

In an effort to cash in on The Monkees phenomenon, a pre-Monkees recording by Micky Dolenz, "Don't Do It," had surfaced and was released by Challenge Records.

First two LP releases from Germany. The album above contained side 1 of "The Monkees" and side 2 of "More Of The Monkees," the one below contained side 1 of "More Of The Monkees" and side 2 of "The Monkees."

29

1967

The Monkees' theme song was released in Italy, but government rules required all TV theme songs be recorded in Italian. Micky redubbed the track phonetically.

In between takes, David takes a quick cigarette and cola break.
Photo courtesy Edmag Archives.

February 13 NBC-TV renewed "The Monkees" for a second season.

February 18 Grammy nominations were announced in Los Angeles, and "Last Train To Clarksville" received two nominations: "Best Contemporary R&R Recording" and "Best Contemporary R&R Group Performance." In England, Davy appeared on "The Rolf Harris Show" and sang "Consider Yourself" from "Oliver!". He had also taped a segment of "Junior Point of View," which aired in England on February 24.

February 23 The Monkees returned to Hollywood to begin an intense six-week session recording their third album, "Headquarters." Whereas the first two albums had been cut at night after long days filming the TV series, this time The Monkees were able to devote their entire attention and time to the music. This was to be *their* album, the one where they made all the decisions, played all the instruments, and exercised all the creative control. Much had changed in the weeks that they'd been away. Kirshner and all his staff had been cleared out and everything recorded under them had been shelved. From this point on, only tracks produced by The Monkees or a producer of their choosing (in this case Chip Douglas) could be released, and then only with The Monkees' complete approval.

"The Monkees gave one of the engineers [Hank Cicalo] a song [that they'd written]. And Hank bought his home with the receipts. Bought a *house* with it, and they just *gave* it to him! They said, 'We were ashamed of the song'."
Lester Sill

February 28 *Variety* reported that Davy Jones planned to decline all personal appearances for a while. The pace of the last six months had reduced him to only 109 pounds.

Imitation is the highest form of flattery. In 1967, everyone cashed in on the Monkees phenomenon by releasing cover versions of Monkees hits. These are just a few. The two albums on Wyncote were by a Monkees sound-alike group, and included a few cover versions as well as parodies of Monkees tunes.

1967

Who can scream the loudest? .... Micky and Peter try to find out.
Photo courtesy Edmag Archives.

"Chicago Tribune TV Week," March 25, 1967.

MARCH 1967

March 2 David and Peter attended the Grammy Awards ceremony. The Monkees lost out, however, when "Monday, Monday," by The Mamas & The Papas, defeated "Last Train To Clarksville" in the category of "Best Contemporary R&R Group Performance." "Last Train To Clarksville" also lost to "Winchester Cathedral," by The New Vaudeville Band, in the category of "Best Contemporary R&R Recording."

March 8 The Monkees' third single, "A Little Bit Me, A Little Bit You," went into release. The Nesmith composition, "The Girl I Knew Somewhere," replaced "She Hangs Out" on the flip side. The single was certified gold by the RIAA at the time of its release, due to the 1.5 million advance orders.

March 13 The National Association of Record Merchants honored The Monkees as the "Best Selling American Vocal Group with the Best Selling LP and Top Single," "I'm A Believer."

March 15 In New York, Don Kirshner filed a $35.5 million suit against Screen Gems-Columbia for being fired without cause from his position as President of Colgems Records. *Variety* reported that "it's understood (David) Jones is the only member of The Monkees siding with Kirshner. Others, Mike Nesmith, Micky Dolenz, and Peter Tork are reportedly going along with manager Schneider."

March 20 The Monkees invaded American jukeboxes with the release of their first jukebox EP.

March 21 The TV show reached its Nielsen ratings peak of number twenty-eight against all other prime time shows for the week.

March 25 Davy Jones announced the launching of his own record label, Davy Jones Records, with the intent of discovering new talent. The first artist signed was Vinnie Basile. Davy's manager, Hal Cone, would handle operations, and Jack Angel and Lee Young would be East and West Coast representatives, respectively.

The ultimate attempt to cash in on The Monkees' name appeared. A company in New Jersey, Entertainment International, began franchising "Monkees Soft Drink Night Clubs," which featured music and non-alcoholic refreshments for teenagers under the drinking age.

The task of covering *all* The Monkees news became too overwhelming for the teen magazine, *Tiger Beat*. They released the first issue of a new publication known as *Monkee Spectacular*, the only magazine to cover The Monkees exclusively. The demand from fans carried the new publication through the next year and a half.

The Monkees remained in the studio throughout the month, experimenting with sounds and generally enjoying the freedom they'd wanted for so long and had finally found.

First issue.

Only three records were known to have been released on the Davy Jones label. Each featured his likeness on the label and picture sleeve.

33

1967

Micky and David reviewing next week's script.
Photo courtesy Edmag Archives.

"They were playing the theme from Warner Brothers, the music at the end of the cartoons, with a steel guitar and they were playing it a bunch of times, and one section of this whole time we would take this down on tape. Peter and Mike did it on steel guitars and Micky was playing it very fast on the drums, and the two were not fitting together exactly."

Chip Douglas
on "Band Six"
Tiger Beat, August 1967

"There were water pistol fights; I think the Jefferson Airplane and some of Question Mark & The Mysterians, some couple of bands were recording at RCA at the time we were recording "Headquarters," and there were some water pistol fights. We painted the control room windows with little bits and pieces and things. I did a little Chinese thing, I was in my Zen at the time. Everybody had these paintings, the graffiti and drawings, sketches, and stuff."

Peter Tork

APRIL 1967

With April, The Monkees finished the recording of their third album. The days of setting their own hours and growing beards were over. The time had come to return to the grueling pace of filming the television show all week and doing concert tours on the weekends. Recording took a back seat, while studio time was devoted to mixing and remixing the "Headquarters" tracks.

"The first three or four weeks in the second season, I remember Ward Sylvester coming up to me and saying, 'You guys want to do this again [for a third season]?' At that time we were still doing leftover scripts from the first year, rejects from the first year. I said, 'If this is all the better we're gonna get, I don't want to do it [a third season].' I said no and that was the last I heard about it."

Peter Tork

April 1-2 The Monkees invaded Canada for the first time, doing two concerts. The Canadian fans went wild. Each concert seemed to be accompanied by progressively more hysteria and pandemonium than its predecessor.

"In Toronto we got a chartered plane, and a limo came right out onto the runway. We stepped right out on the runway, into the cars, and were escorted by this motorcade of cops who brought us into town through rush hour, who pulled everyone off the freeway. It was really a big deal. I remember the crowd control was really the most unique in Toronto at Maple Leaf Gardens. Uniformed nurses with trays with stacks of wet towels, and they'd go up and down the rows and slap wet towels in [hysterical] girls' faces."

Bobby Hart

Early promotional photographs of the guys linked them with studio starlets.
All photos courtesy Edmag Archives.

1967

Phyliss Nesmith seems to be telling an amusing story to Michael.
Photo by Bill Chadwick.

"Headquarters" as released in Argentina.

April 8   *Billboard's* "Music on Campus" survey rated The Monkees as the Number 1 Best Selling Group. "The Monkees" LP was "Number 1 Top Product on Campus" and "Number 1 Best Contemporary Pop LP." On the list of "Tops on Collegiate Picks, Popular," The Monkees came in at Number 3 behind The Mamas & The Papas and the Young Rascals, who were Number 1 and Number 2 respectively.

April 29   At a music industry gathering in Argentina, The Monkees were named "Best New International Artists" for their album, "The Monkees."

MAY 1967

May 8   Don Kirshner officially exited his post as head of Screen Gems-Columbia Pictures Music. He claimed that ever since he'd been discharged from Colgems Records, his superiors had instituted "a program of harassment designed to force me out of the music department."

May 20   "Headquarters," The Monkees' first record sans Kirshner, was released to over one million copies in advance orders. The RIAA immediately certified it as a Gold Record. The record sold over 2,000,000 copies in two weeks.

Fun with the wool hat on the road in '67.
Photos by Henry Diltz.

1967

Recording Engineer Hank Cicalo and Producer Douglas Farthing Hatlelid

▲ Over three million copies of the first pressing of "Headquarters" erroneously identify the recording engineer on the left as Hank Cicalo instead of Dick Bogert. No correction was ever issued, and the repressing was released ▼ with a different photo altogether.

Seated: Recording Engineer Hank Cicalo; Standing (L to R): Peter Tork, Producer Douglas Farthing Hatlelid, Davy Jones, Micky Dolenz, Mike Nesmith

From a Boston newspaper. Note the price!

May 23   Michael Nesmith underwent surgery for a chronic tonsil condition that occasionally reduced his voice to a whisper. It was reported that Mike's tonsils had been liberated from the hospital by a fan less than an hour after their removal. A May 27 concert in San Jose was cancelled while Mike recovered from the operation.

May 28   Davy appeared on "Secombe & Friends" on British TV.

JUNE 1967

June 4   "The Monkees" TV series received two awards at the presentation of the annual Emmy Awards, the highest praise the community of the television industry has to offer. It was voted "Best Comedy Show," and James Frawley received the award for "Outstanding Directorial Achievement" for the debut episode, "Royal Flush."

June 9   After months of honing their concert act to a fine precision, The Monkees were prepared to perform for the first time for their home audience of tough Los Angeles critics and music industry figures.

Photo by Bill Chadwick.

"Micky said, 'I want to do something that's really gonna make a big splash to set this tour off to a good start.' That was the beginning of the 1967 tour. So, about three-fourths of the way through his James Brown number, he signaled over to us to kill the lights on the water fountain [separating the stage from the audience]. So, I killed the lights and there was this small break during the middle of the song and he said, 'I'm gonna jump in the pond.' At the end of the song, in total craziness, he did this flip into the pond. If he hadn't told me he was gonna do it, nobody would have ever seen it because the lights would never have been there. He and I were the only ones that weren't surprised when it happened. The Hollywood Bowl people were thoroughly upset with us for doing it. One of the prime things is to stay out of the pond."
                                                  Bill Chadwick

The Monkees entered the studio in earnest for the first time since March, spending two weeks recording the tracks for their fourth album before departing for their summer concert tour.

Meanwhile, Davy was busy promoting his new record label. He and Davy Jones Records executives spent $25,000 on a contest promotion run by fifty radio stations across the United States. Teenage contest entrants wrote essays on "Why Davy Jones is Your Favorite Monkee." The fifty winners and their parents attended dinner and recording sessions with Davy in California. Davy produced the recording session.

1967

Photo by Bill Chadwick.

June 16-18 Monterey, California, was the site of one of the first big outdoor music festivals, attracting acts from all over the pop world. The weekend-long pop festival formula became a trademark of the late sixties and the hippie movement. Peter and Micky attended, Micky in his Indian chief's headdress, and Peter onstage to introduce a few acts, including Lou Rawls and Buffalo Springfield.

June 24-28 The Monkees arrived in Paris and checked into the prestigious Hotel George V. They and their crew enjoyed a couple days of sightseeing before beginning filming for the "Monkees In Paris" TV episode.

June 24 They'd said it couldn't happen. A Monkees record made by The Monkees without Don Kirshner couldn't possibly make it to Number 1, but "Headquarters" zoomed to the top spot in its third week on Billboard's LP chart. The following week it was topped by the Beatles' masterpiece concept album, "Sgt. Pepper's Lonely Hearts Club Band," but "Headquarters" remained at the Number 2 spot behind "Sgt. Pepper" for eleven weeks.

June 29 The Monkees arrived in England to kick off their summer tour with a series of five concerts at Wembley's Empire Pool in London. The Monkees held a press conference in the Buckingham Suite Ballroom of Kensington's Royal Garden Hotel. Reportedly, more journalists attended The Monkees' event than were at Winston Churchill's press conference at the end of World War II. Micky made an appearance on "The Top of The Pops" TV show.

June 30-31 The Monkees' concerts at Empire Pool drew 10,000 fans each. A few days before, Rolling Stones Mick Jagger and Keith Richards had been convicted on a drug rap, so Micky and Mike wore black armbands in sympathy. Pictures of Jagger and Richards were included in the barrage of images flashed on the screen above the stage during the concert.

Afterwards, the boys partied at a London nightclub with such pop culture luminaries as George Harrison, Pattie Boyd, Brian Jones, Jeff Beck, Pete Townsend, Keith Moon, Lulu, and Spencer Davis. Micky was accompanied by "Top of The Pops" model, Samantha Juste.

▶ The landing at London's Heathrow Airport, June 1967, was almost a disaster due to sudden wind shear. The edge was taken off the moment, however, when TV crews announced that they were not quite ready and requested that the Monkees go back into the plane and wait for a cue.
Photo by Bill Chadwick.

Photo by Bill Chadwick.

1967

Micky in the Monkee equivalent of a kid in a candy store.
Photo by Henry Diltz.

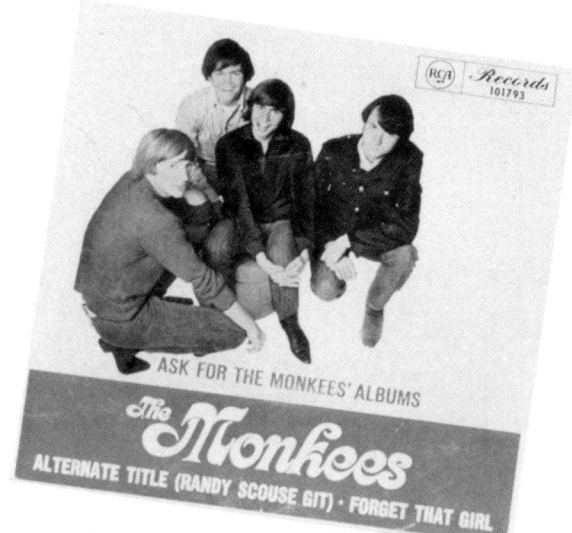

Australian pressing with sleeve. Many foreign countries released it as a single, but the U.S. did not.

JULY 1967

July 1   To coincide with the massive publicity surrounding The Monkees' concert in London, RCA released a track from the new "Headquarters" album as a single in Britain, "Randy Scouse Git," written by Micky.

"The only big hit I had I wrote here in England when I was over here and I met the Beatles, and it inspired me to write a song called 'Randy Scouse Git,' which I heard on that show 'Til Death Do Us Part'."

Micky Dolenz

The slang phrase, which was a harmless piece of nonsense to Micky, was translatable in England as "horny Liverpudlian bastard," and British record executives knew they would have a tough time getting the record played on the air under that title. They replaced the offensive phrase with "Alternate Title," and the single zoomed up the charts.

▶ Sound check prior to opening concert, Wimbledon, England, July 1967.
Photos by Bill Chadwick.

1967

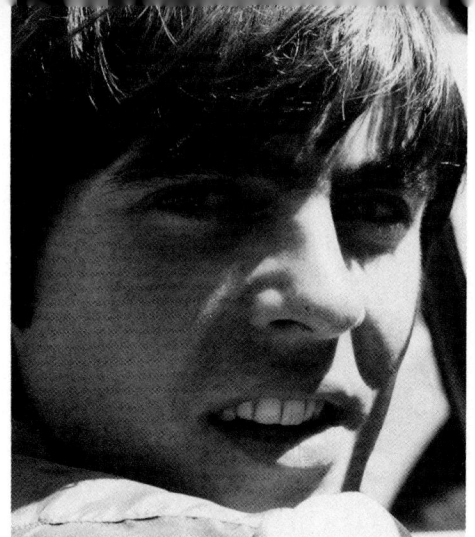
Photo by Bill Chadwick.

July 7 The Monkees appeared on "The Top of The Pops" TV show and screened an excerpt from their London press conference. The opening show of the American concert tour had been scheduled for this date in Atlanta, but The Monkees had begged for more time off after the English gigs. The first American date was the following night in Florida.

July 10 "Pleasant Valley Sunday" was released.

July 14-16 The Monkees invaded New York City for a three-date concert at Forest Hills Tennis Stadium. This was *the* most important stop on the U.S. tour, with a potential attendance of 42,522 over the three nights. Actual attendance was 36,192, as threatening weather held back the crowds. *Billboard* said that "The Monkees demonstrated they could carry a live show and maintain the level of excitement throughout."

"When we went out to do Forest Hills concert, the first day it was really crazy. The second day Neko [Cholis], Charlie [Rocket], David [Price], David Pearl, Rick Klein, and I got these machine gun versions of squirt guns. You could just squirt and squirt, and they held probably about two quarts of water and they lasted a pretty good long time, and we used them for the crowd control. That worked great the first day. The next day they all came back and *they* had squirt guns!"
Bill Chadwick

Jimi Hendrix, the experimental guitar virtuoso, had joined the Monkees' tour as one of the opening acts. Micky had discovered Hendrix in England on one of his trips there, and the two were reunited at Monterey when Hendrix performed in the pop festival. Micky was impressed with his music and invited him along on the tour. Hendrix, who was well known in England but sorely needed stateside exposure, agreed. Unfortunately, The Monkees' fans were not so agreeable. They were too anxious to see The Monkees to appreciate any opening act, and their parents were offended by Hendrix's onstage antics. At Forest Hills, Jimi Hendrix was booed off the stage and, by mutual consent, he and The Monkees parted company. The Monkees were left with two opening acts for the remainder of the tour, The Sundowners, and Australian singer Lynn Randell.

Monkees' fans set up camp around the guys' hotel in New York City, frantically trying any and all methods to meet the boys. None could maneuver past the first floor security force. Finally, a truckman delivered a large crate labeled "Love Gift," addressed to Michael Nesmith. When the boys pried off the lid, out popped a young female Monkeemaniac who flung herself at Michael!

July 29 A concert scheduled in Detroit was cancelled due to the riots and curfew there, but was re-scheduled for a matinee on August 13.

When they were not performing live shows or hiding from crazed fans in hotel rooms, The Monkees were busy in the recording studio. In New York, Davy put the finishing touches to "Star Collector" and a new version of "She Hangs Out," and Micky cut the harmony for "Daydream Believer." At recording sessions in Chicago, the guys cut "Salesman," "Cuddly Toy," and "Ríu Chíu." They also went into Fred Niles' film studio there to film segments for the television series, musical numbers done against a rainbow background. These were added to the end of the second season episodes, although unrelated to the plot.

Meanwhile, the first season Monkees episodes were in their summer reruns. The weekly shows had already served very successfully as half-hour commercials for the first two albums. Now there were new records on the market to be plugged. Cleverly, the producers replaced the original soundtracks to the episodes with cuts from the new records.

AIR DATE	NEW SONG ADDED	EPISODE TITLE
May 1, 1967	"A Little Bit Me, A Little Bit You"	Monkee See, Monkee Die
May 8, 1967	"You Told Me" "The Girl I Knew Somewhere"	Royal Flush
May 15, 1967	"A Little Bit Me, A Little Bit You" "The Girl I Knew Somewhere"	Your Friendly Neighborhood Kidnappers
May 22, 1967	"You Told Me"	Monkee vs. Machine
May 29, 1967	"Shades Of Gray"	Success Story
June 19, 1967	"Randy Scouse Git"	The Spy Who Came In From The Cool
June 26, 1967	"For Pete's Sake"	I've Got A Little Song Here
July 10, 1967	"Words"	Here Come The Monkees-- The Pilot
July 17, 1967	"Pleasant Valley Sunday"	The Case of The Missing Monkee
July 31, 1967	"Words"	Monkee Chow Mein
August 7, 1967	"Pleasant Valley Sunday"	Captain Crocodile
August 14, 1967	"Forget That Girl"	One Man Shy (Peter & The Debutante)
August 21, 1967	"You Just May Be The One"	The Chaperone

The producers replaced the original soundtrack songs in some rerun episodes with cuts from new records.

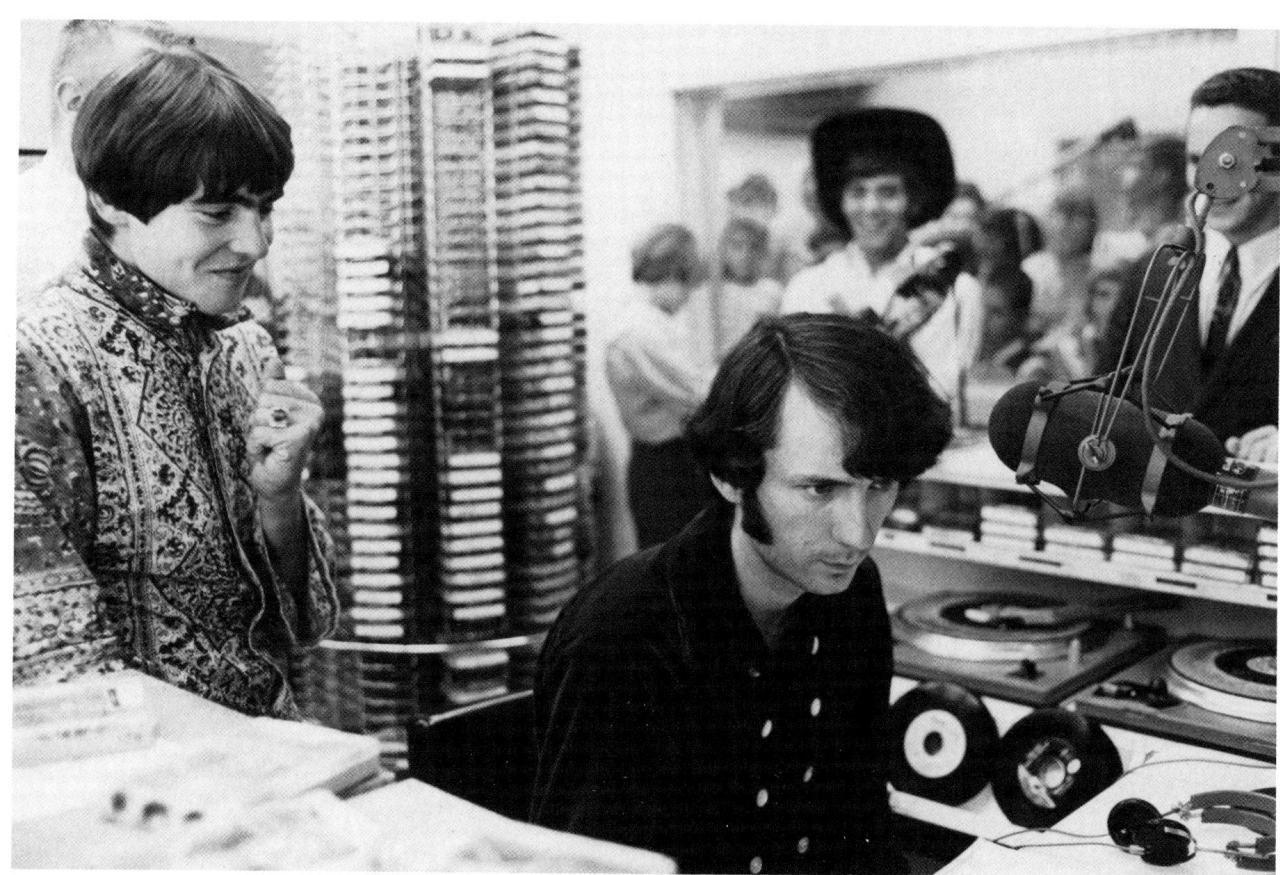

◀ Micky and Davy in the studio with Bill Chadwick.
Photo by Henry Diltz.

AUGUST 1967

August 2 In Milwaukee, a second concert was cancelled due to violence, and could not be re-scheduled.

August 4 After a gig in Minneapolis, a female fan stowed away on The Monkees' tour plane. It took off for St. Louis, and her father threatened to bring charges against everyone for transporting a minor across state lines, a felony.

August 12 *Billboard* reported that "Shades of Gray" was being aired as a single in Milwaukee. Two weeks later *Billboard* reported that RCA had just rush-released "You Just May Be The One" as the latest Monkees single. In fact, no single from the "Headquarters" album was ever released in the United States.

◀ Each tour stop included a visit to the radio station hosting the concert.
Photo by Henry Diltz.

August 25-27 The Monkees played the last three dates on their 1967 tour in the Pacific Northwest. All three concerts were recorded, with the intent of releasing a live Monkees album at a later date.

Screen Gems-Columbia decided to attempt a follow-up to The Monkees' enormous success with another group, The Lewis & Clarke Expedition. This was also a "packaged" act, with carefully designed Old West wardrobe, convenient pseudonyms for band members, and a clever logo the group's name shaped to fit the silhouette of the continental U.S., not unlike the way The Monkees' name had been designed in the shape of an electric guitar. Lewis & Clarke were the first group since the Monkees to release a record on Colgems, and their first single, "I Feel Good," was greatly hyped and a moderate success.

1967

Photo by Henry Diltz.

SEPTEMBER 1967

The Monkees returned to Hollywood after their grueling summer tour to finish filming the second season episodes. By this time, filming had become the most routine and easiest part of their job. They were also able to return to a lifestyle that was somewhat "private," at least when compared to the previous two months of being trapped in hotel rooms due to the pandemonium outside.

Recording was neglected, as they had done enough during the tour to tide them over for a while. There was still lots of material on the shelf awaiting release.

▶ All photos by Bill Chadwick.

1967

Photo by Henry Diltz.

Monkees second and final appearance on the cover of "TV Guide."
Reprinted with permission from "TV Guide®" magazine. Copyright © 1967 by Triangle Publications, Inc., Radnor, Pennsylvania.

September 11 "The Monkees" TV show began its second season on NBC against brand new competition, "Cowboy in Africa" on ABC, and the long-running ratings winner, "Gunsmoke," on CBS. *Billboard* tagged the Monkees' season debut "inane even by their standards." They were saddled with leftover scripts from the first season; in fact, all the episodes filmed before the boys left for their summer tour were done with first year rejects. When filming resumed this month, however, things had changed.

"The scripts got better . . . the writers had settled down, had vacations, and got into the scripts. They were a lot realer, a lot more meaty. There's more about who we were, reality, less contrived situations, less pure situation comedy, and more on what could *The Monkees* really get into, who were these guys. I thought the sense of humor was much meatier, too."

Peter Tork

Photo by Bill Chadwick.

OCTOBER 1967

With "Pleasant Valley Sunday" falling off the charts, the time had come to release another single to keep The Monkees constantly at the attention of the record-buying public. "Love Is Only Sleeping," another cut from the forthcoming fourth album, was slated as the next single, with "Daydream Believer" as the B side. RCA wanted it released simultaneously in England and the United States. Unfortunately, a foul-up occurred in the shipment of the tapes to the United Kingdom and they did not arrive in time for the record to be pressed. Meanwhile, in the states, RCA executives expressed concern that the song's title would be cause for censorship by radio station programmers, especially in the conservative Bible belt. The ill-fated release was scrapped totally.

October 20   Davy Jones ventured into another area of business with his own boutique, "Zilch," in New York City's trendy Greenwich Village section. It opened with all the fanfare of a major Hollywood premiere. Television and rock personalities attended, along with a throng of fans who jammed the narrow side street, drawn by the massive promotion from a New York radio station. Zilch sold most psychedelic clothes available, Nehru jackets, boots, love beads, etc. Many items were designed exclusively for the store by Davy's artist friends. The Flower Power era had arrived over the summer, and The Monkees were at the center of it. Their visits to London and Paris, the headquarters of pop fashion, had helped expand their wardrobes. When they had resumed filming in the fall, they had worn their own togs before the cameras, rejecting the by now stale Monkee garb that was Hollywood's idea of hip. Davy wanted Zilch to be a place where the fans could find at reasonable prices psychedelic clothes their idols wore. Initially, there was such a demand for the free mail-order catalogs that the staff fell hopelessly behind after only a few weeks.

Psychedelic sticker sold exclusively at Davy's store, Zilch.

1967

Photo by Bill Chadwick.

October 25 "Daydream Believer" appeared as The Monkees' fifth single, with "Goin' Down," a group-penned effort, on the flip side. The record was released with a spoken introduction, an exchange between Davy and the producer, which must have driven disc jockeys crazy.

"When you're in a studio, most people say, 'This is a take, David, Take 1.' Hank [Cicalo] was slightly different in that he'd call his takes 1A, 2A, 3A, and so on. We were making an album, and Chip Douglas, the producer, brought us the song 'Daydream Believer.' It was the final song and we were tired when we got it. We were making a mess of it and got up to 7A. That was the take they used, and you can tell from the vocal that I was pissed off. I didn't want 'Daydream Believer' to be on the album and I thought they were quite wrong when they decided to put it out as a single."

David Jones

Nevertheless, "Daydream Believer" added more Gold to The Monkees' treasure trove within a week of release.

NOVEMBER 1967

November 11   *Billboard* reported that since August 1966 The Monkees had sold more than ten million albums and nearly seven million singles.

November 14   The Monkees released their fourth album, "Pisces, Aquarius, Capricorn & Jones, Ltd." The psychedelic era had inspired great interest in the zodiac and other things mystical, so the guys had combined their astrological signs into the title. Micky was the Pisces; Peter, the Aquarian; and, as Mike and Davy were both Capricorns, Davy's name was substituted for his sign to fill out the title. The album's sales totaled over one million dollars prior to release, earning it another gold disc. *Billboard's* review said, "Make room at the top of the charts for this one," and sure enough, it debuted at Number 1. The album was also notable for being one of the first pop albums to feature the sounds of the synthesizer on "Star Collector" and "Daily Nightly." Synthesizer pioneer Paul Beaver played the melodic synthesizer part on the former, and Micky experimented wildly on the latter.

"Micky was having a ball on this tune, so we let him go four times with it and just kept over-dubbing stuff all over the place. Then, later, we sorted it out on the tape. I just brought up the best parts on the final track."

Chip Douglas
Monkee Spectacular, Number 14

Photo by Henry Diltz.

1967

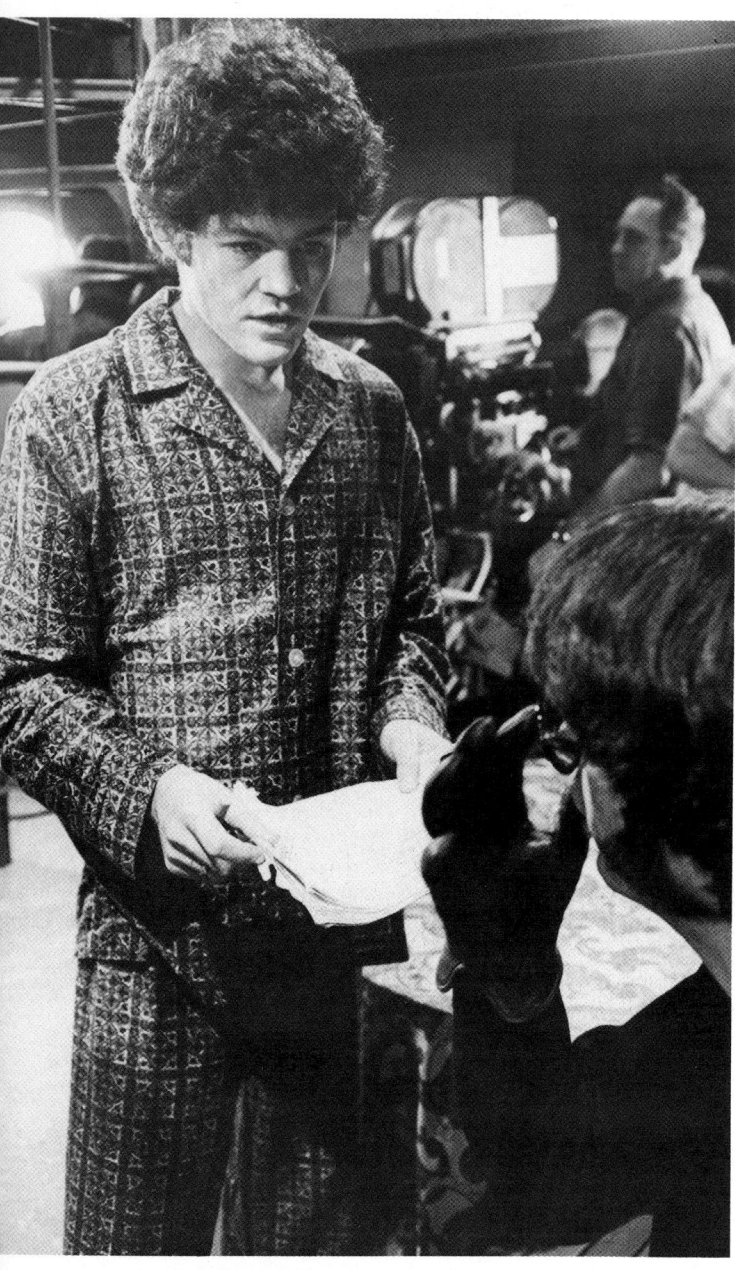

Micky gives Mike direction in
"The Frodis Caper."
Photo by Henry Diltz.

November 18-19 With $75,000 of his own money, Michael Nesmith went into the recording studio in Hollywood with a fifty-eight piece band of studio musicians known collectively as The Wichita Train Whistle. He'd assembled them to do an album of instrumentals of his own compositions for Dot Records. Nesmith served as conductor and producer, and had the whole session catered by the prestigious Los Angeles restaurant, Chasen's.

November 27 Micky took the reins of The Monkees' TV show for a week, writing and directing the episode that came to be known as "The Frodis Caper." Its official title was "Mijacogeo," an acronym Micky had developed as a child for his family - MIcky, his mom JAnelle, his sister COco, and dad GEOrge.

Meanwhile, The Monkees were back in the studio, recording in quantity for the first time since June.

November 30 *Variety* reported that Davy Jones instituted a $150,000 damage suit against Hal Cone, his former manager and head of Davy Jones Records. He demanded an accounting of all funds derived from Jones merchandise over the past year. Apparently, Davy had broken off his contract with Cone in the summer, only a few months after Davy Jones Records began operations.

▶ Photos by Henry Diltz.

1967

Peter H. Thorkelsen directing.
Photo by Henry Diltz.

DECEMBER 1967

December 4   Peter took his turn behind the camera directing an episode, "Monkees Mind Their Manor."

December 12   The Monkees appeared in a pre-recorded clip on "Ed Stewart's Christmas Request Show" in England.

▶ Photo by Bill Chadwick.

1967

Davy takes a break from filming the episode "Monkees Marooned."
Photo by Bill Chadwick.

December 22 The Monkees completed filming the last episode of their television series, "Some Like It Lukewarm."

December 25 The Monkees appeared in a clip on "Meet The Kids" in England.

December 29 *Variety* reported that Bert Schneider and Bob Rafelson would become executive producers of "The Monkees" TV series for its third season. Replacing them as producer was Ward Sylvester, at 26, the youngest producer ever at Screen Gems. Sylvester had been Davy's pre-Monkee manager and production executive on "The Monkees" since its inception.

CASHBOX TOP 50 ALBUMS OF 1967
  #4   "More of The Monkees"
  #8   "The Monkees"
  #9   "Headquarters"

December 30 *Billboard* published its year-end music survey issue. In the Top 100 for 1967, "I'm A Believer" came in at Number 5, "Pleasant Valley Sunday" was Number 74, and "Daydream Believer" ranked Number 94.

In The Top LPs for 1967, "More of The Monkees" was Number 1, "The Monkees" ranked Number 2, and "Headquarters" placed at Number 45.

The Monkees were also named Top Single Artists and Top Album Artists of the year, with six singles in the Hot 100 and three LPs in the Top Album chart. On the Top Group list, The Monkees were unquestionably Number 1.

The Monkees were named Top International Artists for their phenomenal worldwide popularity.

COUNTRY	MONKEES' RANK
Malaysia	14
Mexico	1
Netherlands	4
New Zealand	1
Norway	1
Philippines	2
Puerto Rico	2
Singapore	8
South Africa	7
Spain	9
Sweden	3
United Kingdom	2

The Monkees had the most Gold Records of any group for 1967, three singles and three albums. Tied for second place were the Beatles (three singles and two albums) and The Rolling Stones (one single and four albums). [At the time, Gold Singles had to sell a million, while Gold Albums had to sell one million dollars worth at the manufacturers level.]

Photo by Henry Diltz.

Peter and George Harrison.
Photo by Bill Chadwick.

1968

JANUARY 1968

The Monkees entered 1968 at the apex of their profession. They had topped the charts for 1967 as a recording group; they had completed two successful seasons as a television show; they had packed houses on two continents as a live concert act; and now they were about to conquer new territory as the stars of their first theatrical feature.

This month found them in the recording studio, diligently putting down tracks for their next album and for the soundtrack of their movie. These cuts were all catalogued as having been produced by "The Monkees."

"Each track was produced by whoever sang it or wrote it. Mike produced all his stuff; Davy, his, etc."

Peter Tork
Aware Magazine, March 1982

January 4 During Christmas vacation, Peter visited England and made an appearance on "Top of The Pops."

FEBRUARY 1968

February 6 The *New York Daily News* reported that The Monkees had grown tired of the current format of their series and that they wanted to change it to keep pace with their ever-changing audience. The Monkees themselves outlined a format for their third TV season. It included something different for each week: variety shows to showcase young talents known and unknown; documentaries on the background and family life of each Monkee; visits to Monkees recording sessions; interviews with young people The Monkees encountered in their world travels; and straight dramas, hour-long westerns and science fiction stories. The article also reported that The Monkees had sold 19,556,000 records to date, reflecting sales of five singles and four albums.

February 9 Davy's ex-manager, Hal Cone, was found guilty of multiple counts of grand theft, forgery, receiving stolen property, and conspiracy.

On the set of the Monkees' movie.
Photo by Bill Chadwick.

1968

Photo by Henry Diltz.

February 11 The Monkees movie, then known as "Untitled," was scheduled to begin shooting. With Jack Nicholson and Bob Rafelson, the four guys had written the script over the course of one wild weekend at a rented house in Ojai, California, by throwing ideas into a tape recorder. When plans for the movie were confirmed, it became apparent that The Monkees would be denied screen credit for their part in the writing. Davy, Micky, and Mike rebelled and refused to show up for work on the first day of the movie. Only Peter appeared.

"The first thing they were going to shoot was that scene where the girl kisses each one of the guys as it comes up from out of the aquarium. They said, 'The boys aren't here so we're gonna run it for color and lights and we're going to see about setting it up,' so they did it with the stand-ins! They didn't film me, they just did it with the stand-ins, that was all. I watched and I didn't do anything that day, as I recall."

Peter Tork

February 17 The Monkees were again nominated for two Grammy Awards, in the categories of "Best Performance by a Vocal Group" and "Best Contemporary Group Performance," both for "I'm A Believer."

February 21 The Monkees did their first location shooting for their first movie, still "Untitled." The cast and crew headed for Bronson Canyon to film the war sequence. On the same day, NBC-TV officially cancelled eight of its programs, including "The Monkees."

"Most people thought that we were cancelled. The fact is that we told NBC that we didn't want to do the same old thing."

Michael Nesmith
New York Post, July 12, 1968

February 29 The Monkees were again defeated in the Grammy Awards ceremony. Both categories in which The Monkees were nominated were won by The Fifth Dimension's "Up, Up & Away."

▶ Photo by Bill Chadwick.

1968

Photo by Bill Chadwick.

In Japan, "Valleri" was released with a picture sleeve which folded out into a poster calendar.

MARCH 1968

March 2 The Monkees' sixth single, "Valleri," was released. It was already well known to Monkee audiences in an alternate version as a part of the first season TV soundtrack.

"They came to us when it hadn't worked all that well, since they took the reins to record. They needed a hit and they knew that one ["Valleri"] was, they felt it was, and they asked us to go back. They couldn't use the one that was on the tape [from the Kirshner session], which was great. They had to go back in so that on the union contracts it didn't say it was produced by Boyce & Hart, and tried to re-create it once again."

Bobby Hart

"Valleri" never made Number 1, but it still earned The Monkees their tenth Gold Record.
Meanwhile, The Monkees were busy filming "Untitled," venturing only briefly into the recording studio to cut a few tracks.

APRIL 1968

Again, the filming schedule for their movie occupied most of the guys' time. One of the more notable scenes was Davy's big dance number, filmed in black on white and then white on black to give a positive/negative effect. The dance had to be recreated exactly step-for-step to obtain the desired effect. Rehearsals took seven days and filming took another three, so the other three Monkees got a nice ten-day "vacation" during this period. The number was choreographed by Toni Basil, who danced it onscreen with Davy.

> "Originally, my song 'If You Have The Time' was supposed to have been used. I would play it for Davy on guitar so he could practice the dance steps. At the end, Nilsson's tune 'Daddy's Song' was substituted, which was almost identical in feel."
>
> Bill Chadwick

April 22 The Monkees fifth album, "The Birds, The Bees & The Monkees," was released. Within a few weeks it had been awarded a Gold Record, The Monkees' eleventh in a row.

"The Birds, The Bees & The Monkees" was the last Monkees LP to be pressed in mono. RCA and the rest of the recording industry dropped monophonic pressings in favor of stereo, the wave of the future. Only a few copies of this album were released in mono, but the mono version contains different mixes on some tracks, making it one of the most highly sought after of Monkees collectibles.

MAY 1968

May 19 At the Emmy Award Ceremony, the only nomination "The Monkees" series had was for "Outstanding Directorial Achievement in a Comedy Series" for the episode "The Devil and Peter Tork," directed by James Frawley. Unfortunately, the show lost out to "Get Smart!" for the episode entitled "Maxwell Smart, Private Eye," directed by Bruce Bilson.

May 21 The Monkees finished up their movie with the filming of the concert scene at Valley Auditorium in Salt Lake City, Utah. They did several takes of "Circle Sky" for the movie and performed some other songs for the highly cooperative volunteer audience of teenagers. Nesmith wasn't happy with the live version, however, and saw to it that his own studio cut replaced it on the soundtrack album.

May 23 Micky took off for England, where he and Samantha Juste appeared together on "The Top of The Pops." The rest of The Monkees went into the recording studio for about a week.

"Cashbox" cover, May 11, 1968.

65

1968

JUNE 1968

June 1 Davy appeared on the "Dee Time" TV show on BBC1 in England. On the same day, with teaser ads in *Billboard* the promo campaign began for the following week's release of Nesmith's "Wichita Train Whistle" project.

June 6 Davy appeared on "The Top of The Pops" in England. He brought with him a promo clip for "D. W. Washburn" that he and friends had filmed especially for broadcast on the show.

June 8 "D. W. Washburn" was released. The ad in *Billboard* read, "Which side of The Monkees' new single will get to No. 1 first?" Actually, neither did. "D. W. Washburn" faltered in the charts after reaching Number 19, and the flip side, "It's Nice To Be With You," peaked at Number 51.

"[We] just didn't record it right. We lost the feel. I think it was a negative kind of a song. The guy is really a gutter bum. But it had such a great feel as a demo that I thought we could pull it off. The boys liked it and I liked it. And after it was finished I said, 'This is really, really a negative song,' but I lost the fact it was negative because of the feel to it."

Lester Sill

"I'm A Believer" and "A Little Bit Me, A Little Bit You" received awards from BMI as the "Most Performed BMI Songs of 1967."

June 22 *Billboard* reported that Michael Nesmith had produced and recorded six songs at RCA Victor in Nashville under the guidance of Felton Jarvis. The songs were unique in sound, describable only as "folk-country-rock." The studio musicians used on the cuts were members of Area Code 615. The six tunes were to be included on an upcoming Monkees double album, where each Monkee would be featured on an entire side or on six cuts. [It's notable that this LP was conceived *before* the Beatles' "White Album."] The double album never materialized, but the cuts eventually ended up on Nesmith's first solo album, "Magnetic South," with the exception of "Listen To The Band," released under the name of The Monkees.

▶ Photo by Bill Chadwick.

1968

Photos by Bill Chadwick.

SEPTEMBER 1968

1968 was the Chinese Year of the Monkey, so it seemed only appropriate that The Monkees should choose that year to tour the Far East. They took off for Australia and New Zealand, their only major concert tour of the year, where Monkeemania was reaching its frenzied peak.

"When I was in Australia with The Monkees the first time, it was the first time I had the feeling, you know, it's coming to the end of this now! On the tarmac people were chasing the plane as it was pulling out and there's thousands of kids at the airport, and the tears came in my eyes then and I thought, 'It can't go on like this, it's ridiculous'."
David Jones
Monkee Business Fanzine, June 1984

In Japan, one of the concerts was filmed and later broadcast there as a two-part special in the time slot of "The Monkees" TV show.

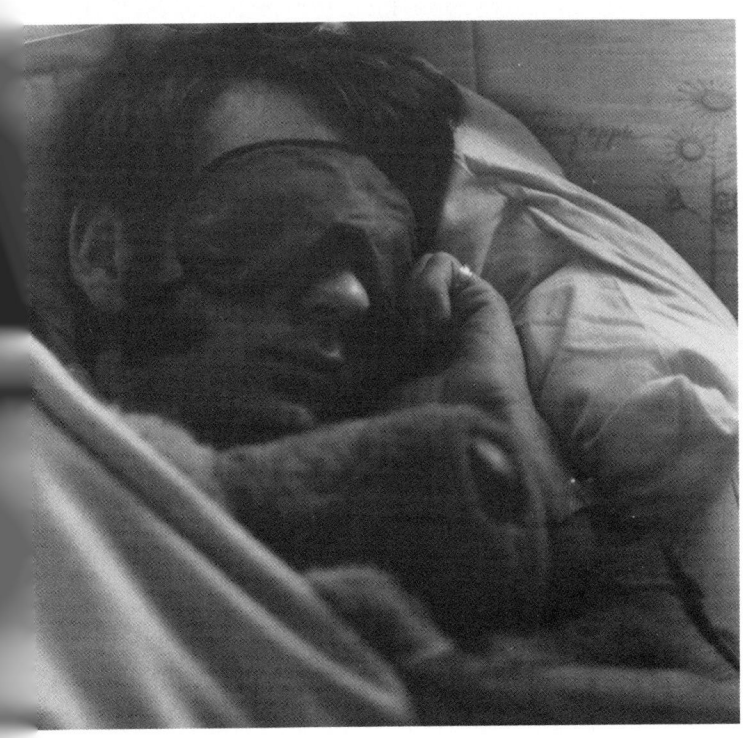

Life on the road makes for strange bedfellows. In flight between Sydney and Tokyo, September 1968, Davy with an inflatable rabbit, and Michael with a stuffed koala bear.
Photos by Bill Chadwick.

1968

The "Head" pressbook indicated that an interview album about the movie would be available to radio stations.

OCTOBER 1968

October 5   "Porpoise Song," the theme song from "Head," was issued as a single. Unlike the other tunes from the film, selected from among many submissions, "Porpoise Song" was written specifically for the opening scene and its lyrics neatly summarized the concept of the movie.

October 8 In Japan, The Monkees played their last live concert as a quartet, after which they returned to Hollywood to begin their next project, their first television special for NBC.

October 26   *Billboard* reported that independent record producer Bones Howe would be taking the reins of The Monkees music: "I want to get The Monkees out of their TV image musically and into a more contemporary rhythm & blues - country & western vein."

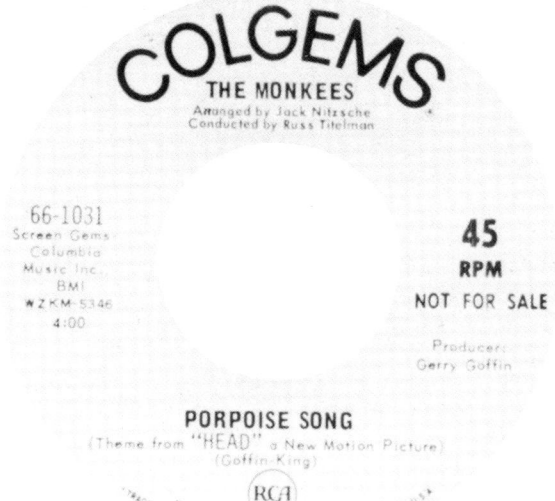

Two promo versions of "Porpoise Song" were released: one at 2:31 for AM radio, and a 4:00 version for FM.

In late October, the ad campaign began for "Head." The powers-that-be had an interesting problem. They had suddenly discovered that The Monkees were a turn-off for a lot of people. This had always been true, but in the past there had been a sufficient quantity of frenzied fans to offset the effects of the group's detractors. By the time the movie was ready to debut, however, the TV show had been off the air for over two months and it had been six months since they'd had a Top 10 single in the U.S. The Monkees were quickly becoming old news.

Peter and Reine Stewart.
Photo by Bill Chadwick.

NOVEMBER 1968

November 6   The Monkees' movie, "Head," premiered in New York, followed by openings in Washington, DC, San Francisco, and Boston.

November 19   "Head" premiered officially on the West Coast at the Vogue Theater in Hollywood. Reviews were mixed, but generally the public stayed away in droves.

> "The ad campaign for 'Head' was not designed to get either the heads or the teenyboppers. The heads didn't want to see a Monkees movie and the teenyboppers didn't want to see a head movie. So, we got nobody."
> Peter Tork
> *Blitz Magazine,* May 1979

The producers felt that they had made a great movie which could stand on its own and become an immense success, if only the public were able to see it without any Monkee-related prejudices. A Columbia advertising consultant, Jon Brodman, designed the campaign specifically to promote the film with no mention of The Monkees.

> ". . . His idea was that we would just put a head on television and elsewhere, with no dialogue, no description, just a minute of total silence in which this head [Brodman's] would appear; and ultimately enough people would be curious to find out what this was and then, when they found out it was connected to a movie, would go out and see the movie."
> Jack Nicholson to Rex Reed
> *New York Times,* March 1, 1970

The plan to intrigue the audience didn't always work. When the CBS-TV affiliate in New York aired the spot, the station was deluged with calls from irate viewers who demanded to know what was wrong with the sound! CBS refused to air the spot thereafter, but Columbia argued that the quiet minute was a public service.

Promotional button.

1968

Photo by Bill Chadwick.

DECEMBER 1968

December 1 The soundtrack album to "Head" was released. It had been delayed a few weeks due to problems with the very unusual album cover.

"On the 'Head' album, Bert [Schneider] insisted on Mylar . . . it was blank. You look at it and see your own head on it. That was the whole idea."
Lester Sill

December 7 *Billboard* reviewed the "Head" album, predicting that "the LP should return the mischievous Monkees to chart stardom."

The Monkees completed production on their TV special, "33 1/3 Revolutions Per Monkee," after which Peter Tork announced his resignation from the group. The musical frustrations hadn't eased as he'd expected; he hadn't felt satisfied with the group's efforts since "Headquarters." Peter bought himself out of his contract with Screen Gems for $160,000 and formed his own company, The Breakthrough Influence Company (Brinco), with the intent of producing both records and movies. He also formed his own band, "Peter Tork & Release," with friends. The other three Monkees spent Christmas week taping segments of the "Hollywood Squares," a daytime game show.

The Monkees were noticeably absent from *Billboard*'s 1968 Top Singles chart. Not one of their songs made it into the Top 100 for the year. "Pisces, Aquarius, Capricorn & Jones, Ltd." was Number 52 in *Billboard's* Top 100 LP's of 1968, and "The Birds, The Bees & The Monkees" ranked Number 54. This did not reflect sales as much as chart stability. "Pisces, Aquarius, Capricorn & Jones, Ltd." also ranked Number 31 in *Cashbox*'s Top 50 Albums of 1968.

JANUARY 1969

As 1969 began, The Monkees suddenly found themselves at loose ends. They'd been in the recording studio to cut the tracks for the TV special, but it seemed that very little new music was coming their way. Not only had they been reduced to a trio due to Peter Tork's departure, but they'd also been practically abandoned by those who had guided them to the top. Rafelson and Schneider had been totally absent from the credits of "33 1/3 Revolutions Per Monkee." They had taken the money The Monkees had made for them and used it to produce new films; "Easy Rider" was their first. Even Ward Sylvester had served only as executive producer of the TV special, leaving the boys to work directly with people who knew little or nothing of their style and abilities.

Micky, David, and Michael were now on their own. They had before them the monumental task of regaining the popularity that had suddenly slipped away from them. The strategy for 1969 was threefold:

1. To spend time recording and experimenting with new sounds and styles in the hope of hitting on the right combination to reestablish themselves in the charts.
2. To keep as visible as possible on television with guest spots on prime-time music and variety shows, in order to compensate for the loss of their weekly TV showcase.
3. To maintain their accessibility to loyal fans and staunch supporters by a series of live concerts, which would also serve as a reminder to detractors of their musical validity.

FEBRUARY 1969

February 5   The Monkees, as a trio, appeared on "The Glen Campbell Goodtime Hour" on CBS-TV.

February 8   "Tear Drop City" was issued. It was actually one of the tracks from the 1966 sessions that had never been released; therefore, it was not really representative of The Monkees' current work. Careful listeners suggested that its instrumental track was nearly identical to that of "Last Train To Clarksville." The record has the historical significance of being the first in a series of stereo 45 rpm singles released by RCA.

Serial numbers for "Tear Drop City" changed from the mono promotional copy (SP-45-191) to the new stereo commercial release (66-5000).

1969

A revised 1969 postcard invited fans who had written to the Monkees to join the fan club.

The various forms in which Monkees music was available in 1969. At lease five Monkees albums were released in the new cassette form that year.

Billboard announced that The Monkees were preparing a U.S. concert tour for early spring to support the single.

February 11 Davy guest starred on "Laugh-In" on NBC-TV.

February 15 The Monkees' seventh album "Instant Replay," was released. *Tiger Beat* magazine called it a collection of "a dozen mouldie oldies Monkee tunes," as many of the tracks were leftovers from earlier recording sessions.

February 16 Davy guested on "This Is Tom Jones" in both England and the United States, singing "Consider Yourself" from "Oliver!".

MARCH 1969

March 22 The Monkees appeared on "Happening '69," a weekly half-hour rock-and-roll show hosted by Mark Lindsay and Paul Revere, members of Paul Revere & The Raiders.

On the same day, *Billboard* released its 1968-1969 Campus Music survey. The Monkees were Number 70 among the "Top Selling LP Artists on Campus," and they ranked Number 41 in the category of "Top Duos and Groups."

March 29 The Monkees set off on their cross-country tour. Opening act and sometimes backing band was Sam and The Goodtimers.

"I put together a band that Davy and Micky found called Sam and The Goodtimers. They were a good band- all black, ex-Ike & Tina Turner and James Brown. We play a Monkees medley, which I gotta tell you sounded terrific. We went to the deep south. It was like my parting shot."
Michael Nesmith to Harold Bronson
Hit Parader, February 1972

▶ Michael relaxing on the set while filming a Kool-Aid commercial.
Photo by Bill Chadwick.

1969

Just two of a few singles Nesmith became involved in producing. The record on the top by Bill Chadwick was the song originally written by Bill and Davy for the Monkees feature film "Head." The one on the bottom included Nesmith's future First National Band members John Ware and John London, as well as Linda Ronstadt.

APRIL 1969

April 12 *Billboard* reported that The Monkees were busy overdubbing the soundtracks of their old TV series with their newer material in preparation for fall reruns of the shows on the CBS network, part of an attempt to update their musical image from "bubblegum" to contemporary. This was the result of a contractual understanding in which the group was allowed freedom in repertoire selection and full creative control over all future product. The Monkees' contract with RCA and Screen Gems required that all recording and music publishing be done together, but it allowed them to pursue other career avenues [like Mike's record producing] individually.

April 14 The Monkees made their farewell appearance as a foursome on the NBC network with the broadcast of their TV special, "33 1/3 Revolutions Per Monkee." Although it had been completed in December, there had been some delay in obtaining a sponsor, so the show went unaired for four months. The special was created and produced by Jack Good, who also wrote the script (with help from director Art Fisher). The Monkees were outnumbered by their musical guest stars, including Jerry Lee Lewis, Fats Domino, Little Richard, The Clara Ward Singers, The Buddy Miles Express, Julie Driscoll, and Brian Auger & Trinity. Unfortunately, "33 1/3" aired opposite the telecast of the Academy Awards on the West Coast, and it received disastrous ratings there. All plans for future specials were immediately scrapped.

April 26 "Someday Man," The Monkees' tenth single, was released. Despite excellent reviews, it fared poorly in the charts. Then someone decided to turn the record over - "Listen To The Band" climbed higher and lasted twice as long in the charts.

April 28 "33 1/3 Revolutions Per Monkee" was aired in Hawaii on a two-week delay.

From "Billboard" magazine.

Newspaper ad for a Monkees concert in Hawaii, held at the same theater where they'd made their concert debut twenty-eight months before.

MAY 1969

May 24 "33 1/3 Revolutions Per Monkee" was broadcast in color in England on BBC2.

The Monkees spent most of the month in the recording studio, the first time since January.

JUNE 1969

June 14 The Monkees first compilation album, "The Monkees Greatest Hits," was released.

June 16 The Monkees appeared on "The Tonight Show starring Johnny Carson" to plug their new act and their new hits album.

June 18 The Monkees' tour hadn't been the overwhelming success they'd expected. In most cities, they were playing to half-empty houses. They had been scheduled to open the 1969 Forest Hills Music Festival on June 21, but were forced to cancel only three days before due to poor ticket sales. Several other dates were cancelled in the same way. Micky shot a promotional film to send to disc jockeys all across the country, alerting them to the "new" Monkees and their "fabulous" concert show. Between concert dates, the boys spent time in the studio recording new material.

79

1969

Photo by Bill Chadwick.

JULY 1969

July 19 The Monkees appeared on "The Johnny Cash Show" on ABC-TV. The Monkees performed live a Nesmith composition entitled "Nine Times Blue," after which they accompanied Johnny Cash on a nonsense song called "Everybody Loves A Nut."

AUGUST 1969

As the popularity of The Monkees as a group waned, only Davy seemed to maintain a faithful following. He kept up a high visibility, much higher than his fellow Monkees, with many solo appearances and guest spots on television. Even the teen magazines managed to find something to write about Davy in each issue, while often omitting Micky and Michael entirely. It began to look like Davy would be the only one to survive The Monkees' experience with a successful solo career. Then *Tiger Beat*, one of the last strongholds of Monkee fandom, delivered the devastating blow. In its September 1969 issue, *Tiger Beat* announced that Davy had been secretly married for twenty months and had a ten-month-old daughter. Most of the remaining die-hard fans were shocked by the news and felt betrayed by Davy. While the magazines got a lot of mileage out of the story, the whole episode only did further damage to The Monkees' already sagging image.

August 30 "33 1/3 Revolutions Per Monkee" was shown in black and white on BBC1 in England.

Photo by Bill Chadwick.

Kool-Aid ad.
Photo by Henry Diltz.

SEPTEMBER 1969

September 6 "Good Clean Fun," single Number 11 for the group, was released. Both *Billboard* and *Cashbox* expressed high hopes that the flip side, "Mommy & Daddy," would reestablish The Monkees on the charts.

September 13 The Monkees' TV series returned to television, part of the CBS network's Saturday morning line-up. New songs had replaced the originals in the soundtrack in the hopes of capturing a new audience. Apparently this succeeded to some extent. The reruns, broadcast at noon, broke all ratings records for a weekend daytime network show. One ratings service reported that over half the households in America with TV sets were watching "The Monkees" in its new time slot.

The trio also starred in a series of TV commercials for "Kool-Aid," "Frosted Flakes," and other kids' products; the ads were aired during the time slot of the show.

September 17 Davy's solo appearance on "Laugh-In" was aired on BBC2 in England.

Colgems tried to give their record label a facelift. The old label showed the Columbia and Screen Gems logos, while the new label replaced them with the Cogems logo.

1969

One of the major merchandise campaigns of late 1969 was for the infamous cereal box records. Here's a newspaper ad promoting them.

OCTOBER 1969

October 6 The Monkees trio guest-starred on "Laugh-In" on NBC-TV, a timely appearance as their new album was due out in a few days.

October 11 The Monkees' second album as a trio, "The Monkees Present Micky, David & Michael," was released. Their individual styles came through more strongly than ever before on the new tracks, although a couple cuts, "Looking For The Good Times" and "Ladies Aid Society," were warmed over from 1966.

"There were things that we shouldn't have cut with them, like 'Ladies Aid Society.' It was that we had some freedom in the studio to fool around with and experiment and [we] took advantage of it. They couldn't believe that one when we sent it in! It was meant to be an 'Octopus's Garden'."

Bobby Hart

NOVEMBER 1969

November 9 Davy appeared on the syndicated show "Music Bag," aired this date in New York City. He sang "Someday Man."

November 24 Davy appeared on "The Tennessee Ernie Ford Show Special" on NBC-TV.

November 30 Mike, Davy, and Micky performed their final concert before 2,000 people. After the concert, Michael announced he was leaving the trio to form his own group, The First National Band. Micky and Davy confirmed that they intended to continue as The Monkees, at least until the end of their contract.

"There was some money that was due to me, and some other things, that in order for me to go on to a solo career I had to abandon, and so I did that. So, that idea sprang up, 'Oh, Nesmith made this move where he bought his contract out!' Basically, I didn't. I made this move where I gave up the contract, the monies that were due to me, in order to get a solo career going."

Michael Nesmith interview with Eric Lefcowitz January 22, 1985

On the same date The Monkees' group appearance on "Laugh-In" was aired on BBC2 in England.

DECEMBER 1969

December 8 Davy began a week-long appearance on the NBC-TV game show, "Love Letters to Laugh-In."

December 22 Davy appeared as guest host of ABC-TV's "Music Scene" special.

December 31 Davy sang "Scarborough Fair" on ITV's "Pea Picker in Picadilly" in England.

Cashbox ranked The Monkees at Number 49 on their list of the "Top 52 Vocal Groups for 1969."

The 70's

1970

The Monkees had begun 1969 as a threesome, but by the start of 1970 they had been reduced to a duo. They'd released three albums and three singles, but none had gone Gold, and their concert tour had been a disappointment.

Micky and Davy decided to make one more attempt to revive The Monkees, spurred by the favorable ratings of the series' reruns. They spent the first few months of the year in the studio with record producer Jeff Barry, recording a new album. The Monkees seemed to have come full circle with the return of Barry as producer, as he was responsible for some of their earlier hits, including "I'm A Believer" and "A Little Bit Me, A Little Bit You." The single "Oh My My" was released in April, but barely cracked the Top 100. The album "Changes" came out in May; it did not make the Top Album chart at all. Nevertheless, *Billboard* stated that "even though [The Monkees] continue to decrease in number, the quality of their sound remains unimpaired . . . with much of the old fire and excitement." Unfortunately, the album served as a swan song for The Monkees as a group. By the end of 1970, even Micky and Davy had gone their separate ways.

1970 may have looked bleak for The Monkees, as one chapter in their careers came to an end, but, as one door closed, another opened, and their solo careers took off.

May 1970 Michael Nesmith and his First National Band debuted their new act, with a distinctly country-western flavor, at the Ice House in Pasadena, California.

Michael's Monkee money was definitely gone. He told *Forbes* magazine that his happiest day was when he turned his $500,000 Bel Air mansion over to his creditors, drove away in a Volkswagen and never looked back. He felt as though he'd escaped and could start afresh.

June 1970 Micky Dolenz starred in the play "Remains To Be Seen" at The Pleasant Run Theatre outside Chicago, June 8 through July 27.

From "Billboard" magazine.

83

1970

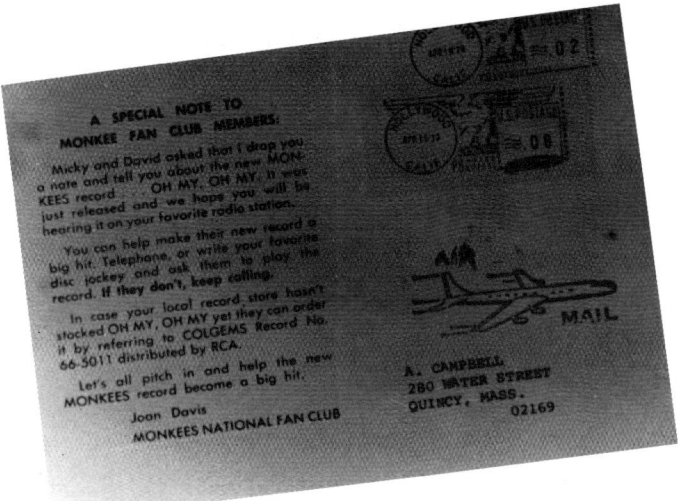

One of the last fan club postcards advising fans of the new record releases.

"Joanne" sheet music.

"Little Red Rider"/"Calico Girlfriend" released in Japan.

July 1970 Michael's debut solo album, "Magnetic South," and the first single from it, "Little Red Rider," were released on the RCA label. "Little Red Rider" unfortunately died on the singles chart. A second single was released from Nesmith's debut album, with the song "Joanne" pushed as the hit side by RCA. It had been Nesmith and the Band's first choice for a single.

August 1970 On August 8th, "Joanne" hit *Billboard's* Hot 100 chart at Number 86. Instead of touring in the United States to support the record, the First National Band was playing in London, where the record never did make a big splash.

With the fall TV season, David Jones was in the spotlight again, appearing on segments of "Make Room For Granddaddy," starring Danny Thomas, and "Love American Style," both of which were shown on ABC-TV.

Quadraphonic 8-track of "Loose Salute."
"Magnetic South" was also released in Quad.

November 1970 Michael Nesmith And The First National Band released their second album, "Loose Salute," following on the heels of their biggest hit to date, "Joanne," which made it in the Top 20 singles chart. The single from their new LP, "Silver Moon," was released, and it pushed on up into the Top 30 Middle-of-the-Road singles chart. Despite the fact "Loose Salute" sold poorly, the album received high critical acclaim. Charlie Burton, critic for *Rolling Stone* magazine, wrote:

"I have never considered myself a real Monkees fan, but I think 'Loose Salute' by Mike Nesmith and The First National Band is one of the hippest country-rock albums in some time, certainly the most listenable. Mike Nesmith? Well, why the hell not?"

Charlie Burton review
Rolling Stone

The song "Silver Moon" was re-recorded later on by Nesmith and his side-kick steel guitar player and First National Band member, Red Rhodes, in Quadrophonic 4 Channel sound (a longer version than the original). In fact, the entire "Loose Salute" LP was recorded for Quadraphonic sound. RCA originally intended to re-release the whole album in Quad, but it never materialized, except as an 8-track cartridge. The First National Band immediately started work on the third LP, "Nevada Fighter," despite the fact that they were having a hard time drawing audiences to their concerts.

Although "Silver Moon" was not released with a picture sleeve in the U.S., other countries were more creative. Pictured here are the sleeves from Spain (top) and Germany (bottom).

1971

"Rainy Jane" from Holland.

"Nevada Fighter" with picture sleeve from Portugal.

January 1971 Colgems decided to make their last big Monkees pitch with a two-album set, "Barrel Full of Monkees," to cash in once more on the interest in the group generated by the Saturday morning reruns.

Davy Jones had gone into the studio and cut an album for Bell Records. A single from the album, "Rainy Jane," was issued. The song had been written for The Monkees by Neil Sedaka around the time the group recorded "Daydream Believer." It was considered for The Monkees' next single, but "Daydream Believer" was chosen instead. Davy decided to hang onto the song for future use. Davy also filed a $2 million suit against his former manager, claiming that more than $3 million was mishandled. He was forced to drop the suit when it became too costly to continue.

May 1971 Michael Nesmith appeared on "American Bandstand" to perform "Joanne" and promote the new "Nevada Fighter" album by his First National Band. Unfortunately, the band had already broken up, so Michael appeared alone.

"Nevada Fighter" was released and spawned three singles during the course of 1971: "Nevada Fighter," "Propinquity," and "Texas Morning," all of which were released and barely making it in the Top 100. The "Nevada Fighter" album completed the trilogy by the First National Band. According to RCA press releases, side 2 of all three albums ("Magnetic South," "Loose Salute," and "Nevada Fighter") played consecutively told the story of the Old West, while side 1 of all three albums presented more contemporary sounds of today intended as hits' single material.

July 1971 Davy Jones appeared on "The Steel Pier Show," a local Atlantic City variety show, to sing "Rainy Jane." Davy also appeared on an episode of "The Brady Bunch" on ABC-TV during the fall season, singing his latest Bell Records single, "Girl." The single was the theme song for Neil Simon's movie "The Star Spangled Girl," and it was Davy who sang it in the opening credits of the movie.

▶ Michael Nesmith and The First National Band (l to r): John London, John Ware, Red Rhodes.
Photo from the collection of Ed Reilly.

Photo by Henry Diltz.

Photo by Bill Chadwick.

September 1971 Micky Dolenz had been frustrated in his attempts to land acting roles after "The Monkees." He found that he was now thought of as a musician, not an actor. He took to doing anonymous voice-overs for animated series instead. The first, "The Funky Phantom," had its broadcast in September for ABC's Saturday morning line-up. Micky was also involved in making a motion picture, "Don't Walk On My Grass." To promote the film, Micky appeared on "Dinah"; unfortunately, the film was only shown in limited release and went virtually unnoticed.

October 1971 Micky released his first solo single after The Monkees, "Oh Someone" backed with "Easy On You." Both tracks were arranged by Micky, David Price, and Peter Tork, and released on the MGM label.

88

Bell Records promotional photo issued in conjuncture with "Rainy Jane" single and Davy's album.
Photo from the collection of Maggie McManus.

1972

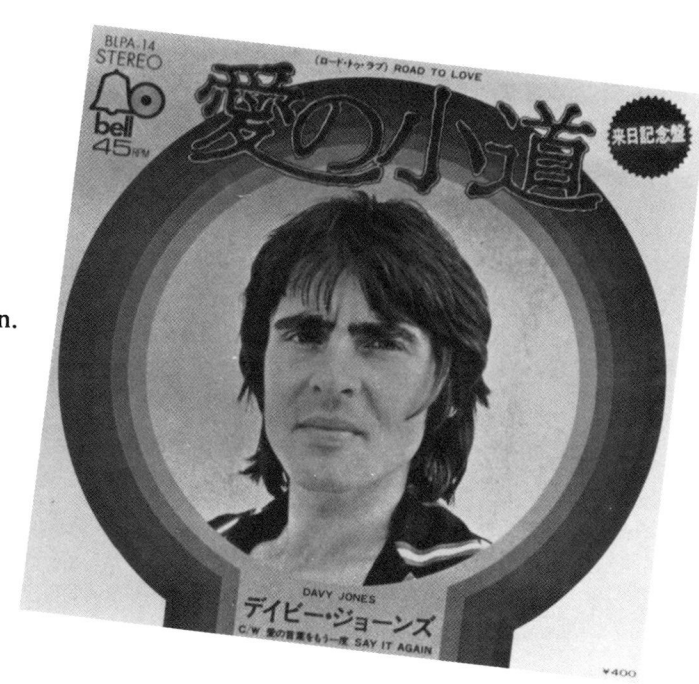

"The Road To Love" from Japan.

Photo from the collection of Maggie McManus.

1972

The first few months of 1972 found Davy making various talk show appearances to promote his new solo recording career. Bell released another single, "I'll Believe in You"/"Road to Love," but it lacked the punch of "Rainy Jane" and never made it to the charts.

February 1972 This month brought the release of the album, "Tantamount to Treason, Volume I," by Michael Nesmith And The Second National Band, a new group of back-up musicians. From the LP, RCA released "Mama Rocker" as a single. With no promotion behind it, "Mama Rocker" did not make it on the charts.

April 1972 Micky appeared in a guest role on "My Three Sons," starring Fred MacMurray.

June 1972 Micky released another single on the MGM label, "Unattended in the Dungeon," backed with a Randy Newman composition known as "A Lover's Prayer."

Davy had also signed to MGM and did two singles for them over the next few months, "Who Was It?"/"You're A Lady" and "Rubberene," which never got beyond the promotion stage and never carried a B side track.

July 1972 Nesmith began the new Countryside label for Electra Records. He served as president, producing new artists including Red Rhodes, Steve Fromholtz, Tim Hollbrook and Garland Frady, to name just a few.

Nesmith found the time at Countryside a great learning experience in the actual business of running a record company. Unfortunately, his time there was short-lived. New management at Electra did not share Nesmith's vision, and Countryside Records sank into oblivion, but not until two albums and several singles were released.

August 1972 Michael Nesmith, without any National Band, released his fifth RCA solo album, sarcastically titled, "And The Hits Just Keep On Comin'," and from this LP a single was released, "Roll With The Flow." Like all Nesmith's singles, with little push from either Nesmith or the record company, the single went unnoticed.

September 1972 On September 9, "The Monkees" TV series moved from Saturday morning reruns on CBS-TV to ABC-TV. Bell Records released "Refocus," a Monkees greatest hits LP, to coincide with the move. This month also found Micky busy with TV guest spots on "Adam 12," which aired September 13 on NBC-TV, and "Cannon," September 27 on CBS-TV.

October 1972 Micky, with Michael Lloyd, released the single, "Johnny B. Goode"/"It's Amazing To Me," on Lion Records under the name of Starship.

Peter Tork, meanwhile, had been rather quiet since his departure from The Monkees. He had formed his own band, but they'd soon broken up when no recording contract was imminent. In 1972, Peter was arrested and found guilty of possession of hashish; he spent four months in a federal prison.

About a half dozen singles were released on the Countryside label. Any similarity in label design to the Beatles' Apple label was purely intentional.

As an RCA promotion, Nesmith appeared on this two-album radio show for the U.S. Navy Public Service Radio, talking about and playing tracks from his five RCA solo albums.

1973

One of only two albums released in 1973 on the Countryside label. The second was by Red Rhodes of Michael's First National Band.

1973

July 1973 During this month, Davy appeared on Merv Griffin's show to plug his solo releases. Also during this month, Ian Matthews released an album, "Valley Hi," which was produced by Michael Nesmith and featured Nesmith's troupe of musicians from the Countryside studio. It was a leftover from the Countryside sessions that had not made it into release before the label folded.

September 1973 "The Monkees" series finished its Saturday morning run on ABC. Ironically, this same month a new cartoon series debuted, featuring Micky's voice-overs, "Butch Cassidy And The Sundance Kids," which went for one season on NBC.

October 1973 Micky put in a non-animated appearance on ABC's "Owen Marshall, Counselor at Law," as well as auditioning for the role of Fonzie on "Happy Days." He was turned down because of his Monkees' image. He also appeared in the lead role in a low budget horror flick, "Night of the Strangler," for Howco Pictures.

While Nesmith was at Countryside, Bill Dear, an unknown director of low-budget films, walked into Nesmith's office and asked him to score a film for free. Nesmith was so impressed with Dear's nerve that he agreed. "Northville Cemetary Massacre" was later released on video with Nesmith's score.

Also during this month, Michael Nesmith released his sixth and final solo album for RCA, "Pretty Much Your Standard Ranch Stash." The album returned Michael to his traditional country sound, but spawned no single.

November 1973 Davy appeared as himself in cartoon format and sang one song as special guest star on a segment of Hanna-Barbera's "The New Scooby Doo Movies." During this month, Davy was seen on an episode of "Love American Style" on the ABC network.

1974

Bert Jansch's "L.A. Turnaround" album, produced by Michael Nesmith on the Countryside label.

1974

With his Countryside experience behind him and his contract for RCA fulfilled, Michael formed his own record company, The Pacific Arts Corporation. In the beginning, the staff consisted only of Michael and his second wife, Kathryn, and financial backing was provided by Michael's mom and part of her "Liquid Paper" fortune. Pacific Arts' first project was Michael's experimental book with record, "The Prison," recorded in September. He toured extensively to promote the package with concerts and interviews, finding the most receptive audiences in England and Australia. While on the other side of the Atlantic, Michael took time to produce the "L.A. Turnaround" album for Bert Jansch.

During 1974, Micky did another single for Romar, a subsidiary record company for MGM, entitled "Buddy Holly Tribute," and appeared on a Dick Clark television special to promote the single. Micky also did voice-overs for two TV cartoon series: "Devlin" and "These Are The Days," both of which debuted in September on the ABC network and ran for two seasons on Saturday mornings. He also appeared in a bit part in "Linda Lovelace for President."

1975

1975

While Michael was busy touring and getting his new record company off the ground, his former colleagues were hoping to reactivate The Monkees as a group. Micky and Davy spearheaded the effort and called a summit of the foursome. Michael would only agree to a reunion if a movie deal were involved. There was a possibility of a McDonald's commercial, but neither Peter nor Michael were interested. Micky and Davy logically turned to Tommy Boyce and Bobby Hart, who were as responsible for The Monkees' sound as any of the group's members, and they put together a stage act called "The Great Golden Hits of The Monkees By The Guys Who Sang 'Em And The Guys Who Wrote 'Em."

> "Some promoter wanted us to do a Far East tour, Southeast Asia tour, . . . and everyone said, 'Why not? Let's try it.' So, in the meantime, in the year it took before that Southeast Asia tour came up, another promoter in town heard and said, 'I can book you in the States.' So, we toured that for a year, every amusement park known to man."
>
> Bobby Hart

July 1975 On July 4, Dolenz Jones Boyce & Hart debuted (unfortunately, they could not use the Columbia-owned name, "Monkees") their act at Six Flags Over Mid-America in St. Louis, Missouri, before 12,500 people. The unexpected reception stunned the guys, who decided it was time to go in and cut an album. They made a deal with Capitol Records, but Capitol underwent a shakeup in personnel immediately afterward and the new people in control had no interest in Dolenz Jones Boyce & Hart. The record company was spending all its time and money on a new group they thought would be the new Beatles, The Knack.

Coincidentally, "The Monkees" TV series was released in syndication in 1975 throughout the United States. Suddenly, a whole new generation of Monkees fans sprang up, those who had been too young during the first wave of Monkeemania to remember the group.

Capitol Records promo handout.
Photo from the collection of Maggie McManus.

1976

Nesmith's four-song EP of his RCA cuts, released on his Pacific Arts label in England, distributed by Island Records.

1976

This year found Micky, Davy, Tommy Boyce, and Bobby Hart still together, on the road and in the studio. The early months of the year were spent making various TV appearances to plug their forthcoming album and their forthcoming summer concert series: in January on "Dinah!," in February on "Don Kirshner's Rock Concert" and "The Mike Douglas Show," and in March on "American Bandstand."

April 1976 Micky took time off from his schedule with DJBH and guested on the ABC-TV game show, "Break The Bank." This same month DJBH began their '76 tour with nightclub shows and, with the return of warmer weather, took up the amusement park circuit again. They then headed for the Far East, where they became the first American rock band to perform in Thailand.

May 1976 The Capitol LP, "Dolenz, Jones, Boyce & Hart," was released and spawned two singles. The first was "I Remember The Feeling," which did fairly well on the West Coast, followed by "I Love You (And I'm Glad That I Said It)."

July 1976 On July 4, DJBH performed at Disneyland in California and were joined onstage by a bearded, long-haired Peter Tork, who was at the time living in Venice, California, and working as a school teacher at Pacific Hills School in Santa Monica.

Dolenz, Jones, Boyce & Hart's album fared poorly, due to almost nonexistent promotion by Capitol. The original intent had been to do a second album based on the material from the stage show.

The DJBH Special released on video cassette in Japan.

1976

Sold through a mail-order offer, the Christmas single came complete with mini-poster.

When Capitol nixed a second release, Micky took the initiative and went into the TV studio with the band to film a video version of the concerts with more elaborate sets and costumes. The DJBH TV special was syndicated and aired across the country throughout the next year. It was later released in video cassette form for home purchase in Great Britain and Japan in the early 1980s.

July 1976 Encouraged by the new interest in The Monkees that had arisen from the syndication of the TV series, Arista Records (formerly Bell Records) released "The Monkees Greatest Hits" album, a reissue of "Refocus." It hit the *Billboard* chart on August 7 and stayed in the Top 100 LPs for sixteen weeks. During the same month, RCA compiled a two-record set of Monkees music, and marketed it as a TV offer.

Also this month, *Billboard* magazine published its 1956-1976 Music Survey. On the Best Singles list for those years (the Top 200) were "I'm A Believer" at Number 8, "Daydream Believer" at Number 89 and "Last Train To Clarksville" at Number 199. On the 200 Best Albums list were "More of The Monkees" at Number 85 and "The Monkees" at Number 90. The Monkees ranked 44 (out of 200) as Best Pop Artist. Topping the list were the Beatles, followed by Elvis Presley and Frank Sinatra.

Nesmith's multimedia project, "The Prison," expanded into still another form, as a San Francisco dance troupe presented it as a ballet. Michael provided musical and vocal accompaniment.

December 1976 "Christmas Is My Time Of Year," a track featuring Micky, Davy, and Peter, produced by Chip Douglas, was released as a single on Douglas' private label.

96

1977

1977

February 1977 Michael Nesmith released his "Compilation" LP on Pacific Arts, a collection of some of his best tracks from his RCA solo catalogue.

March 1977 On March 12, Nesmith's "From A Radio Engine to the Photon Wing" album was released on Pacific Arts, his first new material in over two years. Press releases dubbed it "progressive country." The album made it only to Number 209 on the Top LP chart in *Billboard* magazine in the United States. The single from it, "Rio," jumped into the Top 50 in Great Britain for six weeks, peaking at Number 28, and made the Top 10 in Australia. The release of "Rio" marked a turning point in Michael's career. He was asked by the European distributors to make a promotional film for it, beginning his love affair with music video. He was soon telling interviewers that audio-only records were obsolete and video records were the wave of the future. Other artists like Poco and Kim Carnes shared his vision and asked him to produce video clips for them as well.

Meanwhile, Micky and Davy had parted from Tommy and Bobby, but continued touring. They added Micky's sister Coco to the act as a backup singer, and their new backup band was a group called The Laughing Dogs. Together they toured nightclubs all over the country.

May 1977 Davy also took time to appear in a Disney TV movie, "The Bluegrass Special," which aired on the NBC network.

"Rio" released in Holland.

A second single from Nesmith's "Photon Wing" LP was made available only in England and Australia.

1977

Peter Tork joined Micky, Davy and Coco onstage in California. Photo by Henry Diltz.

Program book from "Tom Sawyer."

"The Point" cast album, 1982 Japanese reissue.

July 1977 Peter Tork emerged from "retirement" to play a few concerts at the prestigious CBGB's in New York's Greenwich Village. His appearance received much attention from the press. Peter also began work on his autobiography with a New York area writer.

August 1977 Between August 22 and 28, Micky and Davy appeared together in a musical version of "Tom Sawyer" in Sacramento, California. Davy played the title role and Micky was "Huck Finn."

September 1977 Micky and Davy appeared on "The Tomorrow Show," hosted by Tom Snyder. Another guest was scheduled to appear after the ex-Monkees, but the interview took such fascinating turns that Snyder kept them on for the hour. Immediately afterward, Micky and Davy left for England to begin rehearsals for "The Point."

November 1977 Michael Nesmith stopped at the Palais Theatre in Melbourne, Australia, on November 10, to record his live concert for release as an album. The gig was part of a twelve-date tour of Australia, where he had always been very popular. The twelve-date tour began November 3, running through November 21.

December 1977 The stage version of Harry Nilsson's musical "The Point," opened in London at the Mermaid Theatre on December 22. Davy was cast as the hero, Oblio, and Micky's role of The Count's Kid was specially written in so that the two of them could appear together. A cast album was also released.

1978

Ad for the record from the back cover of Mickey Mouse 50th Birthday Party program book.

1978

February 1978 The final performance of "The Point" was given in London on February 23. Davy and Micky remained in England after the show closed.

May 1978 On May 12, Davy released "Hey Ra Ra, Happy Birthday, Micky Mouse" on the Warner Brothers' label, the official theme song for the gala fiftieth-birthday celebration of the famous mouse.

August 1978 Michael Nesmith's "Live At The Palais" was released on Pacific Arts, and the live version of "Roll With The Flow" came out as a single. Pacific Arts also reissued "The Wichita Train Whistle Sings" and Michael's two most critically acclaimed RCA albums, "And The Hits Just Keep On Comin'" and "Pretty Much Your Standard Ranch Stash."

November 1978 Between November 6 and November 13, Micky appeared at the Japan Music Festival to perform "I'm Your Man," by Brian Robertson. The record of the song was released in Japan only, and was one of the first award winners. Meanwhile, Micky was making business contacts in England and received a few opportunities to direct in television. He had always enjoyed directing and found it to be the perfect alternative to an acting or musical career, where he would always be haunted by his Monkees past.

1979

Promotional handbill from England.

1979

March 1979   On March 30, Chrysalis Records in England released Micky's single, "Love Light." The first 1,000 copies were pressed with a picture sleeve.

May 1979 On May 17, Michael Nesmith released his new solo album, "Infinite Rider on the Big Dogma." The album produced two singles, "Magic" backed with "Dance," and "Cruisin'" backed with "Horserace." Michael made videos of both singles.

July 1979 On July 25, Micky did an interview on the NBC special, "Echoes of the Sixties."

August 1979   Michael Nesmith's "Rio" video was aired on "Don Kirshner's Rock Concert" on August 11.

September 1979   September 1 began Davy's cross-country tour with his new band, Toast. The group featured ex-Seekers Alan Green (a.k.a. Arlan Day) and Peter Doyle. The tour lasted over a month. Earlier in the year, Davy had done a segment of the British TV series, "Horse In The House," and he had served as host on "Hot City Disco," a syndicated disco version of "American Bandstand."

October 1979   Michael performed songs from "Infinite Rider" before a crowd on 7,000 at Compton Terrace, Phoenix, Arizona, on October 28.

December 1979   Beginning December 22, Davy opened a six-week run as the star of the Christmas pantomime, "Jack & The Beanstalk," at Empire Theatre in Liverpool, England.

The 80's

1980

The first few months of 1980 found Peter on the road performing an extensive tour across the United States, backed by a band called Cottonmouth. When asked about his return to show business, Peter explained that he left the business because he couldn't handle the pressures and frustrations. Then he had discovered that every walk of life had its own equivalent frustrations--show business just had more money and personal satisfaction to offer.

In 1980, Davy also toured from March through October throughout the British Isles.

June 1980 Michael's "Cruisin'" video aired on "Don Kirshner's Rock Concert" on June 20.

July 1980 On July 25, Peter made his first appearance in many years on the syndicated "Uncle Floyd Show," doing an interview and lipsynching two songs.

September 1980 On September 6, Micky began directing the "Metal Micky" comedy series in England.

On September 7, Micky, Davy, Peter, and Michael were set to reunite to present the award for "Best Comedy Show" at the annual Emmy Awards in southern California. Unfortunately, the ongoing actors' union strike caused most of the industry's finest to boycott the awards ceremony and The Monkees decided to honor the strike.

On September 25, Peter made a second appearance on "The Uncle Floyd Show."

October 1980 Kodak began broadcasting a new television commercial in Japan which featured the song, "Daydream Believer." The song became an instant hit, as radio stations were deluged with requests for it. Shortly afterward, "The Monkees" TV series went on the air on a daily basis in Tokyo.

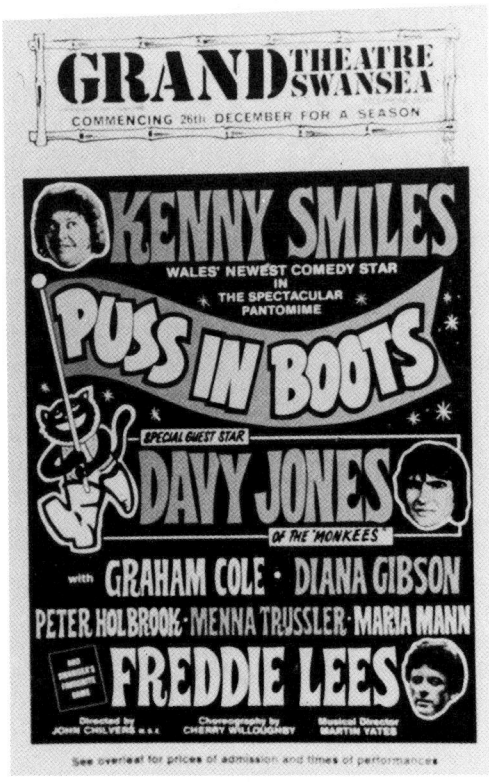

David appeared in the Christmas pantomime of "Puss In Boots" in Swansea, Wales.

1980

Two versions of the "Daydream Believer" picture sleeve: the first reflected the interest in the song generated by the Kodak commercial, the second included a photo of the Monkees issued after their popularity soared.

December 1980 On December 21, Arista Records reissued three albums from The Monkees catalogue in Japan, "More of The Monkees," "The Birds, The Bees & The Monkees," and "The Monkees." "The Birds, The Bees & The Monkees" contained the tune that had started the resurgence of Monkeemania, "Daydream Believer." Within a few weeks, the albums had hit the charts at Number 52, Number 44, and Number 54 respectively. "Daydream Believer" was also released as a single there, backed with "(Theme from) The Monkees."

On December 22, the day following its release, "Daydream Believer" climbed to Number 3 on the charts in Japan.

1981

Japan, 1981.

1981

January 1981 On January 5, Arista Records released a new two-record set called "Monkees Golden Story" in Japan, which reached Number 19 there. On January 25, "I'm A Believer"/"Last Train To Clarksville" was released in Japan as the second single. Also issued in the same week were the "Headquarters" and "Pisces, Aquarius, Capricorn & Jones Ltd." albums.

February 1981 On February 13, Peter and his new band, The New Monks, entered the recording studio to record "Steppin' Stone" and "Higher & Higher." The single was later released on the Claude's Music Works label, named for Peter's then-manager, Claude Hayn. Peter had by this time relocated permanently to New York for career reasons.

Also in February, "I Wanna Be Free"/"Valleri" came out as the third single in Japan, and the "Instant Replay" LP was released.

1981

Program book sold at Davy's concert in Japan.

Peter and the New Monks, 1981 Japan tourbook.

April 1981 Davy Jones traveled to Japan for a week of sold-out concerts there. The hysteria exhibited by fans rivaled that of the early days of Monkeemania. He appeared on the TV interview show, "Ohayo Studios."

May 1981 David's concert on May 1 was recorded and later released as the "Davy Jones Live" LP. His new single, "It's Now," was released.

June 1981 On June 17, Michael Nesmith released his first video cassette, "Michael Nesmith in Elephant Parts," consisting of comedy and music designed wholly for home consumption.

On June 25, Davy released the "Davy Jones Live" LP, as well as a second single, "Dance, Gypsy."

August 1981 Davy made his second tour of Japan. Another live concert was taped for the "Hello Davy" album and a Laserdisc release. Peter Tork and The New Monks toured Japan at the same time, often following Davy into a theatre the very next night. Both ex-Monkees appeared on "Ohayo Studios."

The demand for Monkees-related products was so overwhelming during the summer in Japan that Capitol Records released the five-year-old DJBH album. They also dug into their archives to retrieve a recording of a DJBH concert from Japan from 1976, and released it on LP as well.

October 1981 On October 25, according to the "Whatever Became of . . .?" ABC-TV special, sales of the reissued "Daydream Believer" had passed the 75,000 mark.

November 1981 The Monkees double album, "Golden Story," was released in Great Britain.

December 1981 On December 18, Peter made his third appearance on "The Uncle Floyd Show."

On December 25, Davy paid a Christmas visit to "Ohayo Studios" in Japan.

1982

January 1982   Micky Dolenz became the last of The Monkees to take advantage of the Monkees resurgence in Japan. He was coaxed out of musical retirement by a lucrative offer to do an eight-concert tour of Japan. While there, he appeared on "Ohayo Studios" and released a new single, "To Be Or Not To Be," backed with a composition he wrote called "Beverly Hills."

February 1982   On February 5, Peter appeared for the fourth time on "The Uncle Floyd Show."

On February 24, Michael Nesmith became the first artist to win a Grammy Award in the new category of Best Music Video for "Elephant Parts." The industry's recognition of video music only strengthened further Michael's faith in the new art form. As a result, his Pacific Arts Corporation discontinued manufacture of audio-only records and became Pacific Arts Video Corporation.

On February 25, Davy flew to Chicago to appear on "A.M. Chicago" in a special segment honoring sixties teen idols. Sharing the limelight with him were Peter Noone (of Herman's Hermits) and Mark Lindsay (of Paul Revere & The Raiders).

March 1982   Davy arrived in Japan to promote his new records, "Hello Davy" and "Sixteen," which were released on March 27, and to participate in the Tokyo Music Festival on March 28.

Also in March, Peter's New Monks broke up while on the road, and Peter returned to New York alone.

April 1982   Davy appeared on the "Coronation Street" TV special in England, a sort of reunion for those actors who, like Davy, had begun their careers on this long-running serial.

June 1982   Peter's second post-Monkees record was issued, "I Truly Understand," part of the folk anthology record-magazine, "The Co-op."

July 1982   On July 8, Peter Tork made his first network post-Monkees TV appearance on NBC-TV's "Late Night With David Letterman."

October 1982   In the U.S., Arista Records released "More Greatest Hits of The Monkees" album. With no fanfare or announcement, the album went virtually unnoticed.

On October 9 and October 30, Peter put in two appearances on "The Uncle Floyd Show," which was now being carried (for a short time) by the NBC network late at night.

This same month Peter also taped the pilot for a new TV game show, "It's Rock 'n' Roll," as a guest panelist.

November 1982   On November 15, Michael Nesmith appeared as a judge on the 1982 National Cable Television Association's Awards for Cable-Casting Excellence, aired on cable superstation WTBS.

Also this month, Rhino Records, a small distributing record company from southern California, released "Monkee Business," a picture disc album featuring some rare versions of well-known Monkees songs.

December 1982   On December 2, NBC's "Today" provided a comprehensive update on the activities of the ex-Monkees, demonstrating that even sixteen years later there was still a great amount of interest in the group.

1983

Peter performing with the "Peter Tork Project" at Irving Plaza, New York City, December 1983.
Photo from the collection of Maggie McManus.

1983

January 1983 Michael Nesmith's new feature film, "Timerider," for which he served as executive producer, writer and score composer, went into national release. Nesmith made several TV appearances to promote the film, including interviews on the national "Late Night With David Letterman" on NBC, "People Now" on WTBS, and local shows like "A.M. Chicago."

April 1983 Michael attended the first annual presentation of The American Video Awards in California, and presented the first AVA Hall of Fame Award to Paul McCartney on April 6.

May 1983 "Timerider," which hadn't been a smash at the box office, was released on video cassette from Pacific Arts. Within less than a month, it had hit Number 8 on the *Billboard* video cassette rental charts. On May 25, the stage musical "Bugsy Malone" opened in London. Micky directed the show, adapted the script from the screenplay, and co-wrote the score with Paul Williams. Micky made several TV appearances in England to promote the show, and Michael Nesmith flew to London for the opening night.

June 1983 This month Peter and his new band, The Peter Tork Project, began several months of touring, appearing in major rock clubs up and down the East Coast. Between gigs with the band, Peter managed to continue his solo concert series, which consisted of acoustic folk-rock material.

July 1983 Micky and his family were shown at home on England's "Breakfast Television" show.

Movie poster.

August 1983 Michael served as Producer of Lionel Richie's "All Night Long." The four-minute video cost under $115,000, and was directed by Bob Rafelson.

September 1983 The infamous Monkeemobile, created and owned by custom car designer George Barris, was auctioned off in Los Angeles with eighty-five other Barris creations. Top bid was $26,000, a paltry sum when compared to the Batmobile's price tag of $77,000. The winning bidder for the Monkeemobile never appeared to pay for the car, which is still stored in Barris' North Hollywood showroom.

Also in September, Micky began filming a new TV series in England, "Luna," adapted from a story he wrote as a teenager. He was also nominated for two awards by the Society of West End Theatres for Best Direction and Best Script Adaption for "Bugsy Malone." The show received four nominations altogether. A cast single was released from the show in England, "Fat Sam's Grand Slam," backed with Micky's rendition of "Tomorrow."

October 1983 On October 22, Peter and the Project began a tour of the Midwest United States which lasted a month. Upon their return to New York, they spent time in the recording studio putting much of their original music on tape.

December 1983 On December 19, Davy began a four-week run in the Christmas pantomime, "Dick Whittington," at Westcliffe Pavilion, Southend-on-Sea, Essex, in England. He starred in the lead role.

Promotional flyer from England.

1984

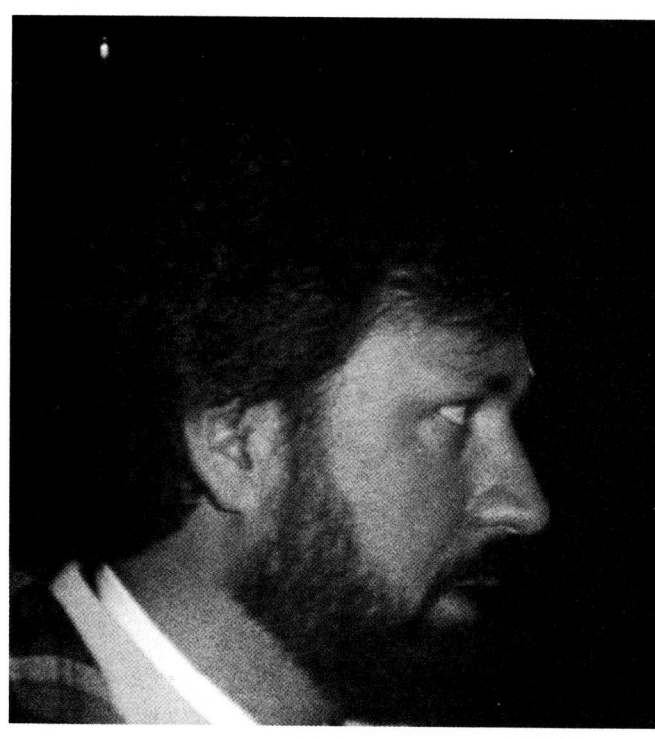

Michael Nesmith in New York promoting "Timerider." Mike stopped by to chat with fans after an interview.
Photo by Fred Velez.

David relaxing while visiting long-time friend, Bill Chadwick.
Photo by Bill Chadwick.

1984

January 1984   Michael Nesmith was asked by NBC entertainment chief Brandon Tartikoff to do a sequel to "Elephant Parts" for network television, and this month he filmed the one-hour comedy-music special, "Michael Nesmith Television Parts." NBC-TV scheduled it to be aired in the spring.

February 1984   Rhino Records released their second album on The Monkees, "Monkee Flips."

Peter Tork's Project played their last concert together before splitting due to lack of a recording deal.

April 1984   During April 4 through the 7, after a series of TV appearances during the first few months of the year, Davy opened his new nightclub act at England's number one night spot, "The Lakeside Country Club" in Surrey.

On April 9, Davy sailed from England on the Queen Elizabeth II ocean liner as one of the guest performers on the cruise. He arrived in New York on April 14 and spent a few days putting in TV appearances on "The Morning Show," a local ABC talk show hosted by Regis Philbin, "The Uncle Floyd Show," and NBC-TV's "Today" show, before returning on the QE II.

On April 28, Michael was inducted into the American Video Association's Hall of Fame at the Second Annual American Video Awards in California.

Scoop 33 EP.

Poster ad for Davy's three-week appearance in "Cinderella."

June 1984 On June 8, David sailed again to New York as a performer on the QE II. On July 17, David appeared in England in a tribute to the actress who'd played his grandmother in "Coronation Street."

July 1984 This month brought out a six-song Monkees EP from England on a small independent label known as Scoop 33, which is a subsidiary of Pickwick Records.

September 1984 Davy's ten-part children's serial, "Puzzle Trail," aired on the BBC in England for two weeks. It was so successful that David was asked to make many guest appearances on various British TV shows in the weeks that followed.

December 1984 On December 22, Davy appeared for three weeks in the pantomime of "Cinderella" at Camberley Civic Theatre, and released a limited edition single from the show, "I'll Love You Forever"/"When I Look Back On Christmas."

Peter on the phone being interviewed by a local radio station, Bethlehem, Pennsylvania.
Photo by Maggie McManus.

1985

VHS video of Michael Nesmith's "Television Parts."

Promotional poster.

1985

March 1985 After a year's delay, the premiere special of "Michael Nesmith in Television Parts" was aired on NBC-TV. It had been reduced to a half hour. Michael appeared on "Today" show and "Entertainment Tonight" to plug the show.

Rhino Records reissued "Head," "The Birds, The Bees & The Monkees," and "Present" under license from Arista Records, the first albums in their projected re-release of the entire Monkees catalogue. During this month, Peter, between solo gigs, began his own business as a pop music coach.

May 1985 Rhino Records reissued "Instant Replay" on May 22.

June 1985 On June 14, "TV Parts" began its weekly run on NBC-TV, lasting a total of five weeks.

On June 27, "Michael Nesmith in Television Parts Home Companion," the home version of the TV series, was issued on video cassette.

July 1985 On July 29, Davy opened in the lead role in a new production of "Godspell" at the Theatre Royal in Norwich. The show toured

David backstage after his performance in "Godspell."
Photo by Maggie McManus.

from city to city in England for the next five months, and David made many local and national TV appearances to promote the show.

November 1985 Peter put in several gigs, both solo and with bands of various members, up and down the East Coast of the U.S.

December 1985 On December 16, Davy and the cast of "Godspell" invaded the Fortune Theatre in London for a four-week run.

Peter in concert.
Photo by Maggie McManus.

1986

1986

Twenty years after it all began, Monkeemania happened all over again, right here in the United States.

Plans for a 20th Anniversary celebration were being formed as early as the fall of 1985. While fans were planning to commemorate the occasion with a Monkees Convention, the Monkees themselves were contemplating a 20th Anniversary reunion, as presented by tour promoter David Fishof. Fishof had been responsible for regrouping several sixties rock-and-roll bands and putting them on the road for the Happy Together concert tours of the eighties. Peter had attended one of these concerts in New York City and went backstage afterwards to see some old friends who were on tour. He had been impressed with the spirit of the concert and expressed a wish for the Monkees to do the same sort of thing. David Fishof took the hint and made arrangements for himself and Peter to fly to England to begin the task of convincing Micky and David to participate in such a reunion. Certain that he would succeed, Fishof licensed the Monkees name and logo from Columbia Pictures for 1986.

January 1986 David Jones had finished his run in "Godspell" in England and was being approached to reunite for a cross-country tour in the United States. Micky Dolenz was also approached. He initially declined the offer but reconsidered the second time around, seeing the tour as a unique opportunity to show his family the United States.

February 1986 Interest in the Monkees reunion grew quickly when cable network MTV purchased the rights to the Monkees series and aired 22 1/2 consecutive hours of Monkee episodes on what was known as "Pleasant Valley Sunday," February 23.

David Jones and Peter Tork toured Australia with their "The Sounds of the Monkees" show from February 25 to March 19, playing to full houses everywhere.

March 1986 Reacting to the overwhelming viewer response towards their Monkee marathon, MTV aired the series twice a day, seven days a week.

Press conference at the
Hard Rock Cafe, June 1986.
Photo by Maggie McManus.

April 1986 Monkee episodes on MTV were increased to three times a day. During the last two weeks of the month, MTV broadcast "I Was A Teenage Monkee," a weekday series of segments produced by MTV lasting about two minutes each. Included were interviews from Micky, Peter, Rhino Records executive Harold Bronson, original series producer Bob Rafelson, character actor and almost considered a fifth Monkee Monte Landis, author Eric Lefcowitz and others.

In the meantime, Peter and Micky entered into the recording studio in New York City to record new music.

May 1986 To cap off the three-month long salute to the Monkees, MTV brought in Micky and Peter to serve as guest VJ's, each for an entire day, May 3 and 4. The finale on May 4 was the one-hour "I Was A Teenage Monkee" special, a compilation of many of the segments from their mini-specials.

The month also saw the re-release of two of the group's hottest albums from Rhino Records, "Headquarters" and "More of The Monkees." Each album in a week's time of release sold over 10,000 copies.

Unofficially, the Monkees tour began in upstate New York with two weeks of rehearsals at a Catskill Mountains resort, where the Monkees played their "dress rehearsal" first concert on May 24. The tour was officially launched the weekend of May 30 in Atlantic City, New Jersey. A press conference on May 28 in New York City made the official announcement that Micky, David, and Peter would begin a 100+ city cross-country tour.

1986

Promotional 12-inch copy for radio stations.

Arista's "That Was Then, This Is Now" (45).

The first of the group's new material was released with a single, "That Was Then, This Is Now" on June 27. The single climbed the charts steadily, peaking at Number 20 on the *Billboard* charts in September, but capturing the Number 1 spot in some cities. MTV aired the "Last Train To Clarksville" marathon of twenty-three hours of Monkee episodes on June 22.

By the end of the month, eighty-seven independent television stations around the country had picked up the Monkees' series in syndication for its summer run, and Rhino Records had re-released "The Monkees" and "Pisces, Aquarius, Capricorn and Jones Ltd." Arista Records released its newest addition to its Monkees catalogue, "Then and Now . . . The Best Of The Monkees." The fourteen-track album contained three newly-recorded songs by Peter and Micky, including their single, "That Was Then, This Is Now." Arista originally planned a two-album set, but scrapped the idea when Peter and Micky decided to record some new tunes. The two-album set already pressed later became available as a TV offer.

July 1986 With the tour in full swing and every concert sold out, Monkeemania had hit big. Radio stations around the country were now jumping on the band wagon. A ninety-minute radio special was aired across the country by various stations on July 13, celebrating the history of The Monkees.

David at the Official Monkees Convention in Philadelphia.
Photo by George Massina.

August 1986 With the momentum of Monkeemania still growing and no end in sight, Philadelphia, Pennsylvania, on August 1, 2, and 3, hosted the first-ever sold-out Monkees Convention. With David, Micky, and Peter stopping by, the highlight of the weekend came when the thousand-plus fans who attended the convention had the chance to see them in concert the final night of the convention. Fans from as far away as Australia, Japan, England, Canada, and Scotland all congregated under one roof to celebrate the Monkees 20th Anniversary. Not to be left out, *Goldmine* magazine, a record collectors' bible, released a cover story on the guys in their August 15 issue. On August 8, MTV debuted the Monkees' video for "That Was Then, This Is Now." The video was recorded at the Great Adventure Amusement Park in New Jersey on July 25.

The month closed on a good note: Arista Records released "Then And Now . . . The Best Of The Monkees" as a commemorative twenty-five track compact disc. Included in this special edition were true stereo versions of "Goin' Down" and "The Girl I Knew Somewhere," the first time ever for both.

115

1986

The backstage pass used for the 1986 concert tour.

September 1986 Another milestone of the 20th Anniversary Tour came September 7 when, during the Monkees' performance at the legendary Greek Theatre in Los Angeles, Michael Nesmith appeared on stage with them. This was the first time all four had performed together in eighteen years. Michael joined for the encore of "Pleasant Valley Sunday" and the finale, "Listen To The Band," Michael's own composition.

Taking full advantage of the new market for the Monkees material, RCA/Columbia released two tapes in their series of original Monkees episodes available on video cassette, two episodes per tape, on their Musicvision label. Columbia also released the group's only feature film, "Head," on home video on September 18.

▶ Michael surprised everyone by appearing on stage at the Greek Theatre in Los Angeles to accompany the other guys on "Pleasant Valley Sunday" and his own composition, "Listen To The Band."
Photo by Stan Brick, P.O. Box 9483, Trenton, NJ 08650.

With the enormous success of the tour, the records, and the TV series, Monkeemania has left its mark on 1986. The future for the Monkees and their fans seems assured. History has proven that Peter, David, Micky, and Michael will always be remembered, thanks to their lasting legacy of film, video, and audio recordings. Micky has become a respected and well-known director in England. David is an all-around entertainer with concert, recording, theatre, and television credits. Peter an established songwriter, musician, and performer, and Michael honored for his creativity and pioneering in the video art. No matter what their latest work has been, however, their greatest recognition comes from having been a part of The Monkees, a twenty-year-old phenomenon still going strong.

"This morning I went to this house that a man had built all by himself. And I really got hung up on it 'cause when I was a kid I used to build a lot of things. And I know I've got a lot going for me, with the music and the show and everything, but still someday I'd like to make something, something that'll last, something really important, something I can say is my own."
Micky Dolenz from the episode "Monkees On Tour" 1967

Arista's compact disc.

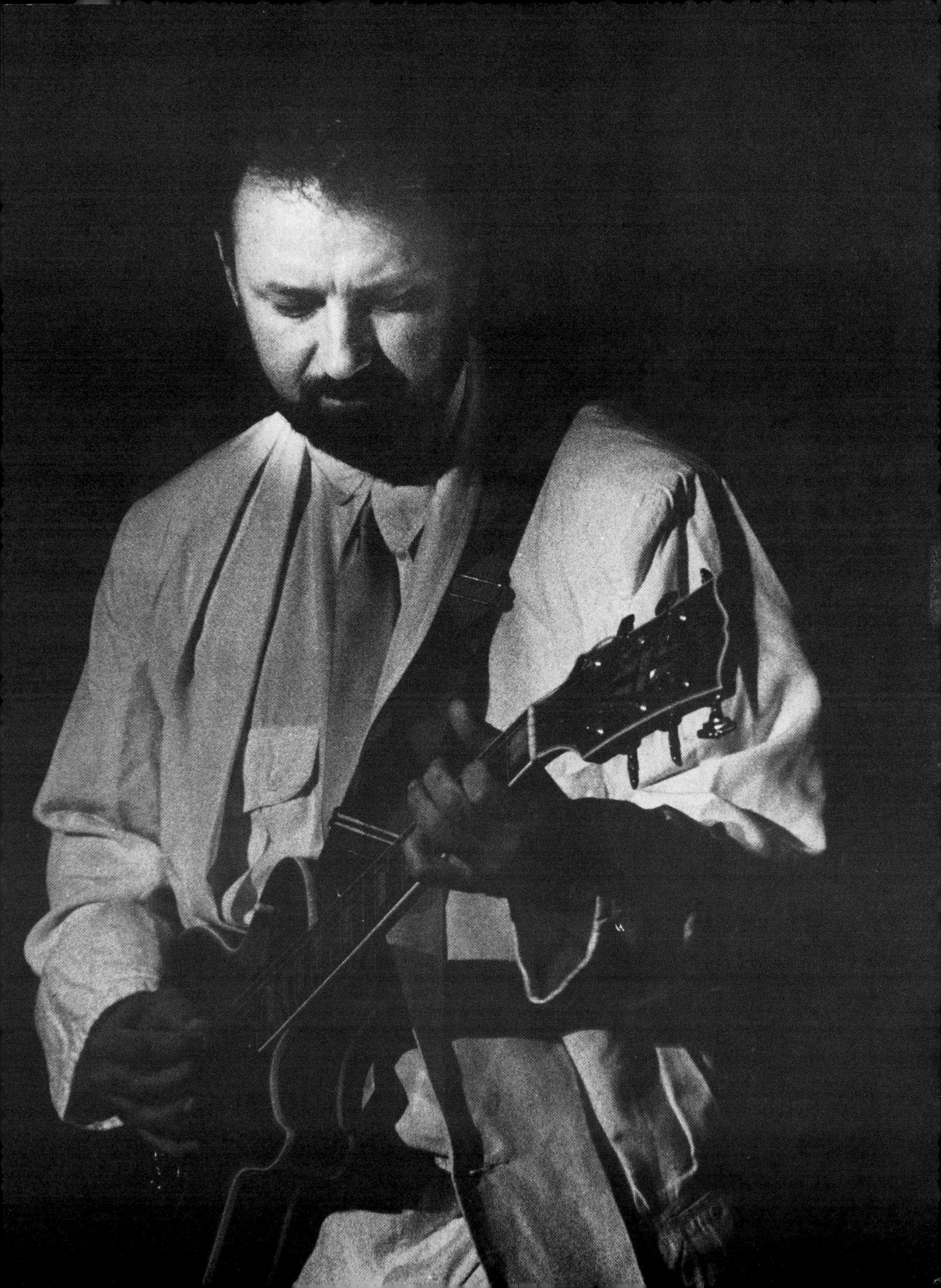

The Monkees In Concert: A Complete Tour List

Onstage in 1967.
Photo by Bill Chadwick.

◀ PAGES 118-119
Peter, David, Michael and Micky are reunited onstage for the first time in over eighteen years. These are The Monkees!
Photo by Stan Brick, P.O. Box 9483, Trenton, NJ 08650.

1966 TOUR SCHEDULE

Sat.	Dec 3	Honolulu, HI	Honolulu International Center Arena
Mon.	Dec 26	Denver, CO	Denver Coliseum
Tues.	Dec 27	Memphis, TN	Mid-South Coliseum
Wed.	Dec 28	Louisville, KY	Freedom Hall
Thurs.	Dec 29	Winston-Salem, NC	Winston-Salem Coliseum
Fri.	Dec 30	Pittsburgh, PA	Civic Arena
Sat.	Dec 31	Cincinnati, OH	Cincinnati Gardens

1967 TOUR SCHEDULE

Sun.	Jan 1	Nashville, TN	Municipal Auditorium
Mon.	Jan 2	Tulsa, OK	Assembly Center Arena
Sat.	Jan 14	Detroit, MI	Olympia Stadium
Sun.	Jan 15	Cleveland, OH	Public Auditorium
Sat.	Jan 21	Phoenix, AZ	The Coliseum
Sun.	Jan 22	San Francisco, CA	Cow Palace
Sat.	Apr 1	Winnipeg, Canada	The Arena
Sun.	Apr 2	Toronto, Canada	Maple Leaf Gardens
Sat.	May 6	Wichita, KS	Field House-State Univ.
Fri.	Jun 9	Hollywood, CA	Hollywood Bowl
Fri.	Jun 30	London, England	Wembley Pool
Sat.	Jul 1	London, England	Wembley Pool
Sun.	Jul 2	London, England	Wembley Pool
Sat.	Jul 8	Jacksonville, FL	Sports Coliseum
Sun.	Jul 9	Miami Beach, FL	Miami Beach Convention Hall
Tues.	Jul 11	Charlotte, NC	The Coliseum
Wed.	Jul 12	Greensboro, NC	The Coliseum
Fri.	Jul 14	New York, NY	Forest Hills Stadium
Sat.	Jul 15	New York, NY	Forest Hills Stadium
Sun.	Jul 16	New York, NY	Forest Hills Stadium
Thurs.	Jul 20	Buffalo, NY	Memorial Auditorium
Fri.	Jul 21	Baltimore, MD	Memorial Auditorium
Sat.	Jul 22	Boston, MA	Boston Garden
Sun.	Jul 23	Philadelphia, PA	Civic Center
Thurs.	Jul 27	Rochester, NY	Rochester War Memorial
Fri.	Jul 28	Cincinnati, OH	Cincinnati Gardens
Sun.	Jul 30	Chicago, IL	The Stadium
Fri.	Aug 4	St. Paul, MN	Municipal Auditorium
Sat.	Aug 5	St. Louis, MO	Kiel Auditorium
Sun.	Aug 6	Des Moines, IA	Veterans Memorial Auditorium
Wed.	Aug 9	Dallas, TX	Memorial Auditorium
Thurs.	Aug 10	Houston, TX	Sam Houston Coliseum
Fri.	Aug 11	Shreveport, LA	State Fair Coliseum
Sat.	Aug 12	Mobile, AL	Municipal Auditorium
Sun.	Aug 13	Detroit, MI	Olympia Stadium
Thurs.	Aug 17	Memphis, TN	Mid-South Coliseum

The Monkees arrival in Australia on their 1968 concert tour.

Oakland Coliseum poster, 1969 tour.

Fri.	Aug 18	Tulsa, OK	Assembly Center Arena
Sat.	Aug 19	Oklahoma City, OK	State Fair Arena
Sun.	Aug 20	Denver, CO	The Denver Coliseum
Fri.	Aug 25	Seattle, WA	Seattle Center Coliseum
Sat.	Aug 26	Portland, OR	Memorial Coliseum
Sun.	Aug 27	Spokane, WA	The Coliseum

1968 TOUR SCHEDULE

Tues.	May 21	Salt Lake City, UT	Valley Auditorium
Wed.	Sep 18	Melbourne, Australia	Festival Hall
Thurs.	Sep 19	Melbourne, Australia	Festival Hall
Sat.	Sep 21	Sydney, Australia	Sydney Stadium
Mon.	Sep 23	Brisbane, Australia	Festival Hall
Fri.	Sep 27	Adelaide, Australia	Adelaide Centennial Hall
Sat.	Sep 28	Sydney, Australia	Sydney Stadium
Sun.	Sep 29	Sydney, Australia	Sydney Stadium
Thurs.	Oct 3	Tokyo, Japan	Budokan Hall
Fri.	Oct 4	Tokyo, Japan	Budokan Hall
Sat.	Oct 5	Kyoto, Japan	Kyoto Kaikan Hall
Mon.	Oct 7	Osaka, Japan	Festival Hall
Tues.	Oct 8	Osaka, Japan	Festival Hall

1969 TOUR SCHEDULE

Sat.	Mar 29	Vancouver, Canada	The Coliseum
Sun.	Mar 30	Seattle, WA	Seattle Center Coliseum
Fri.	Apr 11	Birmingham, AL	Municipal Auditorium
Sat.	Apr 12	Charleston, WV	Civic Center Arena
Sun.	Apr 13	Augusta, GA	Bell Auditorium
Thurs.	Apr 17	Honolulu, HI	Honolulu International Center Arena
Sat.	Apr 26	Chicago, IL	Auditorium
Sat.	May 3	Jackson, MS	The Coliseum
Sun.	May 4	Houston, TX	Coliseum
Fri.	May 9	Albuquerque, NM	Albuquerque Civic Auditorium
Sat.	May 10	Wichita, KS	Convention Hall
Fri.	Jun 20	W. Springfield, MA	Coliseum, Eastern States Exposition
Sun.	Jun 22	Milwaukee, WI	First Annual Pops Festival
Fri.	Jul 18	Madison, WI	4-H Dane County Junior Fair
Sat.	Jul 19	Lake Geneva, WI	
Sat.	Jul 26	West Palm Beach, FL	
Fri.	Aug 1	Tampa, FL	Curtis Hixon Hall
Thurs.	Aug 28	Pueblo, CO	Colorado State Fair
Fri.	Aug 29	Pueblo, CO	Colorado State Fair
Fri.	Oct 17	Raleigh, NC	North Carolina State Fair

1986 tour.
All photos by Stan Brick, P.O. Box 9483, Trenton, NJ 08650.

| Sun. | Nov 30 | Oakland, CA | Oakland Coliseum |

1986 TOUR SCHEDULE

Sat.	May 24	Kiamesha Lake, NY	Concord Hotel
Fri.	May 30	Atlantic City, NJ	Tropicana Hotel
Sat.	May 31	Atlantic City, NJ	Tropicana Hotel
Sun.	Jun 1	Atlantic City, NJ	Tropicana Hotel
Tues.	Jun 3	Erie, PA	Warner Theatre
Wed.	Jun 4	Utica, NY	Stanley Theatre
Thurs.	Jun 5	Elmira, NY	Samuel Clemens Center
Fri.	Jun 6	Jackson, NJ	Great Adventure
Sat.	Jun 7	Cleveland, OH	State Theater
Sun.	Jun 8	Wilkes-Barre, PA	The Woodlands
Tues.	Jun 10	Columbus, OH	Newport Music Hall
Wed.	Jun 11	Columbus, OH	Newport Music Hall
Thurs.	Jun 12	Santa Teresa, NM	Santa Teresa Country Club
Fri.	Jun 13	El Paso, TX	Fort Bliss Army Base
Sat.	Jun 14	Omaha, NE	Omaha Civic Auditorium
Sun.	Jun 15	North Platte, NE	Nebraska Land Days
Tues.	Jun 17	Wichita, KS	Cotillion Ballroom
Wed.	Jun 18	Kansas City, MO	Sandstone
Thurs.	Jun 19	Hannibal, MO	Riverfront Amphitheatre
Fri.	Jun 20	Burlington, IA	Steamboat Days
Sat.	Jun 21	Des Moines, IA	Des Moines Civic Center
Sun.	Jun 22	Arlington, TX	Arlington Stadium
Tues.	Jun 24	Corpus Christi, TX	Bayfront Arena
Wed.	Jun 25	San Antonio, TX	Sunken Gardens
Thurs.	Jun 26	Austin, TX	Frank Erwin Center
Fri.	Jun 27	Houston, TX	Southern Star Amphitheater
Sat.	Jun 28	Beaumont, TX	Beaumont Civic Center
Sun.	Jun 29	New Orleans, LA	Audubon Zoo
Tues.	Jul 1	Memphis, TN	Mud Island Amphitheatre
Wed.	Jul 2	Nashville, TN	Starwood Amphitheatre
Thurs.	Jul 3	Albany, GA	Albany Civic Center
Fri.	Jul 4	Sarasota, FL	Robarts Arena
Sat.	Jul 5	Clearwater, FL	Ruth Eckerd Hall
Sun.	Jul 6	Miami, FL	Flagler Greyhound Track
Tues.	Jul 8	Vienna, VA	Wolftrap Park
Wed.	Jul 9	Pittsburgh, PA	Pittsburgh Civic Center
Thurs.	Jul 10	Cuyahoga Falls, OH	Blossom Music Festival
Fri.	Jul 11	Chautauqua, NY	Chautauqua Institute
Sat.	Jul 12	Toronto, Canada	Ontario Place
Sun.	Jul 13	Ottawa, Canada	Ottawa Congress Center
Mon.	Jul 14	Lake Canadaigua, NY	Fingerlakes Performing Arts Center
Thurs.	Jul 17	Wantagh, NY	Jones Beach Theater
Fri.	Jul 18	Warwick, RI	Warwick Musical Theatre
Sat.	Jul 19	Cohasset, MA	South Shore Music Circus

Sun.	Jul 20	Wallingford, CT	Oakdale Music Theater
Mon.	Jul 21	Hyannis, MA	Cape Cod Melody Tent
Tues.	Jul 22	New York, NY	Pier 84
Wed.	Jul 23	Saratoga Springs, NY	Saratoga Performing Arts Center
Fri.	Jul 25	Jackson, NJ	Great Adventure
Sat.	Jul 26	Wantagh, NY	Jones Beach Theater
Tues.	Jul 29	Hampton Beach, NH	Club Casino
Wed.	Jul 30	Hampton Beach, NH	Club Casino
Thurs.	Jul 31	Vienna, VA	Wolftrap Park
Fri.	Aug 1	Baltimore, MD	Pier Six Pavillion
Sat.	Aug 2	Holmdel, NJ	Garden State Arts Center
Sun.	Aug 3	Philadelphia, PA	Mann Music Center
Tues.	Aug 5	Clarkston, MI	Pine Knob Music Theatre
Wed.	Aug 6	Clarkston, MI	Pine Knob Music Theatre
Thurs.	Aug 7	Hoffman Estates, IL	Poplar Creek Music Theatre
Fri.	Aug 8	Cincinnati, OH	Riverbend
Sat.	Aug 9	Grand Haven, MI	Mulligan's Hollow
Sun.	Aug 10	Milwaukee, WI	Wisconsin State Fair
Tues.	Aug 12	Peoria, IL	Peoria Civic Center
Wed.	Aug 13	St. Louis, MO	Powell Hall
Fri.	Aug 15	Waterloo, NE	Douglas County Fair
Sat.	Aug 16	Aberdeen, SD	Brown County Fair
Sun.	Aug 17	Grand Island, NE	Hall County Fair
Tues.	Aug 19	Sioux Falls, SD	Sioux Empire Fair
Wed.	Aug 20	Bloomington, MN	Carlton Celebrity Theatre
Thurs.	Aug 21	Bloomington, MN	Carlton Celebrity Theatre
Wed.	Aug 27	Denver, CO	Red Rocks Amphitheatre
Fri.	Aug 29	Salt Lake City, UT	The Lagoon
Sat.	Aug 30	Portland, OR	Civic Stadium
Sun.	Aug 31	Santa Clara, CA	Marriott's Great America
Mon.	Sep 1	Santa Clara, CA	Marriott's Great America
Thurs.	Sep 4	Costa Mesa, CA	Pacific Amphitheatre
Fri.	Sep 5	Los Angeles, CA	Greek Theatre
Sat.	Sep 6	Los Angeles, CA	Greek Theatre
Sun.	Sep 7	Los Angeles, CA	Greek Theatre
Mon.	Sep 8	Las Vegas, NV	Hilton Hotel
Tues.	Sep 9	Las Vegas, NV	Hilton Hotel
Wed.	Sep 10	Las Vegas, NV	Hilton Hotel
Thurs.	Sep 11	Las Vegas, NV	Hilton Hotel
Fri.	Sep 12	Las Vegas, NV	Hilton Hotel
Sat.	Sep 13	Las Vegas, NV	Hilton Hotel
Sun.	Sep 14	Las Vegas, NV	Hilton Hotel
Mon.	Sep 15	Phoenix, AZ	Memorial Coliseum
Wed.	Sep 17	Madison, WI	Dane County Arena
Thurs.	Sep 18	Indianapolis, IN	Marketplace Arena
Fri.	Sep 19	Oklahoma City, OK	Oklahoma State Fair
Sat.	Sep 20	Philadelphia, PA	Veteran's Stadium
Sun.	Sep 21	Devon, PA	Valley Forge Music Fair
Tues.	Sep 23	Bloomsburg, PA	Bloomsburg Fair
Wed.	Sep 24	Buffalo, NY	War Memorial Arena

Thurs.	Sep 25	Hartford, CT	Hartford Civic Center
Fri.	Sep 26	Foxboro, MA	Sullivan Stadium
Sat.	Sep 27	Atlantic City, NJ	Trump Plaza
Sun.	Sep 28	Westbury, NY	Westbury Music Fair
Mon.	Sep 29	Binghamton, NY	Broome City Arena
Tues.	Sep 30	Syracuse, NY	Landmark Theatre
Wed.	Oct 8	Pittsburgh, PA	Pittsburgh Civic Center
Thurs.	Oct 9	Johnstown, PA	Cambria War Memorial Coliseum
Fri.	Oct 10	Troy, NY	Rensselaer Polytechnic Institute Fieldhouse
Sat.	Oct 11	Fairfax, VA	Patriot Center
Sun.	Oct 12	Norfolk, VA	Scope Convention Center
Tues.	Oct 14	Secaucus, NJ	Brendan Byrne Arena, Meadowlands
Wed.	Oct 15	Baltimore, MD	Baltimore Civic Center
Thu.	Oct 16	Richmond, VA	Richmond Coliseum
Fri.	Oct 17	Chapel Hill, NC	Dean Dome, University of North Carolina
Sat.	Oct 18	Atlanta, GA	The Omni
Sun.	Oct 19	Gainesville, FL	O'Connell Center
Wed.	Oct 22	New Orleans, LA	Superdome
Thurs.	Oct 23	Jackson, MS	Jackson Coliseum
Fri.	Oct 24	Mobile, AL	Mobile Municipal Auditorium
Sat.	Oct 25	Little Rock, AR	Barton Coliseum
Sun.	Oct 26	Ruston, LA	Louisiana Tech
Wed.	Oct 29	Chattanooga, TN	Chattanooga Arena, Univ. of Tenn.
Thu.	Oct 30	Knoxville, TN	Civic Coliseum
Fri.	Oct 31	Dayton, OH	University of Dayton Arena
Sat.	Nov 1	Evansville, IN	Roberts Stadium
Sun.	Nov 2	Rosemont, IL	Rosemont Horizon
Tue.	Nov 4	St. Louis, MO	Kiel Auditorium
Wed.	Nov 5	Peoria, IL	Peoria Civic Center
Thurs.	Nov 6	Cedar Rapids, IA	Five Seasons Center
Fri.	Nov 7	La Crosse, WI	La Crosse Center
Sat.	Nov 8	Duluth, MN	Duluth Arena
Mon.	Nov 10	Fort Wayne, IN	Fort Wayne Coliseum
Tues.	Nov 11	South Bend, IN	Athletic Center at Notre Dame Univ.
Fri.	Nov 11	Toledo, OH	Centennial Hall
Wed.	Nov 12	Green Bay, WI	Brown County Arena
Fri.	Nov 14	Toledo, OH	Centennial Hall
Sat.	Nov 15	Kalamazoo-Battle Creek, MI	Wing Stadium
Sun.	Nov 16	Pontiac, MI	Silverdome
Mon.	Nov 17	Cleveland, OH	Richfield Stadium
Thurs.	Nov 20	Worcester, MA	Centrum
Fri.	Nov 21	Portland, ME	Cumberland County Civic Center

Sat.	Nov 22	Bangor, ME	Bangor Auditorium
Sun.	Nov 23	Providence, RI	Providence Civic Center
Mon.	Nov 24	Utica, NY	Utica War Memorial
Tues.	Nov 25	Rochester, NY	Rochester War Memorial
Fri.	Nov 28	Hershey, PA	Hershey Arena
Sat.	Nov 29	Roanoke, VA	Roanoke Civic Center
Sun.	Nov 30	Charlotte, NC	Charlotte Coliseum
Mon.	Dec 1	Charleston, WV	Civic Center Arena
Wed.	Dec 3	Bethlehem, PA	Stabler Arena

Part two

The Monkees On Film

Michael Nesmith and Frank Zappa in the opening segment of "Monkees Blow Their Minds."
Photo by Henry Diltz.

TV: The Series and The Special

Beginning on September 12, 1966, and continuing through August 19, 1968, the majority of the teenagers in the United States were tuned into their local NBC affiliate every Monday night to watch "The Monkees." The following is a complete listing of the fifty-eight half-hour episodes, plus the one-hour special which aired April 14, 1969. (Different songs were often substituted in summer reruns.)

1. **SEPTEMBER 12, 1966** (Series debut)
   Title: "Royal Flush"
   Writers: Peter Meyerson and Robert Schlitt
   Director: James Frawley
   Description: Uncle Otto plans the untimely demise of his niece, Princess Bettina, but the Monkees have a plan all their own.
   Additional
   Cast: Princess Bettina - Katherine Walsh
   Otto - Theo Marcuse
   Sigmund - Vincent Beck
   Chambermaid - Ceil Cabot
   Songs: "Take A Giant Step"
   "This Just Doesn't Seem To Be My Day"
   "Last Train To Clarksville"

   This episode was awarded an Emmy in 1967 for "Best Direction."

Photo courtesy Edmag Archives.

2. **SEPTEMBER 19, 1966**
   Title: "Monkee See, Monkee Die"
   Writers: Treva Silverman
   Director: James Frawley
   Description: Visions of great wealth draw the Monkees to a haunted house on a fog shrouded island to claim their inheritance.
   Additional
   Cast:
      Madame Roselle - Lea Marmer
      Ellie - Stacey Maxwell
      Ralph - Milton Parsons
      Babbit - Henry Corden
      McQuinney - Oliver McGowan
      Policeman - Vince Howard
      Captain - George Perina
   Songs:
      "Tomorrow's Gonna Be Another Day"
      "Last Train To Clarksville"

3. **SEPTEMBER 26, 1966**
   Title: "Monkee vs. Machine"
   Writers: David Panich
   Director: Robert Rafelson
   Description: In a computerized toy factory, the Monkees - behind in their rent, as usual - put it all on the line. Assembly, that is.
   Additional
   Cast:
      Daggert - Stan Freberg
      Guggins - Severn Darden
      Pop Harper - Walter Janowitz
      Mrs. Zukerman - Dorothy Konrad
      Secretary - Elaine Fielding
   Songs:
      "Last Train To Clarksville"
      "Saturday's Child"

All photos courtesy Edmag Archives.

4. **OCTOBER 3, 1966**
   Title: "Your Friendly Neighborhood Kidnappers"
   Writers: Dave Evans
   Director: James Frawley
   Description: Publicity is the name of the game when it comes to the entertainment business. But how far is too far? A phony kidnapping?

   A short interview with Michael Nesmith finishes off this episode.
   Additional
   Cast:
      Trump - Andre Phillippe
      George - Vic Tayback
      Horace - Louis Quinn
      Contest Manager - David Hull
      Swine #1 - Ken Del Conte
   Songs:
      "Last Train To Clarksville"
      "(I'm Not Your) Steppin' Stone"

5. **OCTOBER 10, 1966**
   Title: "The Spy Who Came In From The Cool"
   Writers: Gerald Gardner and Dee Caruso
   Director: Robert Rafelson
   Description: Look out James Bond, here come the Monkees. It's high intrigue and high comedy as the boys are mistaken for spy contacts.
   Additional
   Cast:
   Madame Olinsky - Arlene Martel
   Boris - Jacques Aubuchon
   Honeywell - Don Penny
   The Chief - Booth Coleman
   Midget - Billy Curtis
   Genie - Arlene Charles
   Yakimoto - Lee Kolima
   Songs: "The Kind of Girl I Could Love"
   "All The King's Horses"
   "(I'm Not Your) Steppin' Stone"
   "Last Train To Clarksville"

Photo courtesy Edmag Archives.

6. **OCTOBER 17, 1966**
   Title: "Success Story"
   Writers: Gerald Gardner, Dee Caruso, and Bernie Orenstein
   Director: James Frawley
   Description: In an effort to impress his visiting grandfather, Davy takes on the role of the rich country gentleman.

   At the conclusion of the show David Jones is interviewed about his first visit back to England since the series began.
   Additional
   Cast: Grandfather - Ben Wright
   Messenger - Ray Ballard
   Rolls Owner - Donald Foster
   Ice Cream Man - Charlie Callas
   Old Woman - Ceil Cabot
   Songs: "I Wanna Be Free"
   "Sweet Young Thing"

Photos courtesy Edmag Archives.

7. **OCTOBER 24, 1966**
   Title: "Monkees In A Ghost Town"
   Writers: Robert Schlitt and Peter Meyerson
   Director: James Frawley
   Description: Out of gas and out of luck, the Monkees are held prisoner by a gang of bank robbers in a deserted ghost town.
   Additional
   Cast: Lenny - Lon Chaney, Jr.
   Lady - Rose Marie
   George - Len Lesser
   First Cop - Hollis Morrison
   Songs: "(Theme From) The Monkees" (with Rose Marie)
   "Tomorrow's Gonna Be Another Day"
   "Papa Gene's Blues"

8. **OCTOBER 31, 1966**
   Title: "Don't Look a Gift Horse in the Mouth"
   Writers: Dave Evans
   Director: Robert Rafelson
   Description: The excitement begins when Davy receives a pony as a gift, but it will be a horse of a different color when their landlord finds out.
   Additional
   Cast: Dr. Mann, the Veterinarian - Jerry Colonna
   Babbit - Henry Corden
   Mrs. Purdy - Jesslyn Fax
   Farmer Fisher - Jim Boles
   Jenkins - Chuck Bail
   Jonathan - Kerry MacLane
   Songs: "Papa Gene's Blues"
   "All The Kings Horses"

9. **NOVEMBER 7, 1966**
   Title: "The Chaperone"
   Writers: Gerald Gardner and Dee Caruso
   Director: Bruce Kessler
   Description: General Vandenburg falls for Micky in a big way when Micky dresses as a female chaperone so that Davy can date the general's daughter.
   Additional
   Cast:
   Vandenburg - Arch Johnson
   Leslie - Sherry Alberoni
   Babbit - Henry Corden
   Mrs. Weifers - Diana Chesney
   Cynthia - Judy Murdock
   Songs: "This Just Doesn't Seem To Be My Day"
   "Take A Giant Step"

Photo courtesy Edmag Archives.

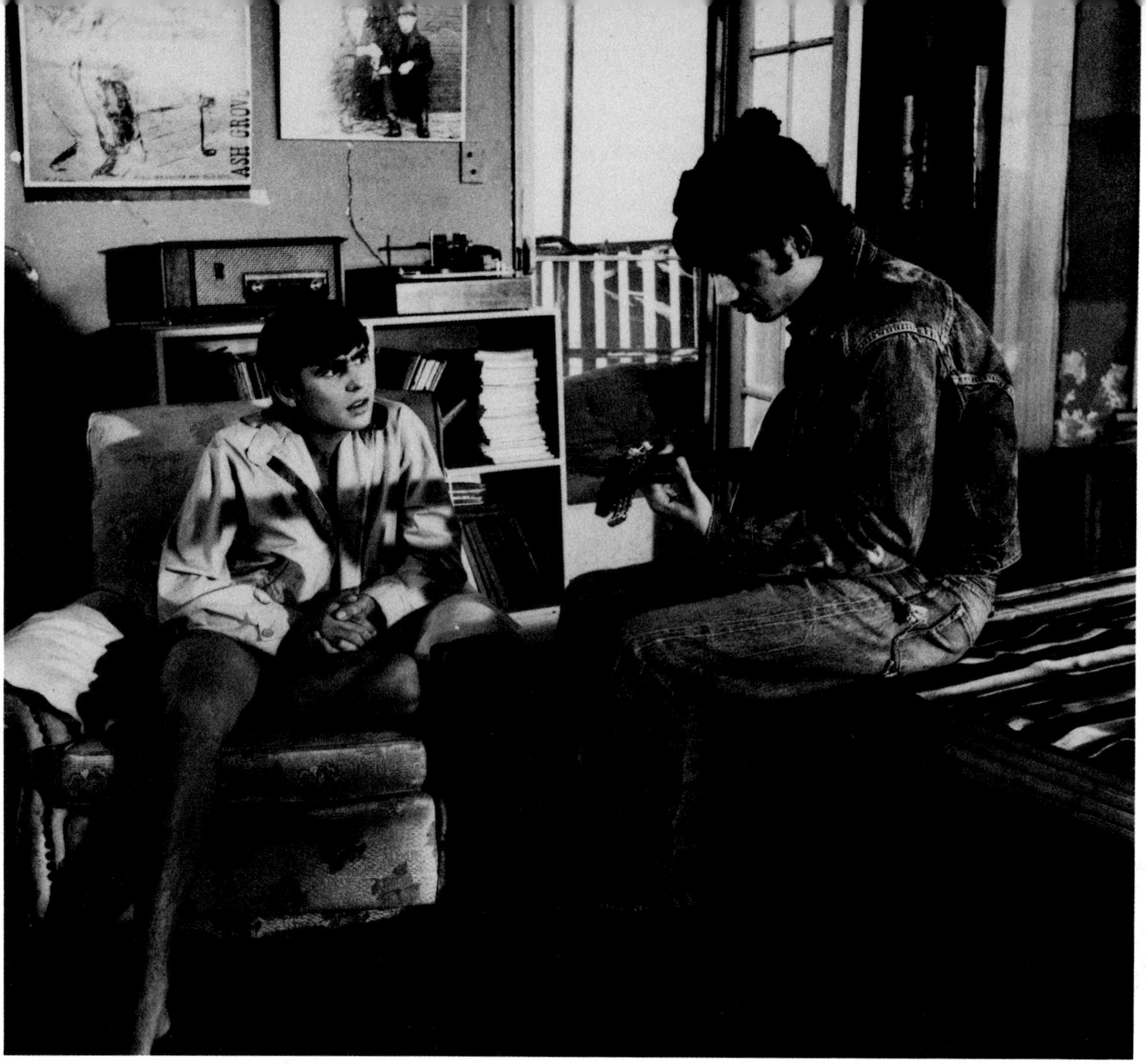

Photo courtesy
Edmag Archives.

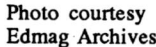

10. **NOVEMBER 14, 1966**
    Title: "Here Come The Monkees - The Pilot"
    Writers: Paul Mazurky and Larry Tucker
    Director: Mike Elliot
    Description: Before her parents will let the Monkees play at her sweet sixteen party, Vanessa must pass her history exam. Are Professors Mike, Peter, Micky, and Davy up to the test?

    As a postscript, the original screen tests of Michael Nesmith and David Jones are shown.

    Additional
    Cast: Vanessa - Robyn Millan
    Mr. Russell - Richard St. John
    Rudy - Bing Russell
    Jill - Jill Van Ness
    Dr. Turner - Larry Tucker
    T.V. Interviewer - Paul Mazurky
    Guard - Joe Higgins
    Mrs. Russell - June Whitley Taylor
    Songs: "I Wanna Be Free"
    "Let's Dance On"

11. **NOVEMBER 21, 1966**
    Title: "Monkees A La Carte"
    Writers: Gerald Gardner, Dee Caruso, and Bernie Orenstein
    Director: James Frawley
    Description: The Monkees pose as "The Purple Flower Gang" to save their favorite Italian restaurant from being taken over by the mob.
    Additional
    Cast:
    Fuselli - Harvey Lembeck
    Rocco - Karl Lukas
    Inspector - Dort Clark
    Red - Paul Sorensen
    Flora - Helene Winston
    Paddy - Jon Kowal
    Benny - Mousy Garner
    Pop - Paul Deville
    Policeman - Don Kennedy
    Songs: (I'm Not Your) Steppin' Stone"
    "She"

Photo courtesy Edmag Archives.

12. **NOVEMBER 28, 1966**
    Title: "I've Got A Little Song Here"
    Writers: Treva Silverman
    Director: Bruce Kessler
    Description: The promises are big and so are the disappointments when Mike is taken in by a phony music publisher.
    Additional
    Cast:
    Bernie - Phil Leeds
    Producer - Irwin Charone
    Joannie - Leigh Chapman
    Harry - Joseph Mell
    Old Man - Owen McGiveney
    Watchman - Buddy Lewis
    Hilda - Mary Foran
    Postman - Bobby Johnson
    Director - Larry Gelman
    Songs: "Gonna Buy Me A Dog"
    "Mary, Mary"

13. **DECEMBER 5, 1966**
    Title: "One Man Shy (Peter and The Debutante)"
    Writers: Gerald Gardner, Dee Caruso, and Treva Silverman
    Director: James Frawley
    Description: When Peter falls for a beautiful young rich girl, with an even wealthier boyfriend, the rest of the boys help him win her heart.
    Additional
    Cast:
    Valerie - Lisa James
    Ronnie - George Furth

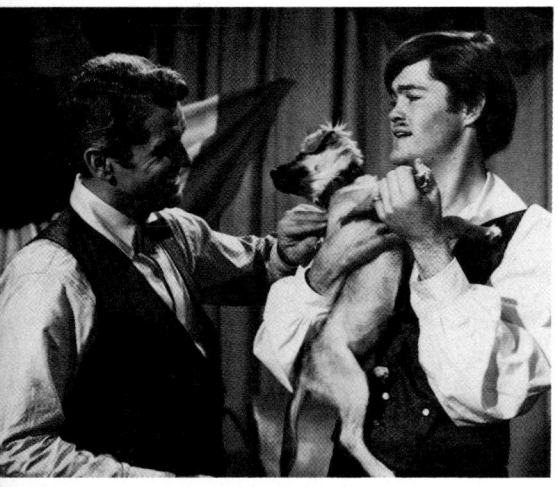

Songs: "You Just May Be The One"
"I'm A Believer"

14. **DECEMBER 12, 1966**
    Title: "Dance, Monkee, Dance"
    Writers: Bernie Orenstein
    Director: James Frawley
    Description: There is a contract out on the Monkees! It's dancing classes for life.
    Additional
    Cast: Renaldo - Hal March
    Miss Buntwell - Karen James
    Timid Man - Stephen Coit
    Woman - Elisabeth Camp
    Smoothie - Derrik Lewis
    Songs: "I'll Be Back Up On My Feet"
    "I'm A Believer"

15. **DECEMBER 19, 1966**
    Title: "Too Many Girls (Davy and Fern)"
    Writers: Dave Evans, Gerald Gardner, and Dee Caruso
    Director: James Frawley
    Description: Will Davy leave the Monkees to team up with the pretty young daughter of a pushy stage mother?
    Additional
    Cast: Mrs. Badderly - Reta Shaw
    Fern - Kelly Jean Peters
    Hack - Jeff De Benning
    Songs: "I'm A Believer"

16. **DECEMBER 26, 1966**
    Title: "Son of Gypsy"
    Writers: Gerald Gardner, Dee Caruso, and Treva Silverman
    Director: James Frawley
    Description: The Monkees are forced to steal "The Maltese Vulture" in order to ransom Peter, who has been kidnapped by the gypsies.
    Additional
    Cast: Rocco - Vic Tayback
    Maria - Jeanne Arnold
    Marco - Vincent Beck
    Zeppo - Gene Dynarski
    Kiko - Mario Roccuzzo
    Madame Rantha - Elisabeth Camp
    Songs: "I'm A Believer"

All photos courtesy Edmag Archives.

JANUARY 1, 1967 - The Monkees' premiere in England

17. **JANUARY 9, 1967**
    Title: "The Case of The Missing Monkee"
    Writers: Gerald Gardner and Dee Caruso
    Director: Robert Rafelson
    Description: Peter kidnapped again? Yes, but this time he faces a mad scientist who's into brain experiments.
    Additional
    Cast: Dr. Marcovich - Vito Scotti
    Bruno - Vincent Gardenia
    Schnitzler - Norbert Schiller
    Nurse - Nancy Fish
    Policeman - Ivan Bonar
    Songs: "(I'm Not Your) Steppin' Stone"

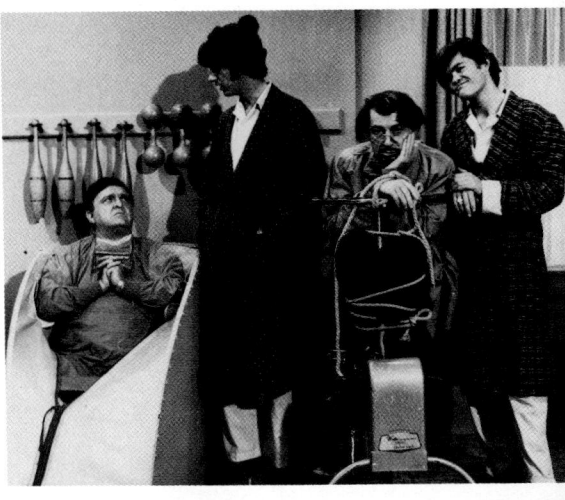

18. **JANUARY 16, 1967**
    Title: "I Was A Teenage Monster"
    Writers: Gerald Gardner, Dee Caruso, and Dave Evans
    Director: Sidney Miller
    Description: The Monkees lose their tempers and almost lose their voices when they are enlisted to give music lessons to the seven-foot tall creation of yet another mad scientist.
    Additional
    Cast: Dr. Mendoza - John Holt
    Monster - Richard Kiel
    Groot - Byron Foulger
    Songs: "Your Auntie Grizelda"

Photos courtesy Edmag Archives.

19. **JANUARY 23, 1967**
    Title: "The Audition (Find The Monkees)"
    Writers: Gerald Gardner and Dee Caruso
    Director: Richard Nunis
    Description: It could be their big chance if the Monkees could just find a way to get into "The Audition."

    A one-minute interview about the guys' feelings on the riots in Los Angeles closes the show.
    Additional
    Cast: Hubbell Benson - Carl Ballantine
    Miss Chomsky - Bobo Lewis
    Masseur - Joe Higgins
    Inspector - Art Lewis
    Songs: "Sweet Young Thing"
    "Papa Gene's Blues"
    "I'm A Believer"

Photo courtesy Edmag Archives.

20. **JANUARY 30, 1967**
    Title: "Monkees in the Ring"
    Writer: Gerald Gardner and Dee Caruso
    Director: James Frawley
    Description: It's the fight of the century when Davy goes for the title. We'll see who is the champ and who is the chump.
    Additional
    Cast:
        Sholto - Ned Glass
        Vernon - Joseph Perry
        The Champ - D'Urville Martin
        Smasher - Robert Lyons
        Fight Announcer - Jerry Hausner
        Ring Announcer - Jimmy Lennon
        Reporter #1 - George Cisar
        Bully - Peter Canon
        Reporter #2 - Richard S. Ramos
    Songs: "Laugh"
        "I'll Be Back Up On My Feet"

21. **FEBRUARY 6, 1967**
    Title: "The Prince And The Paupers"
    Writers: Gerald Gardner, Dee Caruso, and Peter Meyerson
    Director: James Komack
    Description: Davy's resemblance to Prince Ludlow may save the throne, providing Davy doesn't end up a dead ringer.
    Additional
    Cast:
    Count Myron - Oscar Beregal
    Max - Joe Higgins
    Chemist - David Price
    Wendy - Heather North
    Courtier - Donald Foster
    Cardinal - William Chapman
    Jailer - Clegg Hoyt
    Gloria - Linda Kirk
    Songs: "Mary, Mary"

22. **FEBRUARY 13, 1967**
    Title: "Monkees at the Circus"
    Writers: David Panich
    Director: Bruce Kessler
    Description: Love of the big top takes the Monkees to the high wire to save a failing circus.
    Additional
    Cast:
    Victor - Richard Devon
    Susan - Donna Baccala
    Pop - Forrest Lewis
    Sword Swallower - Carl Carlsson
    Strong Man - Gene Rutherford
    Midget - Felix Silla
    Songs: "She"
    "Sometime in the Morning"

23. **FEBRUARY 20, 1967**
    Title: "Captain Crocodile"
    Writers: Dee Caruso, Gerald Gardner, Peter Meyerson, and Robert Schlitt
    Director: James Frawley
    Description: Sometimes your best just ain't good enough, sometimes it's too good. When the Monkees appear on a local TV kids show, the emcee is jealous of their success.
    Additional
    Cast:
    Captain Crocodile - Joey Forman
    Junior Pintoff - Joey Baio
    Howard - Phil Roth
    Pintoff - Oliver McGowan
    Secretary - Judy Howard
    Stage Manager - Larry Gelman
    Songs: "Valleri"
    "Your Auntie Grizelda"

Photo from the collection of Maggie McManus.

Photo courtesy Edmag Archives.

24. **FEBRUARY 27, 1967**
    Title: "Monkees A La Mode"
    Writers: Gerald Gardner and Dee Caruso
    Director: Alex Singer
    Description: Articulate? Sophisticated? Well dressed? A teen magazine profiles the Monkees and gets it all wrong.
    Additional
    Cast: Madame Quagmeyer - Patrice Wynmore
    Rob Roy Fingerhead - Eldon Quick
    Toby Willis - Alexandra Hay
    Assistant #1 - Nancy Walters
    Assistant #2 - Carole Williams
    Rob Roy's Asst. - George Stratton
    Songs: "Laugh"
    "You Just May Be The One"

25. **MARCH 6, 1967**
    Title: "Alias Micky Dolenz"
    Writers: Gerald Gardner, Dee Caruso, and Dave Evans
    Director: Bruce Kessler
    Description: Micky's amazing resemblance to a convicted criminal takes him undercover in search of the missing loot.
    Additional
    Cast: Captain - Robert Strauss
    Ruby - Maureen Arthur
    Tony - Jimmy Murphy
    Vince - Mike Wagner
    Patrolman - Don Sherman
    Songs: "The Kind Of Girl I Could Love"
    "Mary, Mary"

26. **MARCH 13, 1967**
    Title: "Monkee Chow Mein"
    Writers: Gerald Gardner and Dee Caruso
    Director: James Frawley
    Description: Look for superspies and superheroes when the Monkees match wits with the Dragonman.
    Additional
    Cast: Dragonman - Joey Forman
    Toto - Gene Dynarski
    Agent Modell - Mike Farrell
    Chang - Kay Shimatsu
    Policeman - Ed Walsh
    Inspector Blound - Davy Barry
    Songs: "Your Auntie Grizelda"

Photo from the collection of Ed Reilly.

27. **MARCH 20, 1967**
    Title: "Monkee Mother"
    Writers: Peter Meyerson and Robert Schlitt
    Director: James Frawley
    Description: When a motherly widow moves in on the Monkees, they try to find her a husband in self-defense.
    Additional
    Cast:
    Milly - Rose Marie
    Larry - William Bramley
    Clarisse - Alexandra Hay
    Arthur - Al Dennis
    Judy - Judy March
    Babbit - Henry Corden
    Songs: "Sometime in the Morning"
    "Look Out (Here Comes Tomorrow)"

28. **MARCH 27, 1967**
    Title: "Monkees on the Line"
    Writers: Gerald Gardner, Dee Caruso, and Coslough Johnson
    Director: James Frawley
    Description: Crossed wires and crossed clients are the result when the Monkees take over a telephone answering service.
    Additional
    Cast:
    Ellen - Susan Browning
    Manny - Milton Frome
    Mr. Smith - Richard O'Brien
    Drehdal - Helene Winston
    Director - Jack Donner
    Arnold - Tom Bellin
    Mrs. Smith - Lea Marmer
    Songs: "Look Out (Here Comes Tomorrow)"

29. **APRIL 3, 1967**
    Title: "Monkees Get Out More Dirt"
    Writers: Gerald Gardner and Dee Caruso
    Director: Gerald Sheppard
    Description: All is fair in love and the laundry as the Monkees compete for the affection of a beautiful woman who runs a laundromat.
    Additional
    Cast:
    April - Julie Newmar
    Dr. Sisters - Claire Kelly
    Man with Paper - Digby Wolfe
    Girl - Patricia Foster
    Cameo - Wally Cox
    Songs: "The Girl I Knew Somewhere"

Photo from the collection of Ed Reilly.

30. **APRIL 10, 1967**
    Title: "Monkees in Manhattan"
    Writers: Gerald Gardner and Dee Caruso
    Director: Russell Mayberry
    Description: On a visit to the "Big Apple," the Monkees come to the aid of a Broadway producer.

    Another informal interview with the Monkees covers the effects of success on them.

    Additional
    Cast: Mackinley Baker - Dick Andrews
    Weatherwax - Philip Ober
    Butler - Doodles Weaver
    Waiter - Olan Soule
    Dr. Corell - Alfred Dennis
    Groom - Geoffrey Deuel
    Bride - Susan Howard
    Conventioneer - Foster Brooks
    Compton - John Graham
    Songs: "The Girl I Knew Somewhere"
    "Look Out (Here Comes Tomorrow)"
    "Words"

31. **APRIL 17, 1967**
    Title: "Monkees at the Movies"
    Writers: Gerald Gardner and Dee Caruso
    Director: Russell Mayberry
    Description: While working as extras on a beach party film, the Monkees find that it is not all fun and games.

    The Monkees talk about playing their own instruments in an interview with Bob Rafelson.

    Additional
    Cast: Frankie Catalina - Bobby Sherman
    Kramm - Jerry Lester
    Philo - Hamilton Camp
    Reporter - David Frank
    Songs: "When Love Comes Knockin' At Your Door"
    "Valleri"
    "Last Train To Clarksville"

Photo courtesy Edmag Archives.

32. **APRIL 24, 1967**
    Title: "Monkees On Tour"
    Writers: Robert Rafelson
    Director: Robert Rafelson
    Description: Filmed footage of a live concert performance in Phoenix, Arizona, highlights this look at the Monkees first tour.
    Songs: "Randy Scouse Git"
    "Words"
    Medley: "Last Train To Clarksville"/ "Sweet Young Thing"/ "Mary, Mary"/"Cripple Creek"/"You Can't Judge A Book By It's Cover"/"I Wanna Be Free"/"I Got A Woman"/ "(I'm Not Your) Steppin' Stone"

The Monkees' series was awarded an Emmy for "Best Comedy Series, 1966-1967" for its first season.

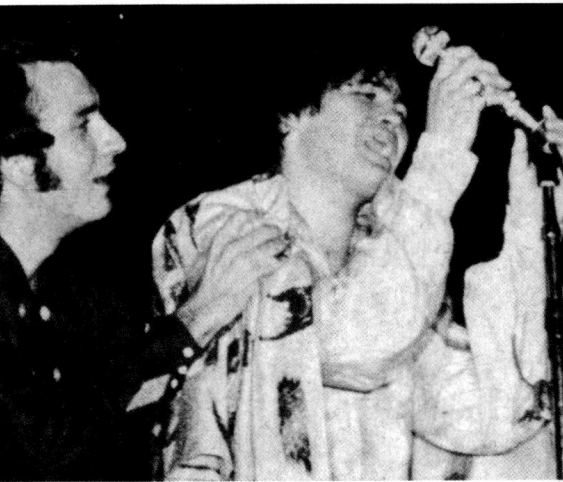
Photo from the collection of Ed Reilly.

33. **SEPTEMBER 11, 1967** (Second season debut)
    Title: "It's A Nice Place To Visit"
    Writers: Treva Silverman
    Director: James Frawley
    Description: A trip south of the border turns sour when Davy is taken prisoner by Mexican banditos.
    Additional
    Cast: El Diablo - Peter Whitney
    Angelita - Cynthia Hull
    Jose - Nate Esformes
    Lupe - Pedro Gonzalez
    Bandit - Arthur Ambrosio
    Parking Attendant - Godfrey Cambridge
    Songs: "What Am I Doing Hangin' 'Round"

Photo from the collection of Ed Reilly.

34. **SEPTEMBER 18, 1967**
    Title: "The Picture Frame (The Bank Robbery)"
    Writers: Jack Winter
    Director: James Frawley
    Description: It is up to Peter to keep the boys out of jail when an acting job turns out to be a cover for a bank robbery.
    Additional
    Cast: J. L. - Cliff Norton
    Judge - Elisabeth Fraser
    D. A. - Henry Beckman
    Harvey - Jonathan Harper
    Sergeant - Dort Clark
    Vice President - Donald Foster
    Lawyer - Art Lewis
    Cashier - Joy Harmon
    Cop - Robert Michaels
    Songs: "Pleasant Valley Sunday"
    "Randy Scouse Git"

35. **SEPTEMBER 25, 1967**
    Title: "Everywhere A Shiek, Sheik"
    Writers: Jack Winter
    Director: Alex Singer
    Description: Davy's forced marriage to an Arabian princess spells doom for the Monkees.

    Also, the Monkees sit for a casual interview about their summer activities.
    Additional
    Cast: King - Monte Landis
    Colette - Donna Loren
    Vidaru - Arnold Moss
    Shazer - Norm Pitlik
    Curad - William Bagdad
    Maiden #1 - Cherie Latimer
    Maiden #2 - Anne Randall
    Maiden #3 - Lisa Mitchell
    Songs: "Love Is Only Sleeping"
    "Cuddly Toy"

Photo from the collection of Ed Reilly.

36. **OCTOBER 2, 1967**
    Title: "Monkee Mayor"
    Writers: Jack Winter
    Director: Alex Singer
    Description: Mike runs for mayor in an effort to save the neighborhood from being demolished in the name of progress.
    Additional
    Cast: Zeckenbush - Monte Landis
    Mayor - Irwin Charone
    Mr. Swezey - Peter Brocco
    Mrs. Homer - Violet Carlson
    Mrs. Filchok - Queenie Smith
    Publisher - Walker Edmiston
    Skywriter - Bill Benedict
    Secretary - Kathy Wakefield
    Songs: "No Time"
    "Pleasant Valley Sunday"

37. **OCTOBER 9, 1967**
    Title: "Art, For Monkees' Sake"
    Writers: Coslough Johnson
    Director: Alex Singer
    Description: Peter is the unknowing pawn in a plot to copy a priceless painting and steal the original.
    Additional
    Cast: Duce - Monte Landis
    Chuce - Vic Tayback
    Curator - Arthur Malet
    Artist - Michael Bell
    Cameo - Liberace
    Songs: "Randy Scouse Git"
    "Daydream Believer"

38. **OCTOBER 16, 1967**
    Title: "I Was A 99 Pound Weakling"
    Writers: Gerald Gardner, Dee Caruso, and Neil Burstyn
    Director: Alex Singer
    Description: To win the heart of a beautiful girl, Micky takes a course in body building.
    Additional
    Cast: Shah-Ku - Monte Landis
    Bulk - Dave Draper
    Brenda - Venita Woolf
    Scrawny Young Man - Gary Waynesmith
    Songs: "Sunny Girlfriend"
    "Love Is Only Sleeping"

39. **OCTOBER 23, 1967**
    Title: "Hillbilly Honeymoon"
    Writers: Peter Meyerson
    Director: James Frawley
    Description: Guns and tempers blaze as the Monkees find themselves in the middle of an old family feud and Davy faces a shotgun wedding.
    Additional
    Cast:
    Ella Mae Chubber - Melody Patterson
    Paw Chubber - Dub Taylor
    Maw Weskitt - Billy Hayes
    Judd Weskitt - Lou Antonio
    Preacher - Jim Boles
    Songs: "Papa Gene's Blues"

40. **OCTOBER 30, 1967**
    Title: "Monkees Marooned"
    Writers: Stanley Ralph Ross
    Director: James Frawley
    Description: A tropical island, a buried treasure, and a looney Robinson Crusoe-type all add up to a lot of laughs when the Monkees are marooned.
    Additional
    Cast:
    Major Pshaw - Monte Landis
    Thursday - Rupert Crosse
    Kimba - Burt Mustin
    Sheldon - Don Sherman
    Jane - Georgia Schmidt
    Policeman - Allen Emerson
    Gorilla - John London
    Press Photographer #1 - Nyles Brown
    Press Photographer #2 - David Pearl
    Songs: "Daydream Believer"
    "What Am I Doing Hangin' 'Round"

Photos by Henry Diltz.

41. **NOVEMBER 6, 1967**
    Title: "Card Carrying Red Shoes"
    Writers: Lee Sanford
    Director: James Frawley
    Description: A prima ballerina keeps the Monkees on their toes in this tale of foreign intrigue.
    Additional
    Cast:
    - Ivan - Vincent Beck
    - Natasha - Ondine Vaughn
    - Nicolai - Leon Askin
    - Nyetovich - Robert Cornthwaite
    - Dancer - Gene Otis Shane
    - Blindfolded Man - Jerry Stevenson

    Songs: "She Hangs Out"

42. **NOVEMBER 13, 1967**
    Title: "The Wild Monkees"
    Writers: Stanley Ralph Ross and Corey Upton
    Director: Jon C. Anderson
    Description: Motorcycle madness highlights an encounter with a band of wild bikers.
    Additional
    Cast:
    - Big Butch - Norman Grabowski
    - Blauner - Henry Corden
    - Nan - Carol Worthington
    - Jan - Christine Williams
    - Ann - Ginny Gan

    Songs: "Goin' Down"
    "Star Collector"

Photo by Henry Diltz.

Photos by Henry Diltz.

43. **NOVEMBER 20, 1967**
    Title: "A Coffin Too Frequent"
    Writers: Stella Linden
    Director: David Winters
    Description: A mad scientist and a crazy aunt take over the Monkee's pad for a seance.
    Additional
    Cast: Henry - George Furth
    Mrs. Weatherspoon - Ruth Buzzi
    Boris - Mickey Morton
    Songs: "Daydream Believer"
    "Goin' Down"

44. **NOVEMBER 27, 1967**
    Title: "Hitting The High Seas"
    Writers: Jack Winter
    Director: James Frawley
    Description: An ocean liner is in danger of attack from pirates unless the Monkees come to the rescue.
    Additional
    Cast: Captain - Chips Rafferty
    Frank - Ted De Corsia
    Harry - Norm Pitlik
    Mayberry - Leslie Randall
    Songs: "Daydream Believer"
    "Star Collector"

Photo by Henry Diltz.

45. **DECEMBER 4, 1967**
    Title: "Monkees In Texas"
    Writers: Jack Winter
    Director: James Frawley
    Description: Way out west they are at their best. The Monkees meet Ben Cartwheel and try to head him off at the pass.
    Additional
    Cast: Bart/Ben Cartwheel - Barton MacLane
    Aunt Kate - Jacqueline DeWit
    Lucy - Bonnie J. Dewberry
    Red - Len Lesser
    Sneak - Rex Holman
    Marshall - James J. Griffith
    Bartender - Stuart Nisbet
    Songs: "Words"
    "Goin' Down"

46. **DECEMBER 11, 1967**
    Title: "Monkees On The Wheel"
    Writers: Coslough Johnson
    Director: Jerry Sheppard
    Description: The stakes are higher than usual when the Monkees go to Las Vegas and uncover a ring of crooked gamblers.

    The closing moments are filled with out-takes of Micky Dolenz and Michael Nesmith.
    Additional
    Cast: Hoss - David Astor
    Biggy - Pepper Davis
    Manager - Rip Taylor
    Policeman - Dort Clark
    Zelda - Joy Harmon
    Della - Sharyn Hillyer
    Songs: "The Door into Summer"
    "Cuddly Toy"

47. **DECEMBER 25, 1967**
    Title: "The Christmas Show"
    Writers: Dave Evans and Neil Burstyn
    Director: Jon Anderson
    Description: The Monkees try to bring the spirit of Christmas back into the life of a cynical young boy.
    Additional
    Cast:
    Melvin - Butch Patrick
    Mrs. Vandersnoot - Jeanne Soret
    Salesman - Larry Gelman
    Butler - Burt Mustin
    Salesgirl - Toby Adler
    Songs: "Ríu, Ríu, Chíu"

48. **JANUARY 8, 1968**
    Title: "Fairy Tale"
    Writers: Peter Meyerson
    Director: James Frawley
    Description: A princess (Mike) is held captive in a castle tower. Does Peter of Tork have the key? Will the magic locket unlock it?

    Also, the Monkees chat about Nesmith's role as the princess at the end of the show.
    Additional
    Cast:
    Harold - Murray Roman
    Richard - John Lawrence
    Narrator/Town Cryer - Rege Cordic
    Fairy of the Locket - Diane Shalet
    Horseman #1 - Richard Klein
    Songs: "Daily Nightly"

Photo from the collection of Ed Reilly.

Photo by Henry Diltz.

49. **JANUARY 15, 1968**
   Title: "Monkees Watch Their Feet"
   Writers: Coslough Johnson
   Director: Alex Singer
   Description: Will the real Micky please stand up? Micky is taken prisoner by aliens and replaced by a not-so-exact clone.
   Additional
   Cast: Captain - Stuart Margolin
   Secretary - Pat Paulsen
   The Assistant - Nita Talbot
   Chief - Clark Gordon
   Songs: "Star Collector"

50. **JANUARY 22, 1968**
   Title: "Monstrous Monkee Mash"
   Writers: Neil Burstyn and David Panich
   Director: James Frawley
   Description: A jealous vampire and his werewolf friend are out for Davy's blood.
   Additional
   Cast: Count Dracula - Ron Masak
   Lorelei - Arlene Martel
   Wolfman - David Pearl
   Songs: "Goin' Down"

51. **JANUARY 29, 1968**
   Title: "The Monkey's Paw"
   Writers: Coslough Johnson
   Director: James Frawley
   Description: A has-been magician and an enchanted monkey's paw bring a change in the Monkees' luck, but is it for the better?

   Peter Tork talks about his feelings regarding the hippie movement in another of the now familiar end of show interviews.
   Additional
   Cast: Mendrek the Magician - Hans Conreid
   Daughter - Merri Ashley
   Manager - Henry Beckman
   Psychiatrist - Severn Darden
   Tax Man - Jack Fife
   Songs: "Words"

52. **FEBRUARY 5, 1968**
    Title: "The Devil And Peter Tork"
    Writers: Gerald Gardner, Dee Caruso, and Robert Kaufman
    Director: James Frawley
    Description: When the devil plays "Let's Make A Deal" for Peter's soul, he gets more than he bargained for.
    Additional
    Cast: Judge Roy Bean - Billy Beck
    Devil/Mr. Zero - Monte Landis
    Blackbeard - Ted De Corsia
    Billy The Kid - Peter Canon
    Attila The Hun - Lee Kolima
    Songs: "Salesman"
    "No Time"

Photo by Henry Diltz.

53. **FEBRUARY 12, 1968**
    Title: "Monkees Race Again"
    Writers: Dave Evans, Elias Davis, and David Pollock
    Director: James Frawley
    Description: Hot wheels and hot action combine in this tale of big-time auto racing and small-time hoods.
    Additional
    Cast: Wolfgang - Stubby Kaye
    The Baron - David Hurst
    T. N. Crumpets - William Glover
    Butler - Maurice Dallimore
    Official - Don Kennedy
    Flower Eater - Robert Rafelson
    Songs: "What Am I Doing Hangin' 'Round"

54. **FEBRUARY 19, 1968**
    Title: "The Monkees In Paris"
    Writers: Robert Rafelson
    Director: Robert Rafelson
    Description: Filmed in June 1967 in the week prior to the summer tour, which opened at London's "Wembley Pool" and crossed the U.S., the Monkees are chased by a band of beauties through the streets of Paris and the surrounding countryside.
    Additional
    Cast: Gendarme - Bill Chadwick
    Gendarme - David Price
    Gendarme - Charlie Rocket
    Gendarme - Rick Klein
    Songs: "Goin' Down"
    "Don't Call On Me"
    "Love Is Only Sleeping"
    "Star Collector"

Photo from the collection of Ed Reilly.

154

55. **FEBRUARY 26, 1968**
    Title: "Monkees Mind Their Manor"
    Writers: Coslough Johnson
    Director: Peter H. Thorkelson (Peter Tork)
    Description: When Davy inherits a fabulous estate, the Monkees travel to England to check it out.

    Also, a late Christmas message from Peter Tork ends this show.

    Additional
    Cast: Twiggly - Bernard Fox
    Lance Kibee The Sot - Jack Good
    Butler - Reginald Gardiner
    Mr. Friar - Laurie Main
    Customs Man - Jack H. Williams
    Real Prop Man - Jack H. Williams
    Mary Friar - Myra DeGroot
    Old Man - William Benedict
    Songs: "Star Collector"

Photo by Henry Diltz.

155

Photo from the collection of Ed Reilly.

Photo from the collection of Ed Reilly.

Photo by Henry Diltz.

56. **MARCH 4, 1968**
    Title: "Some Like It Lukewarm (The Band Contest)"
    Writers: Joel Kane and Stanley Z. Cherry
    Director: James Frawley
    Description: Davy dons a dress and wig to supply the one missing ingredient the Monkees need to win a band contest.

    The closing finds Davy and his special guest, Charlie Smalls, talking about soul in music.
    Additional
    Cast: Daphne - Deana Martin
    Himself - Jerry Blavat
    Maxine - Sharon Cintron
    Pierre - Rob Rudelson
    Janitor - Bill McKinney
    Songs: "The Door Into Summer"
    "She Hangs Out"

57. **MARCH 11, 1968**
    Title: "Monkees Blow Their Minds"
    Writers: Peter Meyerson
    Director: David Winters
    Description: A psychic hypnotizes Peter in an attempt to recruit him for a stage act.

    Michael Nesmith and Frank Zappa reverse roles in an opening vignette.
    Additional
    Cast: Oraculo - Monte Landis
    Latham - Milton Frome
    Rudi - James Frawley
    Songs: "Valleri"
    "Daily Nightly"

58. **MARCH 25, 1968**
    Title: "Mijacogeo (The Frodis Caper)"
    Writers: Micky Dolenz, Dave Evans and Jon Anderson
    Director: Micky Dolenz
    Description: This last regularly scheduled show fittingly and satirically depicts the power of television.

    Guest Tim Buckley closes this show with a performance of one of his songs, "Universal Soldier."
    Additional
    Cast: Glick - Rip Taylor
    Otto - Tony Giorgio
    TV Viewer - Nyles Brown
    Cop - Bob Michaels
    Henchman - Rick Klein
    Songs: "Zor And Zam"

Photo courtesy Personality Photos, Inc.,
P.O. Box 50, Midwood Station,
New York, NY, 11230.

APRIL 14, 1969
Title: "33 1/3 Revolutions Per Monkee"
Writers: Jack Good and Art Fisher
Director: Art Fisher
Description: Thirteen months after the last regular episode, The Monkees again assault the American television audience. For this one-hour special, the emphasis is on their music and that of their guests.

Additional
Cast:
- Julie Driscoll and Brian Auger
- The Trinity
- The Clara Ward Singers
- Fats Domino
- Jerry Lee Lewis
- Little Richard
- The Buddy Miles Express
- We Three
- Jools
- Paul Arnold and the Moon Express

Songs:
- "I'm A Believer" - Micky & Julie Driscoll
- "The Only Thing I Believe Is True" - Michael Nesmith
- "Where Time Won't Fly" - David Jones
- "Prithee (Thou Makest Demands On Me)" - Peter Tork
- "I'm A Wind Up Man" - Monkees
- "A String for My Kite" - David Jones
- "At The Hop" - Monkees with Clara Ward Singers
- "I'm Ready" - Fats Domino
- "Whole Lotta Shakin'" - Jerry Lee Lewis
- "Tutti Frutti" - Little Richard
- "Shake A Tail Feather" - Monkees
- "Blue Monday" - Fats Domino
- "Little Darlin'" - Monkees
- "Down The Line" - Jerry Lee Lewis
- "Long Tall Sally" - Little Richard
- "Listen To The Band" - Monkees with entire cast
- "California Here I Come" - Monkees

"Head," 1968.
Photo courtesy Personality Photos, Inc.,
P.O. Box 50, Midwood Station,
New York, NY, 11230.

Head
Columbia Pictures

Cast

The Monkees	Peter Tork, David Jones, Micky Dolenz, Michael Nesmith
Minnie	Annette Funicello
Lord High 'n' Low	Timothy Carey
Officer Faye Lapid	Logan Ramsey
Swami	Abraham Sofaer
I. Vitteloni	Vito Scotti
Inspector Shrink	Charles Macaulay
Mr. & Mrs. Ace	T. C. Jones
Mayor Feedback	Charles Irving
Black Sheik	William Bagdad
Heraldic Messenger	Percy Helton
Extra	Sonny Liston
Private One	Ray Nitschke
Sally Silicone	Carol Doda
The Critic	Frank Zappa
The Jumper	June Fairchild
Testy True	Terri Garr
Lady Pleasure	I. J. Jefferson

and

The Big Victor	Victor Mature

EXECUTIVE PRODUCER:	Bert Schneider
PRODUCED AND WRITTEN BY:	Bob Rafelson and Jack Nicholson
DIRECTOR:	Bob Rafelson
PHOTOGRAPHY:	Michael Hugo
PHOTOGRAPHIC EFFECTS:	Butler-Glouner
SPECIAL EFFECTS:	Chuck Gaspar
SPECIAL COLOR EFFECTS:	Burton Gershfield and Bruce Lane
EDITOR:	Michael Pozen
ART DIRECTION:	Sydney Z. Litwack
SET DIRECTION:	Ned Parsons
SOUND:	Les Fresholtz
COSTUMES:	Gene Ashman
ASSISTANT TO THE PRODUCERS:	Marilyn Schlossberg
PRODUCTION MANAGER:	Harold Schneider
ASSISTANT DIRECTOR:	Jon Anderson
CHOREOGRAPHY:	Toni Basil
INCIDENTAL MUSIC COMPOSED AND CONDUCTED BY:	Ken Thorne

Songs: "Porpoise Song" (Gerry Goffin & Carole King)
"Circle Sky" (Michael Nesmith)
"Can You Dig It" (Peter Tork)
"As We Go Along" (Carole King & Toni Stern)
"Daddy's Song" (Nilsson)
"Long Title-Do I Have To Do This All Over Again" (Peter Tork)

Technicolor, 86 minutes
Filmed in California, 1968

Photo by Bill Chadwick.

The Nielsen Ratings

A lot of attention has been given to The Monkees as a recording group, and to how they compared to other recording acts of their time. However, until now no one has compared them with the other television shows of their day! It is known that the show never got into the Top 25 in the Nielsen ratings, and week-by-week data ranking "The Monkees" with the other shows of the week is no longer available, according to the A. C. Nielsen Company. The only comparison we can make from the information that remains is the Monkees track record against the competition in its own half-hour time slot on Monday nights, shown by average audience, rating, and share.

In its first season (1966-1967), "The Monkees" was in direct competition with "Gilligan's Island" (CBS), also a half-hour show (7:30-8:00 PM EST), and indirectly with "Iron Horse" (ABC), which was one hour (7:30-8:30 PM EST).

In its second season, the competition, "Gunsmoke" (CBS) and "Cowboy in Africa" (ABC), were both an hour long (7:30-8:30 PM EST). Any deviation from normal programming has been noted. A repeat telecast is denoted by (R). A share represents percentage of sets tuned to the show.

DATE		AVERAGE AUDIENCE	RATING	SHARE
SEPTEMBER 12, 1966				
"Iron Horse"	(ABC)	10,820,000	19.7	34.6
"The Monkees"	(NBC)	8,450,000	15.4	28.5
"Gilligan's Island"	(CBS)	8,020,000	14.6	27.0
SEPTEMBER 19, 1966				
"Gilligan's Island"	(CBS)	10,320,000	18.8	33.9
"The Monkees"	(NBC)	9,280,000	16.9	30.5
"Iron Horse"	(ABC)	9,220,000	16.8	29.1
SEPTEMBER 26, 1966				
"Iron Horse"	(ABC)	10,980,000	20.0	33.8
"Gilligan's Island"	(CBS)	9,720,000	17.7	30.9
"The Monkees"	(NBC)	8,620,000	15.7	27.4
OCTOBER 3, 1966				
"Gilligan's Island"	(CBS)	9,940,000	18.1	32.0
"The Monkees"	(NBC)	9,830,000	17.9	31.7
"Iron Horse"	(ABC)	9,610,000	17.5	29.8
OCTOBER 10, 1966				
"Gilligan's Island"	(CBS)	10,270,000	18.7	33.3
"Iron Horse"	(ABC)	9,220,000	16.8	29.0
"The Monkees"	(NBC)	8,670,000	15.8	28.1
OCTOBER 17, 1966				
"Iron Horse"	(ABC)	10,870,000	19.8	33.1
"Gilligan's Island"	(CBS)	10,710,000	19.5	34.1

DATE		AVERAGE AUDIENCE	RATING	SHARE
"The Monkees"	(NBC)	8,840,000	16.1	28.1
OCTOBER 24, 1966				
"Iron Horse"	(ABC)	10,710,000	19.5	32.3
"The Monkees"	(NBC)	9,390,000	17.1	29.2
"Gilligan's Island"	(CBS)	8,840,000	16.1	27.5
OCTOBER 31, 1966				
"Iron Horse"	(ABC)	10,210,000	18.6	33.5
"The Monkees"	(NBC)	9,060,000	16.5	30.5
"Gilligan's Island"	(CBS)	8,180,000	14.9	27.5
NOVEMBER 7, 1966				
"Iron Horse"	(ABC)	10,540,000	19.2	30.7
"The Monkees"	(NBC)	9,770,000	17.8	28.8
"Gilligan's Island"	(CBS)	9,060,000	16.5	26.7
NOVEMBER 14, 1966				
"The Monkees"	(NBC)	10,160,000	18.5	30.5
"Gilligan's Island"	(CBS)	9,830,000	17.9	29.5
"Iron Horse"	(ABC)	9,830,000	17.9	29.2
NOVEMBER 21, 1966				
"The Monkees"	(NBC)	10,930,000	19.9	33.1
"Iron Horse"	(ABC)	10,050,000	18.3	30.1
"Gilligan's Island"	(CBS)	8,780,000	16.0	26.6
NOVEMBER 28, 1966				
"Iron Horse"	(ABC)	10,870,000	19.8	31.0
"The Monkees"	(NBC)	10,320,000	18.8	30.1
"Gilligan's Island"	(CBS)	9,990,000	18.2	29.1
DECEMBER 5, 1966				
"Iron Horse"	(ABC)	10,650,000	19.4	32.3
"The Monkees"	(NBC)	10,050,000	18.3	31.2
"Gilligan's Island"	(CBS)	8,780,000	16.0	27.3
DECEMBER 12, 1966				
"The Monkees"	(NBC)	10,210,000	18.6	31.3
"Iron Horse"	(ABC)	10,210,000	18.6	30.7
"Gilligan's Island"	(CBS)	9,110,000	16.6	27.9

DATE		AVERAGE AUDIENCE	RATING	SHARE

DECEMBER 19, 1966

Non-Report Week

DECEMBER 26, 1966

"Iron Horse"	(ABC)	9,940,000	18.1	33.1
"Gilligan's Island"	(CBS)	9,060,000	16.5	30.8
"The Monkees"	(NBC)	8,840,000	16.1	30.1

JANUARY 2, 1967

The Monkees was not aired. NBC instead televised the Rose Bowl and Orange Bowl games.

JANUARY 9, 1967

"Gilligan's Island"	(CBS)	11,530,000	21.0	32.9
"The Monkees"	(NBC)	10,760,000	19.6	30.7
"Iron Horse"	(ABC)	10,320,000	18.8	29.2

JANUARY 16, 1967

"Gilligan's Island"	(CBS)	11,420,000	20.8	31.3
"The Monkees"	(NBC)	10,930,000	19.9	30.0
"Iron Horse"	(ABC)	9,770,000	17.8	26.5

JANUARY 23, 1967

"Gilligan's Island"	(CBS)	10,710,000	19.5	30.5
"The Monkees"	(NBC)	10,540,000	19.2	30.0
"Iron Horse"	(ABC)	9,220,000	16.8	25.9

JANUARY 30, 1967

"The Monkees"	(NBC)	11,530,000	21.0	31.6(tie)
"Gilligan's Island"	(CBS)	11,530,000	21.0	31.6(tie)
"Iron Horse"	(ABC)	11,360,000	20.7	30.6

FEBRUARY 6, 1967

"The Monkees"	(NBC)	11,970,000	21.8	32.9
"Gilligan's Island"	(CBS)	11,200,000	20.4	30.8
"Iron Horse"	(ABC)	10,760,000	19.6	29.4

FEBRUARY 13, 1967

"The Monkees"	(NBC)	12,080,000	22.0	33.3
"Gilligan's Island"	(CBS)	11,800,000	21.5	31.7
"Iron Horse"	(ABC)	9,720,000	17.7	26.1

DATE		AVERAGE AUDIENCE	RATING	SHARE
FEBRUARY 20, 1967				
"The Monkees"	(NBC)	11,530,000	21.0	32.5
"Iron Horse"	(ABC)	10,380,000	18.9	28.6
"Gilligan's Island"	(CBS)	10,270,000	18.7	28.9
FEBRUARY 27, 1967				
"The Monkees"	(NBC)	11,910,000	21.7	33.3
"Iron Horse"	(ABC)	10,540,000	19.2	28.9
"Gilligan's Island"	(CBS)	9,440,000	17.2	26.4
MARCH 6, 1967				
"The Monkees"	(NBC)	11,360,000	20.7	32.3
"Iron Horse"	(ABC)	10,210,000	18.6	28.7
"Gilligan's Island"	(CBS)	9,990,000	18.2	28.4
MARCH 13, 1967				
"The Monkees"	(NBC)	11,530,000	21.0	34.1
"Iron Horse"	(ABC)	9,940,000	18.1	29.0
"Gilligan's Island"	(CBS)	9,720,000	17.7	28.7
MARCH 20, 1967				
"Gilligan's Island"	(CBS)	11,030,000	20.1	31.8
"The Monkees"	(NBC)	10,600,000	19.3	30.5
"Iron Horse"	(ABC)	10,100,000	18.4	28.7
MARCH 27, 1967				
"The Monkees"	(NBC)	11,860,000	21.6	35.9
"Gilligan's Island"	(CBS)	10,050,000	18.3	30.4
"Iron Horse"	(ABC)	9,330,000	17.0	27.5
APRIL 3, 1967				
"The Monkees"	(NBC)	10,490,000	19.1	34.0
"Gilligan's Island"	(CBS)	9,830,000	17.9	31.9
"Iron Horse"	(ABC)	8,560,000	15.6	26.9
APRIL 10, 1967				
"The Monkees"	(NBC)	10,270,000	18.7	31.4
"Gilligan's Island"	(CBS)	9,000,000	16.4	27.5
"Iron Horse"	(ABC)	7,910,000	14.4	25.7
APRIL 17, 1967				

Non-Report Week

DATE		AVERAGE AUDIENCE	RATING	SHARE
APRIL 24, 1967				
"The Monkees"	(NBC)	11,640,000	21.2	37.3
(R) "Gilligan's Island"	(CBS)	9,390,000	17.1	30.1
(R) "Iron Horse"	(ABC)	7,800,000	14.2	24.1
MAY 1, 1967				
(R) "The Monkees"	(NBC)	8,780,000	16.0	34.1
(R) "Gilligan's Island"	(CBS)	8,070,000	14.7	31.3
(R) "Iron Horse"	(ABC)	7,580,000	13.8	28.2
MAY 8, 1967				
(R) "The Monkees"	(NBC)	10,100,000	18.4	34.6
(R) "Gilligan's Island"	(CBS)	8,180,000	14.9	28.0
(R) "Iron Horse"	(ABC)	8,130,000	14.8	27.1
MAY 15, 1967				
(R) "The Monkees"	(NBC)	9,440,000	17.2	33.9
(R) "Gilligan's Island"	(CBS)	8,670,000	15.8	31.2
(R) "Iron Horse"	(ABC)	7,800,000	14.2	26.9
MAY 22, 1967				
(R) "The Monkees"	(NBC)	8,450,000	15.4	31.4(tie)
(R) "Gilligan's Island"	(CBS)	8,450,000	15.4	31.4(tie)
(R) "Iron Horse"	(ABC)	7,190,000	13.1	25.7
MAY 29, 1967				
(R) "Gilligan's Island"	(CBS)	8,020,000	14.6	31.8
(R) "The Monkees"	(NBC)	7,960,000	14.5	31.6
(R) "Iron Horse"	(ABC)	6,260,000	11.4	23.9

JUNE 5, 1967

The Monkees was not aired. NBC instead televised a baseball game.

DATE		AVERAGE AUDIENCE	RATING	SHARE
JUNE 12, 1967				
(R) "The Monkees"	(NBC)	6,530,000	11.9	30.6
(R) "Gilligan's Island"	(CBS)	5,930,000	10.8	27.8
(R) "Iron Horse"	(ABC)	5,600,000	10.2	24.9

DATE		AVERAGE AUDIENCE	RATING	SHARE
JUNE 19, 1967				
Non-Report Week				
JUNE 26, 1967				
(R) "Gilligan's Island"	(CBS)	6,480,000	11.8	32.5
(R) "The Monkees"	(NBC)	5,710,000	10.4	28.7
(R) "Iron Horse"	(ABC)	5,110,000	9.3	25.1
JULY 3, 1967				
The Monkees was not aired. NBC instead televised a baseball game.				
JULY 10, 1967				
(R) "Gilligan's Island"	(CBS)	6,700,000	12.2	29.8
(R) "The Monkees"	(NBC)	6,640,000	12.1	29.6
(R) "Iron Horse"	(ABC)	6,150,000	11.2	26.6
JULY 17, 1967				
(R) "Gilligan's Island"	(CBS)	6,640,000	12.1	30.8
(R) "The Monkees"	(NBC)	6,310,000	11.5	29.3
(R) "Iron Horse"	(ABC)	5,220,000	9.5	22.9
JULY 24, 1967				
(R) "The Monkees"	(NBC)	6,370,000	11.6	31.0
(R) "Gilligan's Island"	(CBS)	6,090,000	11.1	29.7
(R) "Iron Horse"	(ABC)	5,440,000	9.9	25.3
JULY 31, 1967				
(R) "Gilligan's Island"	(CBS)	6,310,000	11.5	31.3
(R) "The Monkees"	(NBC)	6,260,000	11.4	31.0
(R) "Iron Horse"	(ABC)	5,440,000	9.9	25.4
AUGUST 7, 1967				
(R) "The Monkees"	(NBC)	6,640,000	12.1	31.7
(R) "Gilligan's Island"	(CBS)	5,600,000	10.2	26.7
(R) "Iron Horse"	(ABC)	5,330,000	9.7	24.9

DATE		AVERAGE AUDIENCE	RATING	SHARE
AUGUST 14, 1967				
(R) "The Monkees"	(NBC)	7,140,000	13.0	35.1
(R) "Gilligan's Island	(CBS)	5,930,000	10.8	29.2
(R) "Iron Horse"	(ABC)	5,760,000	10.5	26.9

AUGUST 21, 1967

Non-Report Week

AUGUST 28, 1967				
(R) "The Monkees"	(NBC)	7,780,000	13.9	31.4
(R) "Gilligan's Island"	(CBS)	6,890,000	12.3	27.8
(R) "Iron Horse"	(ABC)	7,170,000	12.8	27.6

SEPTEMBER 4, 1967

The Monkees was not aired. NBC instead televised a baseball game.

SEPTEMBER 11, 1967				
"Gunsmoke"	(CBS)	11,310,000	20.2	38.0
"The Monkees"	(NBC)	8,790,000	15.7	29.5
"Cowboy In Africa"	(ABC)	8,460,000	15.1	27.2

SEPTEMBER 18, 1967				
"Gunsmoke"	(CBS)	10,580,000	18.9	36.6
"Cowboy In Africa"	(ABC)	8,460,000	15.1	28.1
"The Monkees"	(NBC)	8,120,000	14.5	28.1

SEPTEMBER 25, 1967				
"Gunsmoke"	(CBS)	10,920,000	19.5	36.7
"The Monkees"	(NBC)	8,510,000	15.2	28.6
"Cowboy In Africa"	(ABC)	8,180,000	14.6	26.3

OCTOBER 2, 1967				
"Gunsmoke"	(CBS)	9,910,000	17.7	35.0
"The Monkees"	(NBC)	8,230,000	14.7	27.7
"Cowboy In Africa"	(ABC)	7,840,000	14.0	27.7

OCTOBER 9, 1967				
"Gunsmoke"	(CBS)	11,420,000	20.4	35.4
"The Monkees"	(NBC)	9,520,000	17.0	29.5
"Cowboy In Africa"	(ABC)	8,620,000	15.4	26.1

DATE		AVERAGE AUDIENCE	RATING	SHARE
OCTOBER 16, 1967				
"Gunsmoke"	(CBS)	12,150,000	21.7	36.9
"The Monkees"	(NBC)	9,580,000	17.1	29.1
"Cowboy In Africa"	(ABC)	8,680,000	15.5	25.6
OCTOBER 23, 1967				
"Gunsmoke"	(CBS)	13,380,000	23.9	42.0
"The Monkees"	(NBC)	9,020,000	16.1	28.3
"Cowboy In Africa"	(ABC)	7,840,000	14.0	23.8
OCTOBER 30, 1967				
"Gunsmoke"	(CBS)	13,160,000	23.5	38.3
"The Monkees"	(NBC)	8,790,000	15.7	25.6
"Cowboy In Africa"	(ABC)	8,510,000	15.2	24.6
NOVEMBER 6, 1967				
"Gunsmoke"	(CBS)	13,100,000	23.4	37.4
"The Monkees"	(NBC)	9,180,000	16.4	26.2
"Cowboy In Africa"	(ABC)	8,680,000	15.5	24.6
NOVEMBER 13, 1967				
"Gunsmoke"	(CBS)	13,270,000	23.7	37.7
"The Monkees"	(NBC)	9,910,000	17.7	28.1
"Cowboy In Africa"	(ABC)	8,510,000	15.2	23.3
NOVEMBER 20, 1967				
"Gunsmoke"	(CBS)	14,620,000	26.1	42.6
"The Monkees"	(NBC)	10,190,000	18.2	29.7
"Cowboy In Africa"	(ABC)	7,780,000	13.9	22.1
NOVEMBER 27, 1967				
"Gunsmoke"	(CBS)	14,340,000	25.6	39.3
"The Monkees"	(NBC)	11,140,000	19.9	30.6
"Cowboy In Africa"	(ABC)	8,960,000	16.0	24.1
DECEMBER 4, 1967				
"Gunsmoke"	(CBS)	12,710,000	22.7	37.4
"The Monkees"	(NBC)	10,250,000	18.3	30.1
"Cowboy In Africa"	(ABC)	7,390,000	13.2	21.4
DECEMBER 11, 1967				
Special: "National Geographic - Sharks"	(CBS)	13,550,000	24.2	37.6

DATE		AVERAGE AUDIENCE	RATING	SHARE
"The Monkees"	(NBC)	9,520,000	17.0	27.1
"Cowboy In Africa"	(ABC)	8,850,000	15.8	24.5

DECEMBER 18, 1967

Non-Report Week

DECEMBER 25, 1967

"Gunsmoke"	(CBS)	11,090,000	19.8	44.2
"The Monkees"	(NBC)	7,110,000	12.7	28.3
"Cowboy In Africa"	(ABC)	5,320,000	9.5	20.7

JANUARY 1, 1968

The Monkees was not aired. NBC instead televised the Orange Bowl.

JANUARY 8, 1968

"Gunsmoke"	(CBS)	15,680,000	28.0	40.5
Special: "Undersea World of Cousteau"	(ABC)	11,980,000	21.4	30.4
"The Monkees"	(NBC)	9,410,000	16.8	24.3

JANUARY 15, 1968

"Gunsmoke"	(CBS)	16,070,000	28.7	42.8
"The Monkees"	(NBC)	10,080,000	18.0	26.9
"Cowboy In Africa"	(ABC)	8,180,000	14.6	21.3

JANUARY 22, 1968

"Gunsmoke"	(CBS)	16,300,000	29.1	44.4
"The Monkees"	(NBC)	9,740,000	17.4	26.6
"Cowboy In Africa"	(ABC)	7,900,000	14.1	20.9

JANUARY 29, 1968

"Gunsmoke"	(CBS)	15,290,000	27.3	41.2
"The Monkees"	(NBC)	9,860,000	17.6	26.6
"Cowboy In Africa"	(ABC)	8,120,000	14.5	21.3

FEBRUARY 5, 1968

"Gunsmoke"	(CBS)	14,280,000	25.5	39.9
"The Monkees"	(NBC)	9,910,000	17.7	27.7
"Cowboy In Africa"	(ABC)	7,390,000	13.2	20.1

FEBRUARY 12, 1968

"Gunsmoke"	(CBS)	15,960,000	28.5	43.1
"The Monkees"	(NBC)	11,090,000	19.8	29.9

DATE		AVERAGE AUDIENCE	RATING	SHARE
Special: "Winter Olympics"	(ABC)	7,060,000	12.6	18.6

FEBRUARY 19, 1968

"Gunsmoke"	(CBS)	13,550,000	24.2	38.1
"The Monkees"	(NBC)	9,580,000	17.1	26.9
"Cowboy In Africa"	(ABC)	8,230,000	14.7	22.4

FEBRUARY 26, 1968

"Gunsmoke"	(CBS)	14,220,000	25.4	40.1
"The Monkees"	(NBC)	10,530,000	18.8	29.7
"Cowboy In Africa"	(ABC)	7,840,000	14.0	21.3

MARCH 4, 1968

"Gunsmoke"	(CBS)	13,270,000	23.7	37.7
"The Monkees"	(NBC)	11,140,000	19.9	31.7
"Cowboy In Africa"	(ABC)	7,390,000	13.2	20.3

MARCH 11, 1968

"Gunsmoke"	(CBS)	13,440,000	24.0	38.1
"The Monkees"	(NBC)	9,460,000	16.9	26.8
"Cowboy In Africa"	(ABC)	7,560,000	13.5	20.9

MARCH 18, 1968

"Gunsmoke"	(CBS)	13,610,000	24.3	38.7
(R) "The Monkees"	(NBC)	11,030,000	19.7	31.4
"Cowboy In Africa"	(ABC)	7,390,000	13.2	20.1

MARCH 25, 1968

"Gunsmoke"	(CBS)	12,990,000	23.2	38.9
"The Monkees"	(NBC)	9,130,000	16.3	27.3
"Cowboy In Africa"	(ABC)	7,170,000	12.8	20.5

APRIL 1, 1968

The Monkees was not aired. NBC instead televised an address by Senator McCarthy.

APRIL 8, 1968

(R) "Gunsmoke"	(CBS)	13,330,000	23.8	39.1
(R) "The Monkees"	(NBC)	9,630,000	17.2	28.2
(R) "Cowboy In Africa"	(ABC)	7,220,000	12.9	20.3

APRIL 15, 1968

Non-Report Week

DATE		AVERAGE AUDIENCE	RATING	SHARE
APRIL 22, 1968				
(R) "Gunsmoke"	(CBS)	12,380,000	22.1	37.7
(R) "The Monkees"	(NBC)	8,740,000	15.6	28.3
(R) "Cowboy In Africa"	(ABC)	6,100,000	10.9	18.6
APRIL 29, 1968				
(R) "Gunsmoke"	(CBS)	10,530,000	18.8	34.4
(R) "The Monkees"	(NBC)	8,180,000	14.6	28.8
(R) "Cowboy In Africa"	(ABC)	5,100,000	9.1	16.7
MAY 6, 1968				
(R) "Gunsmoke"	(CBS)	11,540,000	20.6	38.6
(R) "The Monkees"	(NBC)	7,280,000	13.0	26.6
(R) "Cowboy In Africa"	(ABC)	4,540,000	8.1	15.2
MAY 13, 1968				
(R) "Gunsmoke"	(CBS)	10,420,000	18.6	35.6
(R) "The Monkees"	(NBC)	7,450,000	13.3	27.5
(R) "Cowboy In Africa"	(ABC)	5,380,000	9.6	18.4

MAY 20, 1968

Non-Report Week

DATE		AVERAGE AUDIENCE	RATING	SHARE
MAY 27, 1968				
(R) "Gunsmoke"	(CBS)	10,860,000	19.4	35.7
(R) "The Monkees"	(NBC)	7,950,000	14.2	28.2
(R) "Cowboy In Africa"	(ABC)	5,150,000	9.2	16.9

JUNE 3, 1968

The Monkees was not aired. NBC instead televised a baseball game.

DATE		AVERAGE AUDIENCE	RATING	SHARE
JUNE 10, 1968				
(R) "Gunsmoke"	(CBS)	9,910,000	17.7	41.2
(R) "The Monkees"	(NBC)	6,440,000	11.5	28.3
(R) "Cowboy In Africa"	(ABC)	3,580,000	6.4	14.9

DATE		AVERAGE AUDIENCE	RATING	SHARE

JUNE 17, 1968

(R) "Gunsmoke"	(CBS)	8,570,000	15.3	34.5
(R) "The Monkees"	(NBC)	6,100,000	10.9	26.0
(R) "Cowboy In Africa"	(ABC)	4,090,000	7.3	16.4

JUNE 24, 1968

Non-Report Week

JULY 1, 1968

(R) "Gunsmoke"	(CBS)	7,780,000	13.9	40.3
(R) "The Monkees"	(NBC)	4,870,000	8.7	26.4
(R) "Cowboy In Africa"	(ABC)	3,980,000	7.1	20.6

JULY 8, 1968

(R) "Gunsmoke"	(CBS)	8,850,000	15.8	43.8
(R) "The Monkees"	(NBC)	5,380,000	9.6	27.8
(R) "Cowboy In Africa"	(ABC)	3,810,000	6.8	18.8

JULY 15, 1968

(R) "Gunsmoke"	(CBS)	9,300,000	16.6	44.5
(R) "The Monkees"	(NBC)	4,590,000	8.2	23.2
Special: "Time for Americans"	(ABC)	no information available		

JULY 22, 1968

The Monkees was not aired. NBC instead televised a baseball game.

JULY 29, 1968

Non-Report Week

AUGUST 5, 1968

The Monkees was not aired. NBC instead televised the Republican National Convention.

AUGUST 12, 1968

(R) "Gunsmoke"	(CBS)	8,960,000	16.0	39.8
(R) "The Monkees"	(NBC)	4,820,000	8.6	22.3
(R) "Cowboy In Africa"	(ABC)	4,140,000	7.4	18.4

DATE			AVERAGE AUDIENCE	RATING	SHARE
AUGUST 19, 1968					
(R) "Gunsmoke"	(CBS)		8,120,000	14.5	36.5
(R) "The Monkees"	(NBC)		6,220,000	11.1	27.2
(R) "Cowboy In Africa"	(ABC)		4,370,000	7.8	18.3

AUGUST 26, 1968

The Monkees was not aired. NBC instead televised the Democratic National Convention.

APRIL 14, 1969 (Based on Eastern Standard Time)

CBS					
"Gunsmoke"	(7:30 - 8:30)		13,510,000	23.7	37.0
"Here's Lucy"	(8:30 - 9:00)		14,080,000	24.7	36.0
NBC					
"33 1/3 Revolutions Per Monkee"	(8:00 - 9:00)		10,430,000	18.3	27.0
ABC					
"The Avengers"	(7:30 - 8:30)		5,240,000	9.2	16.0
"Peyton Place"	(8:30 - 9:00)		7,300,000	12.8	20.0

SUMMARY:

In its first season (1966-1967), "The Monkees" won the time slot twenty-one times out of the forty-four weeks reported and on the air; "Gilligan's Island" won thirteen times, followed by "Iron Horse" with eight wins.

The second season (1967-1968) took its toll on "The Monkees," which held second place almost the entire season, trailing the time slot's top-ranked show, "Gunsmoke."

▶ Photo courtesy Edmag Archives.

Part three
The Monkees On Record

The Songs: A Complete Session List

During his term as President of Screen Gems Music, Lester Sill meticulously kept a personal account of the recording efforts of all Colgems artists, including dates, producers, songwriters, and site of recording. His diary included both released and unreleased tracks. This listing has been combined with an inventory of Monkees master tapes in existence and in storage at Columbia Pictures facility in 1972, prior to the release of the LP "Refocus." Of interest are the unreleased songs by today's major songwriters, the fact that several tracks released on 1969 albums were actually leftovers recorded in previous years, and the fact that some of the most productive recording sessions were those that coincided with the high-pressure filming of the television series.

DATE RECORDED	SONG TITLE	MASTER NUMBER	STUDIO RECORDED	PRODUCER	WRITERS
June 10, 1966	"Let's Dance On"	TZB3-4615	RCA-L.A.	Boyce/Hart & Keller	Boyce-Hart
June 10, 1966	"Take A Giant Step"	TZB3-4520	RCA-L.A.	Boyce-Hart	Goffin-King
June 25, 1966	"The Kind Of Girl I Could Love"	TZB3-4522	RCA-L.A.	Nesmith	Nesmith-Atkins
June 25, 1966	"All The King's Horses"	TZB3-4521	RCA-L.A.	Nesmith	Nesmith
June 25, 1966	"I Don't Think You Know Me"	TZB1-7738	RCA-L.A. RCA-N.Y.	Jeff Barry	Goffin-King
July 5, 1966	"Let's Dance On"	TZB3-4615	RCA-L.A.	Boyce/Hart & Keller	Boyce-Hart
July 5, 1966	"(Theme From) The Monkees"	TZB3-4607	RCA-L.A.	Boyce/Hart & Keller	Boyce-Hart
July 5, 1966	"This Just Doesn't Seem To Be My Day"	TZB3-4606	RCA-L.A.	Boyce/Hart & Keller	Boyce-Hart
July 7, 1966	"Gonna Buy Me A Dog"	TZB3-4608	Western	Boyce-Hart	Boyce-Hart
July 7, 1966	"So Goes Love"	TZB3-4609	Western	Nesmith	Goffin-King
July 9, 1966	"I'll Be True To You"	TZB3-4611	RCA-L.A.	Boyce/Hart & Keller	Goffin-Titleman
July 9, 1966	"Papa Gene's Blues"	TZB3-4612	RCA-L.A.	Nesmith	Nesmith
July 9, 1966	"Saturday's Child"	TZB3-4610	RCA-L.A.	Boyce/Hart & Keller	David Gates
July 9, 1966	"Take A Giant Step"	TZB3-4520	RCA-L.A.	Boyce-Hart	Goffin-King
July 18, 1966	"Sweet Young Thing"	TZB3-4615	RCA-L.A.	Nesmith	Nesmith/Goffin & King
July 18, 1966	"You Just May Be The One"	TZB3-4615	RCA-L.A.	Chip Douglas	Nesmith
July 18, 1966	"I Won't Be The Same Without Her"	TZB3-4613	RCA-L.A.	Nesmith	Goffin-King
July 19, 1966	"I Wanna Be Free"	TZB3-4616	RCA-L.A.	Boyce-Hart	Boyce-Hart
July 23, 1966	"Tomorrow's Gonna Be Another Day"	TZB3-4621	RCA-L.A.	Boyce/Hart & Keller	Boyce-Venet
July 25, 1966	"The Kind Of Girl I Could Love"	TZB3-4522	RCA-L.A.	Nesmith	Nesmith-Atkins
July 25, 1966	"The Last Train To Clarksville"	TZB3-4622	RCA-L.A.	Boyce-Hart	Boyce-Hart
July 25, 1966	"Mary, Mary"	TZB3-4625	Western	Nesmith	Nesmith
July 25, 1966	"Of You"	TZB3-4626	Western	Nesmith	Chadwick
July 26, 1966	"(I'm Not Your) Steppin' Stone"	TZB1-4620	Western	Boyce-Hart	Boyce-Hart
July 26, 1966	"Whatever's Right"	WZB5-5351	Western	Boyce-Hart	Boyce-Hart

DATE RECORDED	SONG TITLE	MASTER NUMBER	STUDIO RECORDED	PRODUCER	WRITERS
August 6, 1966	"Valleri"	TZB3-4727	RCA-L.A.	Boyce-Hart	Boyce-Hart
August 15, 1966	"She"	TZB3-4724	RCA-L.A.	Boyce-Hart	Boyce-Hart
August 23, 1966	"Ladies Aid Society"	TZB3-4725	RCA-L.A.	Boyce-Hart	Boyce-Hart
August 23, 1966	"Teeny Tiny Gnome"	TZB3-4726	RCA-L.A.	Boyce-Hart	Erwin-Castle
September 10, 1966	"Mr. Webster"	UZB3-8374	RCA-L.A.	Boyce-Hart	Boyce-Hart
September 10, 1966	"Through The Looking Glass"	TZB3-4730	RCA-L.A.	Boyce-Hart	Boyce-Hart
October 13, 1966	"Sometime In The Morning"	TZB1-7737	RCA-N.Y.	Jeff Barry	Goffin-King
October 13, 1966	"I Don't Think You Know Me"	TZB1-7738	RCA-N.Y.	Jeff Barry	Goffin-King
October 15, 1966	"I'm A Believer"	TZB1-7744	RCA-N.Y.	Jeff Barry	Diamond
October 15, 1966	"Look Out (Here Comes Tomorrow)"	TZB1-7739	RCA-N.Y.	Jeff Barry	Diamond
October 23, 1966	"Your Auntie Grizelda"	TZB3-4740	RCA-L.A.	Keller-Barry	Keller-Hilderbrand
October 23, 1966	"Look Out (Here Comes Tomorrow)"	TZB1-7739	RCA-N.Y.	Jeff Barry	Diamond
October 23, 1966	"Hold On Girl"	TZB3-4729	RCA-L.A.	Barry-Keller	Keller/Raleigh & Carr
October 25, 1966	"Sometime In The Morning"	TZB1-7737	RCA-N.Y.	Jeff Barry	Goffin-King
October 26, 1966	"Looking For The Good Times"	TZB3-4732	RCA-L.A.	Boyce-Hart	Boyce-Hart
October 26, 1966	"I'll Spend My Life With You"	TZB3-4733	RCA-L.A.	Boyce-Hart	Boyce-Hart
October 26, 1966	"Teardrop City"	TZB3-4731 XZB5-0124	RCA-L.A.	Boyce-Hart	Boyce-Hart
October 28, 1966	"Don't Listen To Linda"	TZB3-4735	RCA-L.A.	Boyce-Hart	Boyce-Hart
October 28, 1966	"Apples, Peaches, Bananas & Pears"	TZB3-4734	RCA-L.A.	Boyce-Hart	Boyce-Hart
October 28, 1966	"I Never Thought It Peculiar"	TZB3-4736	RCA-L.A.	Boyce-Hart	Boyce-Hart
October 29, 1966	"The Day We Fall In Love"	TZB3-4739	RCA-N.Y.	Jeff Barry	Medress/Margo/ Siegal/Margo
November 17, 1966	"Do Not Ask For Love (Prithee)"	TZB4-4627	RCA-L.A.	Nesmith	Murphy
November 17, 1966	"Looking For The Good Times"	TZB3-4732	RCA-L.A.	Boyce-Hart	Boyce-Hart
November 23, 1966	"When Love Comes Knockin' (At Your Door)"	TZB1-8690	RCA-N.Y.	Sedaka-Bayer	Sedaka-Bayer
November 23, 1966	"The Girl I Left Behind Me"	TZB1-8689	RCA-N.Y.	Sedaka-Bayer	Sedaka-Bayer
January 1967	"So Far Out She's In"	UZB3-8184	RCA-L.A.		
January 16, 1967	"All Of Your Toys"	UZB3-8186	RCA-L.A.	Chip Douglas	Martin
January 16, 1967	"The Girl I Knew Somewhere"	UZB3-8185	RCA-L.A.	Chip Douglas	Nesmith
January 21, 1967	"99 lbs. Of Dynamite"	UZB1-4402	RCA-N.Y.	Jeff Barry	Barry
January 21, 1967	"She Hangs Out"	UZB1-4401	RCA-N.Y.	Jeff Barry	Barry-Greenwich
January 21, 1967	"You Can't Tie A Mustang Down"	UZB1-4401 TZB1-4401	RCA-N.Y.	Jeff Barry	Barry/Stoller & Leiber
January 21, 1967	"A Little Bit Me, A Little Bit You"	UZB1-4406	RCA-N.Y.	Jeff Barry	Diamond
January 21, 1967	"Gotta Give It Time"	UZB1-4405	RCA-N.Y.	Jeff Barry	Barry/Levine/ Stoller/Leiber
January 21, 1967	"Love To Love"	UZB1-4403	RCA-N.Y.	Jeff Barry	Diamond
January 22, 1967	"I Didn't Know You Had It In You, Sally"	UZB1-4414	RCA-N.Y.	D. Randell	Linzer-Randell
January 22, 1967	"I Wanna Be Your Puppy Dog"	UZB1-4415	RCA-N.Y.	D. Randell	Linzer-Randell
January 22, 1967	"Love Is On The Way"	UZB1-4413	RCA-N.Y.	D. Randell	Linzer-Randell
January 22, 1967	"Sugar Man"	UZB1-4416	RCA-N.Y.	D. Randell	Linzer-Randell
January 26, 1967	"Poor Little Me"	UZB1-4408	RCA-N.Y.	Jeff Barry	Barry-Kim

DATE RECORDED	SONG TITLE	MASTER NUMBER	STUDIO RECORDED	PRODUCER	WRITERS
January 26, 1967	"Black And Blue"	UZB1-4411	RCA-N.Y.	Jeff Barry	Diamond/Leiber & Stoller
January 26, 1967	"Eve Of My Sorrow"	UZB1-4410	RCA-N.Y.	Jeff Barry	Barry/Levine/Stoller & Leiber
January 26, 1967	"If I Learned To Play The Violin"	UZB1-4409	RCA-N.Y.	Jeff Barry	Levine-Resnick
January 26, 1967	"The Love You Got Inside"	UZB1-4412	RCA-N.Y.	Jeff Barry	Barry/Kim/Stoller & Leiber
January 27, 1967	"Love Is On The Way"	UZB1-4413	RCA-N.Y.	D. Randell	Linzer-Randell
January 27, 1967	"Sugar Man"	UZB1-4416	RCA-N.Y.	D. Randell	Linzer-Randell
February 23, 1967	"Sunny Girlfriend"	UZB3-8374	RCA-L.A.	Chip Douglas	Nesmith
February 24, 1967	"Mr. Webster"	UZB3-8374	RCA-L.A.	Chip Douglas	Boyce-Hart
February 1967	"She'll Be There"	UZB3-8375	RCA-L.A.		
February 1967	"Where Has It All Gone"	UZB3-8377	RCA-L.A.		
March 2, 1967	"Band Six"	UZB3-8378	RCA-L.A.	Chip Douglas	Monkees
March 3, 1967	"Zilch"	UZB3-8381	RCA-L.A.	Chip Douglas	Monkees
March 3, 1967	"You Told Me"	UZB3-8380	RCA-L.A.	Chip Douglas	Nesmith
March 4, 1967	"Randy Scouse Git"	UZB3-0467	RCA-L.A.	Chip Douglas	Dolenz
March 4, 1967	"I'll Spend My Life With You"	UZB3-8372	RCA-L.A.	Chip Douglas	Boyce-Hart
March 7, 1967	"Forget That Girl"	UZB3-8379	RCA-L.A.	Chip Douglas	Douglas
March 1967	"I Had A Dream Last Night"	UZB3-8385	RCA-L.A.		
March 16, 1967	"Shades Of Gray"	UZB3-8383	RCA-L.A.	Chip Douglas	Mann-Weil
March 17, 1967	"Masking Tape"	UZB3-8388	RCA-L.A.		
March 17, 1967	"No Time"	UZB3-8390	RCA-L.A.	Chip Douglas	Cicalo
March 17, 1967	"Blues"	UZB3-8391	RCA-L.A.		
March 17, 1967	"I Can't Get Her Off My Mind"	UZB3-8389	RCA-L.A.	Chip Douglas	Boyce-Hart
March 18, 1967	"I'll Spend My Life With You"	UZB3-8382	RCA-L.A.	Chip Douglas	Boyce-Hart
March 18, 1967	"Rock & Roll Music"	UZB3-8394	RCA-L.A.	Nesmith	Nilsson
March 22, 1967	"Early Morning Blues and Greens"	UZB3-8393	RCA-L.A.	Chip Douglas	Keller-Hilderbrand
March 23, 1967	"For Pete's Sake"	UZB3-8490	RCA-L.A.	Chip Douglas	Tork-Richards
April 26, 1967	"Cuddly Toy"	UZB3-8392	RCA-L.A.	Chip Douglas	Nilsson
May 5, 1967	"A Man Without A Dream"	UZB3-5435	RCA-L.A.	Chip Douglas	Goffin-King
May 29, 1967	"The Door Into Summer"	UZB3-5436	RCA-L.A.	Chip Douglas	Douglas-Martin
June 10, 1967	"Pleasant Valley Sunday"	UZB3-5437	RCA-L.A.	Chip Douglas	Goffin-King
June 10, 1967	"Peter Percival Patterson's Pet Pig"	UZB3-9832	RCA-L.A.	Chip Douglas	Tork
June 14, 1967	"Daydream Believer"	UZB3-5438	RCA-L.A.	Chip Douglas	Stewart
June 14, 1967	"Salesman"	UZB3-5439	RCA-L.A.	Chip Douglas	Smith
June 14, 1967	"Words"	TZB3-4725	RCA-L.A.	Chip Douglas	Boyce-Hart
June 19, 1967	"Love Is Only Sleeping"	UZB3-5441	RCA-L.A.	Chip Douglas	Mann-Weil
June 19, 1967	"Daily Nightly"	UZB3-5440	RCA-L.A.	Chip Douglas	Nesmith
June 20, 1967	"What Am I Doing Hangin' 'Round?"	UZB3-5442	RCA-L.A.	Chip Douglas	Murphy-Castleman
June 20, 1967	"Don't Call On Me"	UZB3-7314	RCA-L.A.	Chip Douglas	Nesmith
June 20, 1967	"Goin' Down"	UZB3-7315	RCA-L.A.	Chip Douglas	Hilderbrand-Monkees
June 21, 1967	"Love Song - Tippy Taylor"	UZB3-7317	RCA-L.A.		
June 22, 1967	"Star Collector"	UZB3-7319	RCA-L.A.	Chip Douglas	Goffin-King
June 22, 1967	"Yours Until Tomorrow"	UZB3-7318	RCA-L.A.	Chip Douglas	Goffin-King
June 1967	"Symphony Is Over"	UZB3-5433	RCA-L.A.	Chip Douglas	
July 21, 1967	"She Hangs Out"	UZB3-7313	RCA-L.A.	Chip Douglas	Barry-Greenwich

DATE RECORDED	SONG TITLE	MASTER NUMBER	STUDIO RECORDED	PRODUCER	WRITERS
August 21, 1967	"Ríu Chíu"	UZB3-7321	RCA-L.A.	Chip Douglas	Public Domain
September 6, 1967	"Hard To Believe"	UZB3-7322	RCA-L.A.	Chip Douglas	Jones/Capti/Brick/Rockett
October 17, 1967	"I'm A Man"	UZB3-7539	RCA-L.A.	Chip Douglas	Mann-Weil
November 4, 1967	"I'm A Man"	UZB3-9781	RCA-L.A.	Monkees	Mann-Weil
November 4, 1967	"The Girl I Left Behind Me"	UZB3-9780	RCA-L.A.		Sedaka-Bayer
November 4, 1967	"We Were Made For Each Other"	UZB3-9779	RCA-L.A.	Monkees	Bayer-Fischoff
November 1967	"Tapioca Tundra"	UZB3-9783	RCA-L.A.	Monkees	Nesmith
November 1967	"Carlisle Wheeling Effervescent Popsicle"	UZB3-9782	RCA-L.A.	Monkees	Nesmith
November 1967	"Ceiling In My Room"	UZB3-9787	RCA-L.A.	Monkees	
November 1967	"My Head"	UZB3-9786	RCA-L.A.	Monkees	
December 3, 1967	"Writing Wrongs"	UZB3-9789	RCA-L.A.	Monkees	Nesmith
December 3, 1967	"Who Will Buy"	UZB3-9790	RCA-L.A.	Monkees	
December 17, 1967	"Lady's Baby"	UZB3-9784	RCA-L.A.	Monkees	Tork
December 17, 1967	"The Surprise"	UZB3-9785	RCA-L.A.	Monkees	
December 17, 1967	"Merry Go Round"	UZB3-9791	RCA-L.A.	Monkees	Tork
December 26, 1967	"P.O. Box 9847"	WZB3-0183	United Recorders	Monkees	Boyce-Hart
December 30, 1967	"Through The Looking Glass"	WZB3-5350	United Recorders	Monkees	Boyce-Hart
December 31, 1967	"Don't Listen To Linda"	WZB3-0187	United Recorders	Monkees	Boyce-Hart
January 6, 1968	"Auntie's Municipal Court" (AKA "Auntie & The Municipal Court")	WZB3-0107	RCA-L.A.	Monkees	Nesmith
January 6, 1968	"Circle Sky"	WZB3-0582	RCA-L.A.	Monkees	Nesmith
January 7, 1968	"Zor & Zam"	WZB3-0108	RCA-L.A.	Monkees	Chadwick-Chadwick
January 9, 1968	"My Share Of The Sidewalk"	UZB3-9795	RCA-L.A.	Monkees	Nesmith
January 10, 1968	"Daddy's Song"	WZB3-0589 WZB3-0110	RCA-L.A.	Monkees	Nilsson
January 10, 1968	"Good Time"	WZB3-0111	RCA-L.A.	Monkees	
January 11, 1968	"Mr. Richland's Favorite Song"	WZB3-0113	RCA-L.A.	Monkees	Nilsson
January 14, 1968	"While I Cried"	WZB3-0114	RCA-L.A.	Monkees	Nesmith
January 15, 1968	"Sound Of The Sunset, Sound Of The Sea"	WZB3-0107	RCA-L.A.	Monkees	Nesmith
January 15, 1968	"I'm Gonna Try"	WZB3-0138	RCA-L.A.	Monkees	Jones-Pitts
January 19, 1968	"Shorty Blackwell"	WZB3-0116	RCA-L.A.	Monkees	Dolenz
January 20, 1968	"Seeger's Theme"	UZB3-9790	Western	Monkees	Seeger
January 22, 1968	"Do I Have To Do This All Over Again"	WZB-0017 WZB3-0591	RCA-L.A.	Monkees	Tork
January 23, 1968	"War Games"	WZB3-0119	RCA-L.A.	Monkees	Jones-Pitts
January 24, 1968	"My Song In 7"	WZB3-0185	Sunset Sound	Monkees	Tork
January 25, 1968	"Empire"	WZB3-0122	RCA-L.A.	Monkees	Nesmith
January 28, 1968	"Can You Dig It?"	UZB3-0123	RCA-L.A.	Monkees	Tork
January 1968	"Tears Of Joy"	WZB3-0120	RCA-L.A.		
February 3, 1968	"Me Without You"	WZB3-3511	United Recorders	Monkees	Boyce-Hart

DATE RECORDED	SONG TITLE	MASTER NUMBER	STUDIO RECORDED	PRODUCER	WRITERS
February 4, 1968	"Long Title (Do I Have To Do This All Over Again)"	WZB3-0115	Western	Monkees	Tork
February 1968	"Alvin"		Western	Monkees	Tork
February 6, 1968	"Tear To Top Off My Head"	WZB3-0184	Western	Monkees	Tork
February 6, 1968	"Dream World"	WZB3-0127	Western	Monkees	Jones-Pitts
February 6, 1968	"Changes"	WZB3-0128	Western	Monkees	Jones-Pitts
February 7, 1968	"It's Nice To Be With You"	WZB3-0129	RCA-L.A.	Monkees	Goldstein
February 8, 1968	"She Calls Herself St. Matthew"	WZB3-0135	RCA-L.A.	Monkees	Nesmith
February 8, 1968	"Come On In"	WZB3-0180	Western	Monkees	Levonsen-Duboff
February 9, 1968	"Nine Times Blue"	WZB3-0125	RCA-L.A.	Monkees	Nesmith
February 1968	"Seasons"	WZB3-0126			
February 15, 1968	"Poster"	WZB3-0136	RCA-L.A.	Monkees	Jones-Pitts
February 15, 1968	"Party"	WZB3-0137	RCA-L.A.	Monkees	Jones-Pitts
February 17, 1968	"D. W. Washburn"	WZB3-0130	RCA-L.A.	Monkees	Leiber-Stoller
February 1968	"Impact"	WZB3-0139			
February 1968	"If I Ever Get To Saginaw Again"	WZB3-0178	RCA-L.A.	Monkees	Nesmith
February 1968	"All The Gray Haired Men"	WZB3-0179			
February 24, 1968	"Shake 'Em Up"	WZB3-0181	RCA-L.A.	Monkees	Leiber-Stoller
February 24, 1968	"Don't Say Nothing Bad"	WZB3-0182	RCA-L.A.	Monkees	
February 28, 1968	"Porpoise Song"	WZB3-3513	California Recorders	Monkees	Goffin-King
February 28, 1968	"Rose Marie"	UZB3-0104	RCA-L.A.	Monkees	Dolenz
March 9, 1968	"Shadow Of A Man"	WZB3-0142	RCA-L.A.	Monkees	Miller/Greenfield
March 9, 1968	"I'll Be Back Up On My Feet"	WZB3-0141	RCA-L.A.	Monkees	Linzer-Randell
March 9, 1968	"I Was Not Born To Follow"	WZB3-0144	RCA-L.A.	Monkees	Goffin-King
March 14, 1968	"Look Down"	WZB4-3515	T.T.G.	Monkees	Stern-King
March 28, 1968	"Music Of The World A-Turnin'"		American	Monkees	Nesmith
April 9, 1968	"Just A Game"	WZB4-3516	Western	Monkees	Dolenz
May 1968	"I Think It's Gonna Rain"	WZB5-5301			
May 1968	"Large As Life"	WZB5-5302			
May 1968	"Hold Me"	WZB5-5303			
May 1968	"Go Away Little Girl"	WZB5-5304			
May 27, 1968	"You & I"	WZB5-5307	Wally Heider	Monkees	Jones-Chadwick
May 27, 1968	"That's What It's Like Lovin You"	WZB5-5308	Wally Heider	Monkees	Jones-Pitts
May 27, 1968	"Smile"	WZB5-5309	Wally Heider	Monkees	Jones
May 29, 1968	"Propinquity"	WZB3-0136	RCA-L.A.	Monkees	Nesmith
		WZA4-3070	Nashville		
May 31, 1968	"Hollywood"	WZA4-3073	RCA-L.A.	Monkees	Nesmith
May 31, 1968	"Don't Wait For Me"	WZA4-3072	RCA-L.A.	Monkees	Nesmith
May 31, 1968	"The Crippled Lion"	WZA4-3071	RCA-L.A.	Monkees	Nesmith
May 31, 1968	"Some of Shelley's Blues"	WZB4-3073	RCA-L.A.	Monkees	Nesmith
May 31, 1968	"How Insensitive"	WZA4-3075	RCA-L.A.	Monkees	
June 1, 1968	"Good Clean Fun"	WZB4-3077	RCA-L.A.	Monkees	Nesmith
June 3, 1968	"Saint Matthew"	WZB4-3076	RCA-L.A.	Monkees	Nesmith
June 3, 1968	"Title Unknown"	WZA4-3086	RCA-L.A.	Monkees	
August 1, 1968	"Tell Your Mommy (Mommy & Daddy)"	WZB5-5349	RCA-L.A.	Monkees	Dolenz

DATE RECORDED	SONG TITLE	MASTER NUMBER	STUDIO RECORDED	PRODUCER	WRITERS
August 3, 1968	"As We Go Along"	WZB5-5342	Original Sound	Monkees	King-Stern
August 3, 1968	"Happy Birthday"	WZB5-5353	RCA-L.A.	Monkees	Lewis
August 1968	"Ditty Diego"	WZB3-0581	RCA-L.A.	Monkees	
August 1968	"Dandruff"	WZB3-0588	RCA-L.A.	Monkees	
August 1968	"Gravy"	WZB3-0588	RCA-L.A.	Monkees	
August 1968	"Opening Ceremony"	WZB3-0579	RCA-L.A.	Monkees	
August 1968	"Poll"	WZB3-0590	RCA-L.A.	Monkees	
August 1968	"Swami: Plus Strings"	WZB3-0592	RCA-L.A.	Monkees	
August 1968	"Supplicio"	WZB3-0598	RCA-L.A.	Monkees	
August 1958	"Superstitious"	WZB3-0586	RCA-L.A.	Monkees	
December 9, 1968	"Listen To The Band"	WZB5-5398	RCA-N.Y.	Monkees	Nesmith
December 1968	"Wind Up Man"	WZB5-5391	RCA-L.A.	Bones Howe	
December 1968	"I Go Ape"	WAB5-5393	RCA-L.A.	Bones Howe	
December 1968	"String For My Kite"	WZB5-5397	RCA-L.A.	Bones Howe	
December 23, 1968	"Me Without You"	WZB3-3511	United	Monkees	Boyce-Hart
December 1968	"Darwin"	WZB5-5392	RCA-L.A.	Bones Howe	
January 11, 1969	"Someday Man"	WZB5-5399	Western	Bones Howe	Williams-Nichols
January 11, 1969	"A Man Without A Dream"	XZB5-0123	Western	Bones Howe	Goffin-King
January 14, 1969	"Mommy & Daddy"	WZB3-5310	RCA-L.A.	Dolenz	Dolenz
January 22, 1969	"My Share Of The Sidewalk"	WZB3-0109	RCA-L.A.	Nesmith	Nesmith
May 1, 1969	"Penny Music"	XZB3-0361	RCA-L.A.	Jones	Leonard
May 1, 1969	"If You Have The Time"	XZB3-0576	RCA-L.A.	Chadwick-Jones	Chadwick-Jones
May 12, 1969	"Today"	XZB5-0510	Western	Chip Douglas	Chip Douglas
May 12, 1969	"Steam Engine"	XZB5-0509	Western	Chip Douglas	Chip Douglas
May 12, 1969	"Kitty Hawk"	XZB5-0575	Western	Chip Douglas	Chip Douglas
May 27, 1969	"You're So Good"	XZB3-0363	RCA-L.A.	Nesmith	Stone
May 27, 1969	"Oklahoma Backroom Dancer"	XZB3-0362	RCA-L.A.	Nesmith	Murphy
May 28, 1969	"Thirteen Is Not Our Lucky Number"	XZB3-0365	RCA-L.A.	Nesmith	Nesmith
May 28, 1969	"Little Red Rider"	XZB3-0364	RCA-L.A.	Nesmith	Nesmith
May 29, 1969	"Calico Sombra Girlfriend"	XZB3-0367	RCA-L.A.	Nesmith	Nesmith
May 29, 1969	"Lynn Harper"	XZB3-0368	RCA-L.A.	Nesmith	Nesmith
May 29, 1969	"Thank You My Friend"	XZB3-0366	RCA-L.A.	Nesmith	Nesmith
May 30, 1969	"Suzanna Sometime"	XZB3-0480	RCA-L.A.	Nesmith	Nesmith
May 30, 1969	"Storybook Of You"	XZB3-0479	RCA-L.A.	Boyce-Hart	Boyce-Hart
May 31, 1969	"Suzanna Sometime"	XZB3-0480	RCA-L.A.	Nesmith	Nesmith
May 31, 1969	"Storybook Of You"	XZB3-0479	RCA-L.A.	Boyce-Hart	Boyce-Hart
June 2, 1969	"Omega"	XZB3-0481	RCA-L.A.	Nesmith	Nesmith
June 2, 1969	"Never Tell A Woman Yes"	XZB3-0369	RCA-L.A.	Nesmith	Nesmith
June 5, 1969	"Good Afternoon"	XZB3-0370	RCA-L.A.	Nesmith	
June 5, 1969	"Down The Highway"	XZB3-0371	RCA-L.A.	Nesmith	King-Stern
June 6, 1969	"London Bridge"	XZB3-0448	RCA-L.A.	Nesmith	Nesmith
June 6, 1969	"The Bus That Never Comes"	XZB3-0447	RCA-L.A.	Nesmith	Keller-Russell
June 9, 1969	"Angel Band"	XZB3-0450	RCA-L.A.	Nesmith	Nesmith
June 9, 1969	"Till Then"	XZB3-0449	RCA-L.A.	Nesmith	
June 10, 1969	"Michigan Blackhawk"	XZB3-0452	RCA-L.A.	Nesmith	Nesmith
June 10, 1969	"Little Tommy Blue"	XZB3-0451	RCA-L.A.	Nesmith	
June 17, 1969	"Little Red Rider"	XZB3-0364	RCA-L.A.	Nesmith	Nesmith
June 26, 1969	"You're So Good"	XZB3-0363	RCA-L.A.	Nesmith	Stone
June 27, 1969	"French Song"	XZB3-0236	RCA-L.A.	Chadwick-Jones	Chadwick

DATE RECORDED	SONG TITLE	MASTER NUMBER	STUDIO RECORDED	PRODUCER	WRITERS
June 27, 1969	"How Can I Tell You"	XZB3-0237	RCA-L.A.	Chadwick-Jones	Chadwick-Jones
June 27, 1969	"If I Knew"	XZB3-0591	RCA-L.A.	Chadwick-Jones	Chadwick-Jones
June 27, 1969	"Opening Night"	XZB3-0360	RCA-L.A.	Jones	Smalls
June 1969	"The Good Earth"	XZB3-0594			
June 1969	"Time & Time Again"	XZB3-0592		Chadwick-Jones	Chadwick-Jones
July 16, 1969	"Midnight Train"	XZB3-0523	RCA-L.A.	Dolenz	Dolenz
July 16, 1969	"Bye Bye Baby Bye Bye (Second Song)"	XZB3-0524	RCA-L.A.	Dolenz	Klein-Dolenz
July 18, 1969	"Steam Engine"	XZB3-0509	RCA-L.A.	Chip Douglas	Chip Douglas
August 14, 1969	"Little Girl"	XZB3-0578	RCA-L.A.	Dolenz	Dolenz
August 14, 1969	"Pillow Time"	XZB3-0577	RCA-L.A.	Dolenz	Scott-Willis
February 5, 1970	"Tell Me Love"	ZZB1-4844	RCA-N.Y.	Jeff Barry	Barry-Kim
February 5, 1970	"I Love You Better"	ZZB1-5712	RCA-L.A.	Jeff Barry	Barry-Kim
February 5, 1970	"Oh My My"	ZZB1-4843	RCA-N.Y.	Jeff Barry	Barry-Kim
March 25, 1970	"You're So Good To Me"	ZZB1-5708	RCA-N.Y.	Jeff Barry	Barry-Bloom
March 25, 1970	"Which Way (Do You Want It)"	ZZB1-5706	RCA-N.Y.	Jeff Barry	Barry-Bloom
March 25, 1970	"Ticket On A Ferry Ride"	ZZB1-5705	RCA-N.Y.	Jeff Barry	Barry-Bloom
March 26, 1970	"Ride Baby Ride"		RCA-N.Y.	Jeff Barry	
March 26, 1970	"Do You Feel It Too?"	ZZB1-5709	RCA-N.Y.	Jeff Barry	Barry-Kim
March 26, 1970	"All Alone In The Dark"	ZZB1-5707	RCA-N.Y.	Jeff Barry	Soles-Albright
March 1970	"Do It In The Name Of Love"		RCA-N.Y.	Jeff Barry	Bloom-Goldberg
March 1970	"Lady Jane"		RCA-N.Y.	Jeff Barry	Barry
April 2, 1970	"Acapulco Sun"	ZZB1-5711	RCA-N.Y.	Jeff Barry	Soles-Albright
April 2, 1970	"It's Got To Be Love"	ZZB1-5712	RCA-N.Y.	Jeff Barry	Goldberg

The Monkees' U.S. Singles

AUGUST 1966
Colgems 66-1001
"Last Train To Clarksville"
*(Boyce-Hart) 2:40
b/w
"Take A Giant Step"
*(Goffin-King) 2:32

NOVEMBER 1966
Colgems 66-1002
"I'm A Believer"
*(Diamond) 2:41
b/w
"(I'm Not Your) Steppin' Stone"
*(Boyce-Hart) 2:25

MARCH 1967
Colgems 66-1004
"A Little Bit Me, A Little Bit You"
*(Diamond) 2:35
b/w
"The Girl I Knew Somewhere"
*(Nesmith) 2:32

JULY 1967
Colgems 66-1007
"Pleasant Valley Sunday"
*(Goffin-King) 3:10
b/w
"Words"
*(Boyce-Hart) 2:47

OCTOBER 1967
Colgems 66-1012
"Daydream Believer"
*(Stewart) 2:57
b/w
"Goin' Down"
*(Hilderbrand-Monkees) 3:57

APRIL 1968
Colgems 66-1019
"Valleri"
*(Boyce-Hart) 2:16
b/w
"Tapioca Tundra"
*(Nesmith) 3:03

*Songwriter

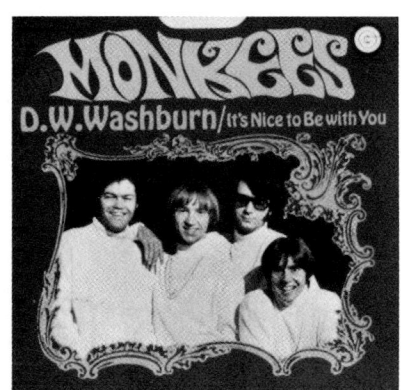

MAY 1968
Colgems 66-1023
"D. W. Washburn"
*(Leiber-Stoller) 2:43
b/w
"It's Nice To Be With You"
*(Goldstein) 2:47

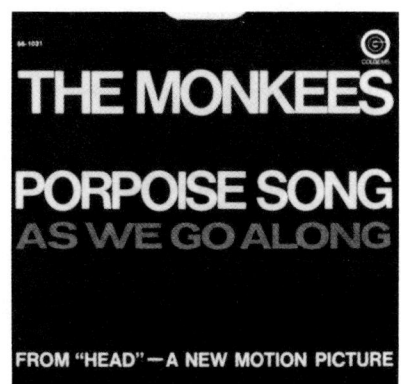

OCTOBER 1968
Colgems 66-1031
"Porpoise Song"
*(Goffin-King) 4:40
b/w
"As We Go ALong"
*(King-Stern) 3:53

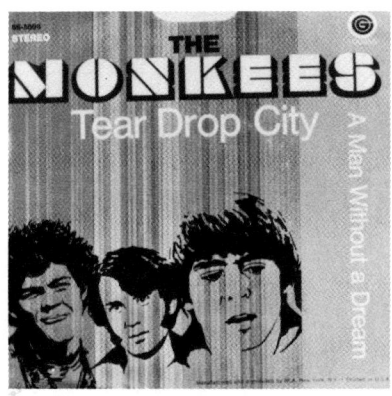

APRIL 1969
Colgems 66-5000
"Tear Drop City"
*(Boyce-Hart) 2:01
b/w
"A Man Without A Dream"
*(Goffin-King) 2:58

JULY 1969
Colgems 66-5004
"Listen To The Band"
*(Nesmith) 2:15
b/w
"Someday Man"
*(Nichols-Williams) 2:38

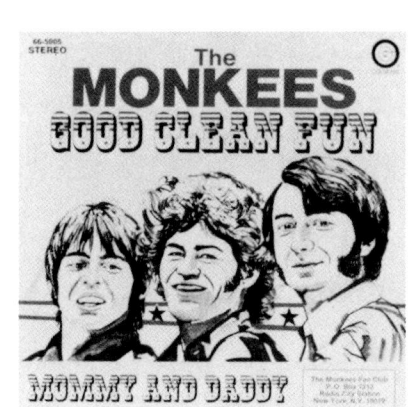

SEPTEMBER 1969
Colgems 66-5005
"Good Clean Fun"
*(Nesmith) 2:15
b/w
"Mommy And Daddy"
*(Dolenz) 2:10

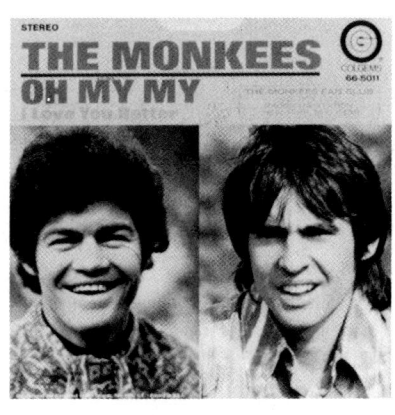

APRIL 1970
Colgems 66-5011
"Oh My My"
*(Barry-Kim) 2:57
b/w
"I Love You Better"
*(Barry-Kim) 2:26

*Songwriter

▶ Photo courtesy Edmag Archives.

The "Billboard" Singles Charts, 1968 - 1986

SINGLE	DATE	CHART POSITION	WEEKS ON CHART
"Last Train To Clarksville"	9/03/66	101	Debut
	9/10/66	67	1
	9/17/66	43	2
	9/24/66	26	3
	10/01/66	18	4
	10/08/66	6	5
	10/15/66	4	6
	10/22/66	3	7
	10/29/66	2	8
	11/05/66	1	9
	11/12/66	2	10
	11/19/66	4	11
	11/26/66	7	12
	12/03/66	10	13
	12/10/66	27	14
	12/17/66	43	15
"I'm A Believer"	12/10/66	44	1
	12/17/66	8	2
	12/24/66	3	3
	12/31/66	1	4
	1/07/67	1	5
	1/14/67	1	6
	1/21/67	1	7
	1/28/67	1	8
	2/04/67	1	9
	2/11/67	1	10
	2/18/67	2	11
	2/25/67	3	12
	3/04/67	10	13
	3/11/67	21	14
	3/18/67	43	15
"(I'm Not Your) Steppin' Stone"	12/10/66	120	Debut
	12/17/66	77	1
	12/24/66	48	2
	12/31/66	32	3
	1/07/67	32	4
	1/14/67	20	5
	1/21/67	28	6
	1/28/67	28	7
	2/04/67	40	8
"A Little Bit Me, A Little Bit You"	3/25/67	32	1

SINGLE	DATE	CHART POSITION	WEEKS ON CHART
	4/01/67	19	2
	4/08/67	9	3
	4/15/67	5	4
	4/22/67	3	5
	4/29/67	2	6
	5/06/67	4	7
	5/13/67	5	8
	5/20/67	20	9
"Pleasant Valley Sunday"	7/22/67	51	1
	7/29/67	24	2
	8/05/67	9	3
	8/12/67	4	4
	8/19/67	3	5
	8/26/67	3	6
	9/02/67	8	7
	9/09/67	13	8
	9/16/67	25	9
	9/23/67	40	10
"Words"	7/22/67	78	1
	7/29/67	46	2
	8/05/67	34	3
	8/12/67	24	4
	8/19/67	15	5
	8/26/67	15	6
	9/02/67	11	7
	9/09/67	12	8
	9/16/67	29	9
"Daydream Believer"	11/11/67	101	Debut
	11/18/67	33	1
	11/25/67	5	2
	12/02/67	1	3
	12/09/67	1	4
	12/16/67	1	5
	12/23/67	1	6
	1/06/68	2	7
	1/13/68	3	8
	1/20/68	6	9
	1/27/68	8	10
	2/03/68	24	11
"Goin' Down"	11/25/67	104	Debut
"Valleri"	3/09/68	24	1
	3/16/68	8	2
	3/23/68	7	3
	3/30/68	3	4
	4/06/68	3	5
	4/13/68	9	6

SINGLE	DATE	CHART POSITION	WEEKS ON CHART
	4/20/68	13	7
	4/27/68	45	8
	5/04/68	45	9
	5/11/68	47	10
"Tapioca Tundra"	3/09/68	73	1
	3/16/68	49	2
	3/23/68	49	3
	3/30/68	34	4
	4/06/68	45	5
	4/13/68	45	6
"D. W. Washburn"	6/08/68	101	Debut
	6/15/68	61	1
	6/22/68	29	2
	6/29/68	29	3
	7/06/68	19	4
	7/13/68	19	5
	7/20/68	31	6
	7/27/68	39	7
"It's Nice To Be With You"	6/08/68	105	Debut
	6/15/68	84	1
	6/22/68	54	2
	6/29/68	54	3
	7/06/68	51	4
	7/13/68	51	5
	7/20/68	51	6
	7/27/68	51	7
"Porpoise Song"	10/12/68	89	1
	10/19/68	62	2
	10/26/68	62	3
	11/02/68	62	4
	11/09/68	62	5
	11/16/68	62	6
"As We Go Along"	10/19/68	106	Debut
	10/26/68	109	1
"Tear Drop City"	2/22/69	87	1
	3/01/69	68	2
	3/08/69	62	3
	3/15/69	56	4
	3/22/69	56	5
	3/29/69	58	6
	4/05/69	66	7
"Someday Man"	5/03/69	133	Debut
	5/10/69	85	1

SINGLE	DATE	CHART POSITION	WEEKS ON CHART
	5/17/69	81	2
	5/24/69	111	3
"Listen To The Band"	5/24/69	101	Debut
	5/31/69	101	1
	6/07/69	97	2
	6/14/69	97	3
	6/21/69	91	4
	6/28/69	73	5
	7/05/69	67	6
	7/12/69	64	7
	7/19/69	63	8
	7/26/69	75	9
"Good Clean Fun"	9/13/69	113	Debut
	9/20/69	100	1
	9/27/69	99	2
	10/04/69	97	3
	10/11/69	91	4
	10/18/69	82	5
"Mommy & Daddy"	9/20/69	110	Debut
"Oh My My"	6/06/70	99	1
	6/13/70	98	2
"That Was Then, This Is Now"	7/05/86	88	Debut
	7/12/86	68	1
	7/19/86	57	2
	7/26/86	46	3
	8/02/86	36	4
	8/09/86	29	5
	8/16/86	25	6
	8/23/86	21	7
	8/30/86	20	8
	9/06/86	23	9
	9/13/86	36	10
	9/20/86	62	11
	9/27/86	75	12
	10/04/86	90	13
"Daydream Believer" (Remix)	11/01/86	90	Debut
	11/08/86	79	1
	11/15/86	79	2
	11/22/86	89	3

The Monkees' U.S. Albums

THE MONKEES Colgems COM/COS 101   October 1966
SIDE 1
(Theme from) The Monkees (2:20) *Boyce-Hart **Boyce-Hart
Saturday's Child (2:44) *Gates **Boyce-Hart-Keller
I Wanna Be Free (2:24) *Boyce-Hart **Boyce-Hart
Tomorrow's Gonna Be Another Day (2:33) *Boyce-Venet **Boyce-Hart
Papa Gene's Blues (1:55) *Nesmith **Nesmith
Take A Giant Step (2:32) *King-Goffin **Boyce-Hart
SIDE 2
Last Train To Clarksville (2:40) *Boyce-Hart **Boyce-Hart
This Just Doesn't Seem To Be My Day (2:08) *Boyce-Hart **Boyce-Hart-Keller
Let's Dance On (2:30) *Boyce-Hart **Boyce-Hart-Keller
I'll Be True To You (2:48) *Goffin-Titleman **Boyce-Hart-Keller
Sweet Young Thing (1:54) *Nesmith-King-Goffin **Nesmith
Gonna Buy Me A Dog (2:38) *Boyce-Hart **Boyce-Hart

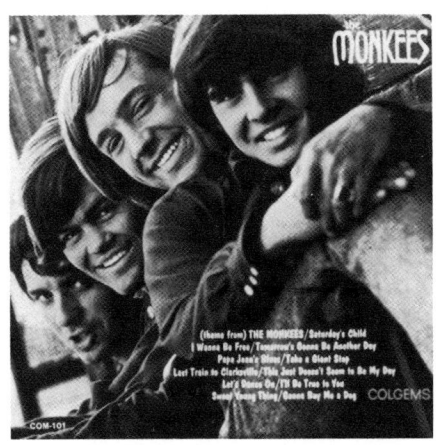

MORE OF THE MONKEES Colgems COM/COS 102   January 1967
SIDE 1
She (2:27) *Boyce-Hart **Boyce-Hart
When Love Comes Knockin' (At Your Door) (1:45) *Sedaka-Bayer **Sedaka-Bayer
Mary, Mary (2:12) *Nesmith **Nesmith
Hold On Girl (2:23) *Keller-Raleigh-Carr **Barry-Keller
Your Auntie Grizelda (2:28) *Keller-Hilderbrand **Barry-Keller
(I'm Not Your) Steppin' Stone (2:25) *Boyce-Hart **Boyce-Hart
SIDE 2
Look Out (Here Comes Tomorrow) *Diamond **Barry
The Kind Of Girl I Could Love (1:50) *Nesmith-Atkins **Nesmith
The Day We Fall In Love (2:20) *Linzer-Randell **Barry
Sometime In The Morning (2:24) *Goffin-King **Goffin-King-Barry
Laugh (2:25) *Medress-Margo-Margo-Seigal **Barry
I'm A Believer (2:41) *Diamond **Barry

THE MONKEES' HEADQUARTERS Colgems COM/COS 103   May 1967
SIDE 1
You Told Me (2:22) *Nesmith **Hatlelid
I'll Spend My Life With You (2:23) *Boyce-Hart **Hatlelid
Forget That Girl (2:21) *Hatlelid **Hatlelid
Band 6 (0:38) *Monkees **Hatlelid
You Just May Be The One (2:00) *Nesmith **Hatlelid
Shades Of Gray (3:20) *Mann-Weil **Hatlelid
I Can't Get Her Off My Mind (2:23) *Boyce-Hart **Hatlelid
SIDE 2
For Pete's Sake (2:10) *Tork-Richards **Hatlelid
Mr. Webster (2:02) *Boyce-Hart **Hatlelid
Sunny Girlfriend (2:31) *Nesmith **Hatlelid
Zilch (1:05) *Monkees **Hatlelid
No Time (2:09) *Cicalo **Hatlelid
Early Morning Blues And Greens (2:00) *Hilderbrand-Keller **Hatlelid
Randy Scouse Git (2:35) *Dolenz **Hatlelid

*Writer
**Producer

PISCES, AQUARIUS, CAPRICORN & JONES LTD
Colgems COM/COS 104 November 1967
SIDE 1
Salesman (2:03) *Smith **Douglas
She Hangs Out (2:33) *Barry **Douglas
The Door Into Summer (2:50) *Douglas-Martin **Douglas
Love Is Only Sleeping (2:28) *Mann-Weil **Douglas
Cuddly Toy (2:45) *Nilsson **Douglas
Words (2:48) *Boyce-Hart **Douglas
SIDE 2
Hard To Believe (2:33) *Jones-Capli-Brick-Rockett **Douglas
What Am I Doing Hangin' 'Round (3:02) *Lewis-Clarke **Douglas
Peter Percival Patterson's Pet Pig Porky *Tork **Douglas
Pleasant Valley Sunday (3:30) *King-Goffin **Douglas
Daily Nightly (2:26) *Nesmith **Douglas
Don't Call On Me (2:28) *Nesmith-London **Douglas
Star Collector (3:30) *King-Goffin **Douglas

THE BIRDS, THE BEES & THE MONKEES Colgems COM/COS 109
April 1968
SIDE 1
Dream World (3:16) *Jones-Pitts **Monkees
Auntie's Municipal Court (3:55) *Nesmith **Monkees
We Were Made For Each Other (2:24) *Fischoff-Bayer **Monkees
Tapioca Tundra (3:03) *Nesmith **Monkees
Daydream Believer (2:58) *Stewart **Douglas
Writing Wrongs (5:06) *Nesmith **Monkees
SIDE 2
I'll Be Back Upon My Feet (2:32) *Linzer-Randell **Monkees
The Poster (2:16) *Jones-Pitts **Monkees
P.O. Box 9847 (3:18) *Boyce-Hart **Monkees
Magnolia Simms (3:42) *Nesmith **Monkees
Valleri (2:16) *Boyce-Hart **Monkees
Zor And Zam (2:08) *Chadwick-Chadwick **Monkees

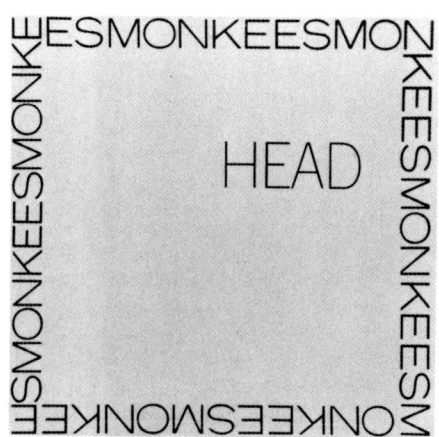

HEAD Colgems COSO 5008 December 1968
SIDE 1
Opening Ceremony (1:19) **Monkees
Porpoise Song (Theme from "Head") (2:56) *Goffin-King **Goffin
Ditty Diego - War Chant (1:27) **Monkees
Circle Sky (2:32) *Nesmith **Monkees
Supplicio (0:49) **Monkees
Can You Dig It (3:19) *Tork **Monkees
Gravy (0:05) **Monkees
SIDE 2
Superstitious (0:06) **Monkees
As We Go Along (3:53) *King-Stern **Monkees
Dandruff? (0:04) **Monkees
Daddy's Song (2:29) *Nilsson **Monkees
Poll (1:12) **Monkees
Long Title: Do I Have To Do This All Over Again (2:37) *Tork **Monkees
Swami - Plus Strings (5:18) *Thorne-Goffin-King **Monkees

*Writer
**Producer

INSTANT REPLAY Colgems COS 113   February 1969
SIDE 1
Through The Looking Glass (2:41) *Boyce-Hart-Baldwin **Boyce-Hart
Don't Listen To Linda (2:45) *Boyce-Hart **Boyce-Hart
I Won't Be The Same Without Her (2:38) *Goffin-King **Nesmith
Just A Game (1:46) *Dolenz **Dolenz
Me Without You (2:08) *Boyce-Hart **Boyce-Hart
Don't Wait For Me (2:34) *Nesmith **Nesmith
SIDE 2
You And I (2:10) *Jones-Chadwick **Jones
While I Cry (2:57) *Nesmith **Nesmith
Tear Drop City (2:01) *Boyce-Hart **Boyce-Hart
The Girl I Left Behind Me (2:40) *Bayer-Sedaka **Bayer-Sedaka
A Man Without A Dream (2:58) *Goffin-King **Howe
Shorty Blackwell (5:42) *Dolenz **Dolenz

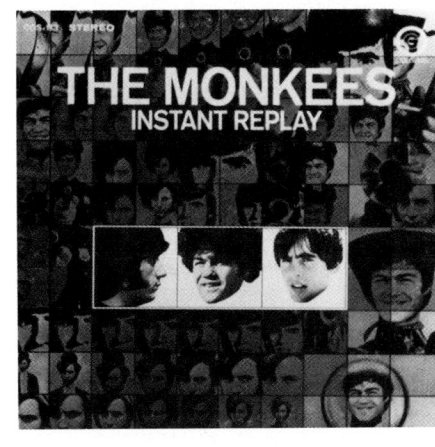

THE MONKEES GREATEST HITS Colgems COS 115   June 1969
SIDE 1
Daydream Believer (2:58) *Stewart **Douglas
Pleasant Valley Sunday (3:10) *Goffin-King **Douglas
Cuddly Toy (2:45) *Nilsson **Douglas
Shades Of Gray (3:20) *Mann-Weil **Douglas
Zor And Zam (2:08) *Chadwick-Chadwick **Monkees
A Little Bit Me, A Little Bit You (2:35) *Diamond **Barry
She (2:27) *Boyce-Hart **Boyce-Hart
SIDE 2
Randy Scouse Git (2:35) *Dolenz **Douglas
I Wanna Be Free (2:24) *Boyce-Hart **Boyce-Hart
I'm A Believer (2:41) *Diamond **Barry
Valleri (2:16) *Boyce-Hart **Monkees
Mary, Mary (2:12) *Nesmith **Nesmith
(I'm Not Your) Steppin' Stone (2:25) *Boyce-Hart **Boyce-Hart
Last Train To Clarksville (2:40) *Boyce-Hart **Boyce-Hart

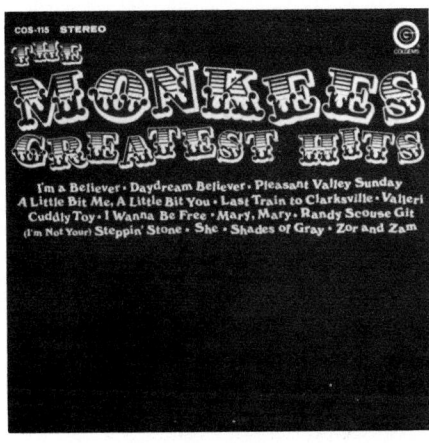

THE MONKEES PRESENT Colgems COS 117   October 1969
SIDE 1
Little Girl (1:59) *Dolenz **Dolenz
Good Clean Fun (2:15) *Nesmith **Nesmith
If I Knew (2:19) *Jones-Chadwick **Jones-Chadwick
Bye Bye Baby Bye Bye (2:17) *Dolenz-Klein **Dolenz
Never Tell A Woman Yes (3:44) *Nesmith **Nesmith
Looking For The Good Times (2:00) *Boyce-Hart **Boyce-Hart
SIDE 2
Ladies Aid Society (2:40) *Boyce-Hart **Boyce-Hart
Listen To The Band (2:45) *Nesmith **Nesmith
French Song (2:23) *Chadwick **Jones-Chadwick
Mommy And Daddy (2:10) *Dolenz **Dolenz
Oklahoma Backroom Dancer (2:34) *Murphy **Nesmith
Pillow Time (2:25) *Scott-Willis **Dolenz

*Writer
**Producer

THE MONKEES GOLDEN HITS   Colgems PRS 329
SIDE 1
(Theme from) The Monkees (2:20) *Boyce-Hart **Boyce-Hart
Valleri (2:16) *Boyce-Hart **Monkees
Forget That Girl (2:21) *Hatelid **Hatelid
I Wanna Be Free (2:24) *Boyce-Hart **Boyce-Hart
Teardrop City (2:01) *Boyce-Hart **Boyce-Hart
Last Train To Clarksville (2:40) *Boyce-Hart **Boyce-Hart
SIDE 2
Pleasant Valley Sunday (3:10) *King-Goffin **Douglas
I'm A Believer (2:41) *Diamond **Barry
The Day We Fall In Love (2:20) *Linzer-Randell **Barry
Mary, Mary (2:12) *Nesmith **Nesmith
Papa Gene's Blues (1:55) *Nesmith **Nesmith
(I'm Not Your) Steppin' Stone (2:25) *Boyce-Hart **Boyce-Hart

Special Edition LP released only through RCA Record Club and Post Cereals.

CHANGES   Colgems COS 119   May 1970
SIDE 1
Oh My My (2:57) *Barry-Kim **Barry
Ticket On A Ferry Ride (3:25) *Barry-Bloom **Barry
You're So Good To Me (2:29) *Barry-Bloom **Barry
It's Got To Be Love (2:20) *Goldberg **Barry
Acapulco Sun (2:46) *Soles-Albright **Barry
99 Pounds (2:25) *Barry **Barry
SIDE 2
Tell Me Love (2:32) *Barry **Barry
Do You Feel It Too? (2:28) *Barry-Kim **Barry
I Love You Better (2:26) *Barry-Kim **Barry
All Alone In The Dark (2:47) *Soles-Albright **Barry
Midnight Train (2:05) *Dolenz **Dolenz
I Never Thought It Peculiar (2:20) *Boyce-Hart **Boyce-Hart

BARREL FULL OF MONKEES   Colgems SCOS-1001   January 1971
SIDE 1
I'm A Believer (2:41) *Diamond **Barry
Cuddly Toy (2:45) *Nilsson **Douglas
Star Collector (3:30) *King-Goffin **Douglas
What Am I Doing Hangin' 'Round (3:02) *Lewis-Clark **Douglas
Pleasant Valley Sunday (3:10) *Goffin-King **Douglas
SIDE 2
Last Train To Clarksville (2:40) *Boyce-Hart **Boyce-Hart
Valleri (2:16) *Boyce-Hart **Monkees
Randy Scouse Git (2:35) *Dolenz **Hatelid
I Wanna Be Free (2:24) *Boyce-Hart **Boyce-Hart
Listen To The Band (2:45) *Nesmith **Nesmith
SIDE 3
(Theme from) The Monkees (2:20) *Boyce-Hart **Boyce-Hart
She Hangs Out (2:33) *Barry **Douglas
Gonna Buy Me A Dog (2:38) *Boyce-Hart **Boyce-Hart
She (2:27) *Boyce-Hart **Boyce-Hart
(I'm Not Your) Steppin' Stone (2:25) *Boyce-Hart **Boyce-Hart

*Writer
**Producer

SIDE 4
Daydream Believer (2:58) *Stewart **Douglas
Your Auntie Grizelda (2:28) *Keller-Hilderbrand **Barry-Keller
A Little Bit Me, A Little Bit You (2:35) *Diamond **Barry
Mary, Mary (2:12) *Nesmith **Nesmith
Shades Of Gray (3:20) *Mann-Weil **Hatelid

REFOCUS Bell 6081 September 1972
SIDE 1
Monkee's Theme (2:20) *Boyce-Hart **Boyce-Hart
Last Train To Clarksville (2:40) *Boyce-Hart **Boyce-Hart
She (2:27) *Boyce-Hart **Boyce-Hart
Daydream Believer (2:58) *Stewart **Douglas
Listen To The Band (2:45) *Nesmith **Nesmith
A Little Bit Me, A Little Bit You (2:35) *Diamond **Barry
SIDE 2
I'm A Believer (2:41) *Diamond **Barry
I Wanna Be Free (2:24) *Boyce-Hart **Boyce-Hart
Pleasant Valley Sunday (3:10) *King-Goffin **Douglas
(I'm Not Your) Steppin' Stone (2:25) *Boyce-Hart **Boyce-Hart
Shades Of Gray (3:20) *Mann-Weil **Hatelid

THE MONKEES RCA/Laurie House LH-8009/DLP2-0188 July 1976
SIDE 1
I'm A Believer (2:41) *Diamond **Barry
Oh My My (2:57) *Barry-Kim **Barry
Good Clean Fun (2:15) *Nesmith **Nesmith
Porpoise Song (2:56) *Goffin-King **Goffin
SIDE 2
Daydream Believer (2:57) *Stewart **Douglas
Valleri (2:16) *Boyce-Hart **Monkees
The Girl I Knew Somewhere (2:32) *Nesmith **Hatelid
Tapioca Tundra (3:03) *Nesmith **Monkees
A Little Bit Me, A Little Bit You (2:35) *Diamond **Barry
SIDE 3
Pleasant Valley Sunday (3:10) *Goffin-King **Douglas
Cuddly Toy (2:45) *Nilsson **Douglas
Tear Drop City (2:01) *Boyce-Hart **Boyce-Hart
Words (2:48) *Boyce-Hart **Douglas
SIDE 4
Last Train To Clarksville (2:40) *Boyce-Hart **Boyce-Hart
Someday Man (2:38) *Nichols-Williams **Howe
(I'm Not Your) Steppin' Stone (2:25) *Boyce-Hart **Boyce-Hart
It's Nice To Be With You (2:47) *Goldstein **Monkees
Listen To The Band (2:45) *Nesmith **Nesmith

This Special Products Edition was released as a TV mail order item only.

*Writer
**Producer

THE MONKEES GREATEST HITS   Arista AL 4089   July 1976
SIDE 1
Monkee's Theme (2:20) *Boyce-Hart **Boyce-Hart
Last Train To Clarksville (2:40) *Boyce-Hart **Boyce-Hart
She (2:27) *Boyce-Hart **Boyce-Hart
Daydream Believer (2:58) *Stewart **Douglas
Listen To The Band (2:45) *Nesmith **Nesmith
A Little Bit Me, A Little Bit You (2:35) *Diamond **Barry
SIDE 2
I'm A Believer (2:41) *Diamond **Barry
I Wanna Be Free (2:24) *Boyce-Hart **Boyce-Hart
Pleasant Valley Sunday (3:10) *King-Goffin **Douglas
(I'm Not Your) Steppin' Stone (2:25) *Boyce-Hart **Boyce-Hart
Shades Of Gray (3:20) *Mann-Weil **Hatlelid

Reissue of "REFOCUS" LP.

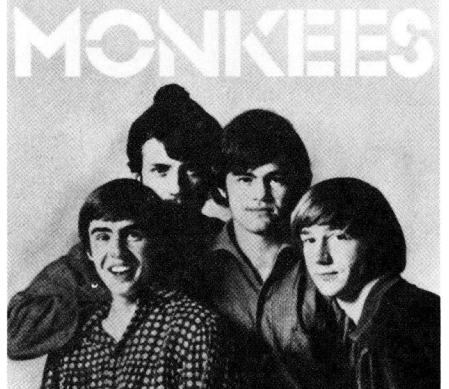

MORE GREATEST HITS OF THE MONKEES   Arista ABM 2007
October 1982
SIDE 1
Take a Giant Step (2:32) *King-Goffin **Boyce-Hart
Mary, Mary (2:12) *Nesmith **Nesmith
Sometime In The Morning (2:24) *Goffin-King **Goffin-King-Barry
Cuddly Toy (2:38) *Nilsson **Douglas
Randy Scouse Git (2:32) *Dolenz **Hatlelid
Words (2:46) *Boyce-Hart **Douglas
SIDE 2
Valleri (2:16) *Boyce-Hart **Monkees
You Just May Be The One (2:00) *Nesmith **Hatlelid
The Girl I Knew Somewhere (2:32) *Nesmith **Hatlelid
Saturday's Child (2:40) *Gates **Boyce-Hart-Keller
Look Out (Here Comes Tomorrow (2:12) *Diamond **Barry
For Pete's Sake (Closing Theme) (2:10) *Tork-Richards **Hatlelid

MONKEE BUSINESS   Rhino RNLP 701   November 1982
SIDE 1
Porpoise Song (4:04) *Goffin-King **Goffin
Star Collector (3:30) *Goffin-King **Douglas
It's Nice To Be With You (2:47) *Goldstein **Monkees
D. W. Washburn (2:47) *Leiber-Stoller **Monkees
Steam Engine (2:21) *Douglas **Douglas
Tema Dei Monkees (2:16) *Boyce-Hart **Boyce-Hart
SIDE 2
Pleasant Valley Sunday (3:12) *Goffin-King **Douglas
What Am I Doing Hangin' 'Round (3:02) *Murphy-Castleman **Douglas
She Hangs Out (2:33) *Barry-Greenwich **Barry
Love To Love (2:35) *Diamond **Barry
Someday Man (2:38) *Nichols-Williams **Howe
Goin' Down (4:27) *Monkees-Hilderbrand **Douglas

*Writer
**Producer

MONKEE FLIPS Rhino RNLP 113 February 1984
SIDE 1
You Told Me (2:22) *Nesmith **Hatlelid
Tear Drop City (2:01) *Boyce-Hart **Boyce-Hart
I Love You Better (2:26) *Barry-Kim **Barry
Forget That Girl (2:21) *Hatlelid **Hatlelid
Love Is Only Sleeping (2:28) *Mann-Weil **Douglas
Good Clean Fun (2:15) *Nesmith **Nesmith
Zor & Zam (2:08) *Chadwick-Chadwick **Monkees
SIDE 2
No Time (2:09) *Cicalo **Hatlelid
Oh My My (2:57) *Barry-Kim **Barry
Dream World (3:16) *Jones-Pitts **Monkees
Circle Sky (2:32) *Nesmith **Monkees
Little Girl (1:59) *Dolenz **Dolenz
Daily Nightly (2:26) *Nesmith **Douglas
Gonna Buy Me A Dog (2:38) *Boyce-Hart **Boyce-Hart

THE MONKEES/HIT FACTORY Pair ARPDL2-1109 December 1985
SIDE 1
Monkees Theme (2:20) *Boyce-Hart **Boyce-Hart
Tomorrow's Gonna Be Another Day (2:33) *Boyce-Venet **Boyce-Hart
I'll Be True To You (2:48) *Goffin-Titleman **Boyce-Hart-Keller
Sweet Young Thing (1:54) *Nesmith-King-Goffin **Nesmith
SIDE 2
When Love Comes Knockin' (1:45) *Sedaka-Bayer **Sedaka-Bayer
Forget That Girl (2:21) *Hatlelid **Hatlelid
D. W. Washburn (2:47) *Leiber-Stoller **Monkees
Can You Dig It? (3:19) *Tork **Monkees
SIDE 3
Last Train To Clarksville (2:40) *Boyce-Hart **Boyce-Hart
Tapioca Tundra (3:03) *Nesmith **Monkees
Through The Looking Glass (2:41) *Boyce-Hart-Baldwin **Boyce-Hart
Shorty Blackwell (5:42) *Dolenz **Dolenz
SIDE 4
Porpoise Song (2:56) *Goffin-King **Goffin
I'll Be Back Up On My Feet (2:32) *Linzer-Randell **Monkees
Little Girl (1:59) *Dolenz **Dolenz
Looking For The Good Times (2:00) *Boyce-Hart **Boyce-Hart

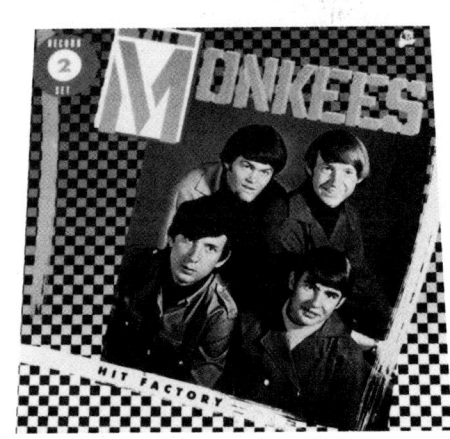

*Writer
**Producer

THEN & NOW . . . THE BEST OF THE MONKEES Arista AL9-8432
June 1986
SIDE 1
(Theme From) The Monkees (2:20) *Boyce-Hart **Boyce-Hart
Last Train To Clarksville (2:40) *Boyce-Hart **Boyce-Hart
Take A Giant Step (2:32) , *King-Goffin **Boyce-Hart
I'm A Believer (2:41) *Diamond **Barry
(I'm Not Your) Steppin' Stone (2:25) *Boyce-Hart **Boyce-Hart
A Little Bit Me, A Little Bit You (2:35) *Diamond **Barry
Anytime, Anyplace, Anywhere (3:53) *Hart-Eastman **Lloyd
SIDE 2
That Was Then, This Is Now (4:00) *Brescia **Lloyd
The Girl I Knew Somewhere (2:32) *Nesmith **Hatelid
Pleasant Valley Sunday (3:13) *King-Goffin **Douglas
What Am I Doing Hangin' 'Round (3:08) *Murphy-Castleman **Douglas
Daydream Believer (2:58) *Stewart **Douglas
Valleri (2:18) *Boyce-Hart **Monkees
Kicks (4:00) *Mann-Weil **Lloyd

THE BEST OF THE MONKEES Silver Eagle SE1048 June 1986
SIDE 1
(Theme From) The Monkees (2:20) *Boyce-Hart **Boyce-Hart
Last Train To Clarksville (2:40) *Boyce-Hart **Boyce-Hart
Take A Giant Step (2:32) *King-Goffin **Boyce-Hart
(I'm Not Your) Steppin' Stone (2:25) *Boyce-Hart **Boyce-Hart
Mary, Mary (2:12) *Nesmith **Nesmith
A Little Bit Me, A Little Bit You (2:35) *Diamond **Barry
SIDE 2
I'm A Believer (2:41) *Diamond **Barry
She (2:27) *Boyce-Hart **Boyce-Hart
Sometime In The Morning (2:24) *Goffin-King **Goffin-King-Barry
The Girl I Knew Somewhere (2:32) *Nesmith **Hatelid
You Just May Be The One (2:00) *Nesmith **Hatelid
Randy Scouse Git (2:35) *Dolenz **Hatelid
SIDE 3
Pleasant Valley Sunday (3:13) *King-Goffin **Douglas
What Am I Doing Hangin' 'Round (3:08) *Murphy-Castleman **Douglas
Words (2:54) *Boyce-Hart **Douglas
Goin' Down (4:25) *Dolenz-Tork-Jones-Nesmith-Hilderbrand **Douglas
Valleri (3:18) *Boyce-Hart **Monkees
Porpoise Song (4:12) *Goffin-King **Goffin
SIDE 4
Daydream Believer (2:58) *Stewart **Douglas
D. W. Washburn (2:48) *Leiber-Stoller **Monkees
Good Clean Fun (2:16) *Nesmith **Nesmith
Tear Drop City (2:01) *Boyce-Hart **Boyce-Hart
Listen To The Band (2:43) *Nesmith **Nesmith
For Pete's Sake (2:10) *Tork-Richards **Hatelid

This special collector's album was released as a television mail order item only. Originally planned as Arista's 20th Anniversary LP.

*Writer
**Producer

The "Billboard" Album Charts, 1968 - 1986

WEEK OF	CHART POSITION	ALBUM	WEEKS ON CHART
October 8, 1966	121	"The Monkees"	1
October 15, 1966	29	"The Monkees"	2
October 22, 1966	18	"The Monkees"	3
October 29, 1966	6	"The Monkees"	4
November 5, 1966	2	"The Monkees"	5
November 12, 1966	1	"The Monkees"	6
November 19, 1966	1	"The Monkees"	7
November 26, 1966	1	"The Monkees"	8
December 3, 1966	1	"The Monkees"	9
December 10, 1966	1	"The Monkees"	10
December 17, 1966	1	"The Monkees"	11
December 24, 1966	1	"The Monkees"	12
December 31, 1966	1	"The Monkees"	13
January 7, 1967	1	"The Monkees"	14
January 14, 1967	1	"The Monkees"	15
January 21, 1967	1	"The Monkees"	16
January 28, 1967	1	"The Monkees"	17
February 4, 1967	1	"The Monkees"	18
February 11, 1967	1	"More of The Monkees"	1
	2	"The Monkees"	19
February 18, 1967	1	"More of The Monkees"	2
	2	"The Monkees"	20
February 25, 1967	1	"More Of The Monkees"	3
	2	"The Monkees"	21
March 4, 1967	1	"More Of The Monkees"	4
	2	"The Monkees"	22
March 11, 1967	1	"More of The Monkees"	5

WEEK OF	CHART POSITION	ALBUM	WEEKS ON CHART
	3	"The Monkees"	23
March 18, 1967	1	"More of The Monkees"	6
	3	"The Monkees"	24
March 25, 1967	1	"More of The Monkees"	7
	3	"The Monkees"	25
April 1, 1967	1	"More of The Monkees"	8
	3	"The Monkees"	26
April 8, 1967	1	"More of The Monkees"	9
	3	"The Monkees"	27
April 15, 1967	1	"More of The Monkees"	10
	3	"The Monkees	28
April 22, 1967	1	"More of The Monkees"	12
	5	"The Monkees"	29
April 29, 1967	1	"More of The Monkees"	13
	6	"The Monkees"	30
May 6, 1967	1	"More of The Monkees"	14
	6	"The Monkees"	31
May 13, 1967	1	"More of The Monkees"	15
	7	"The Monkees"	32
May 20, 1967	1	"More of The Monkees"	16
	7	"The Monkees"	33
May 27, 1967	1	"More of The Monkees"	17
	7	"The Monkees"	34
	200	"The Monkees Song Book"	Debut
	188	"David Jones"	Debut
June 3, 1967	1	"More of The Monkees"	18
	9	"The Monkees"	35
	200	"The Monkees Song Book"	1
	185	"David Jones"	2
June 10, 1967	1	"More of The Monkees"	19
	13	"The Monkees"	36
	197	"Headquarters"	Debut
	193	"David Jones	3
June 17, 1967	4	"More of The Monkees"	19
	6	"Headquarters"	1
	14	"The Monkees"	37
	193	"David Jones"	4
June 24, 1967	1	"Headquarters"	2

WEEK OF	CHART POSITION	ALBUM	WEEKS ON CHART
	7	"More of The Monkees"	21
	16	"The Monkees"	38
	190	"David Jones"	5
July 1, 1967	2	"Headquarters"	3
	8	"More of The Monkees"	22
	21	"The Monkees"	39
July 8, 1967	2	"Headquarters"	4
	8	"More of The Monkees"	23
	20	"The Monkees"	40
July 15, 1967	2	"Headquarters"	5
	9	"More of The Monkees"	24
	17	"The Monkees"	41
July 22, 1967	2	"Headquarters"	6
	10	"More of The Monkees"	25
	30	"The Monkees"	42
July 29, 1967	2	"Headquarters	7
	10	"More of The Monkees"	26
	32	"The Monkees"	43
August 5, 1967	2	"Headquarters"	8
	17	"More of The Monkees"	27
	35	"The Monkees"	44
August 12, 1967	2	"Headquarters"	9
	15	"More of The Monkees"	28
	35	"The Monkees"	45
August 19, 1967	2	"Headquarters"	10
	11	"More of The Monkees"	29
	38	"The Monkees"	46
August 26, 1967	2	"Headquarters"	11
	17	"More of The Monkees"	30
	37	"The Monkees"	47
September 2, 1967	2	"Headquarters"	12
	18	"More of The Monkees"	31
	37	"The Monkees"	48
September 9, 1967	2	"Headquarters"	13
	18	"More of The Monkees"	32
	34	"The Monkees"	49
September 16, 1967	3	"Headquarters"	14
	19	"More of The Monkees"	33
	34	"The Monkees"	50
September 23, 1967	4	"Headquarters"	15

WEEK OF	CHART POSITION	ALBUM	WEEKS ON CHART
	24	"More of The Monkees"	34
	44	"The Monkees"	51
September 30, 1967	5	"Headquarters"	16
	28	"More of The Monkees"	35
	46	"The Monkees"	52
October 7, 1967	6	"Headquarters"	17
	38	"More of The Monkees"	36
	53	"The Monkees"	53
October 14, 1967	7	"Headquarters"	18
	39	"More of The Monkees"	37
	54	"The Monkees"	54
October 21, 1967	8	"Headquarters"	19
	39	"More of The Monkees"	38
	61	"The Monkees"	55
October 28, 1967	10	"Headquarters"	20
	37	"More of The Monkees"	39
	62	"The Monkees"	56
November 4, 1967	10	"Headquarters"	21
	36	"More of The Monkees"	40
	63	"The Monkees"	57
November 11, 1967	13	"Headquarters"	22
	34	"More of The Monkees"	41
	67	"The Monkees"	58
November 18, 1967	15	"Headquarters"	23
	34	"More of The Monkees"	42
	94	"The Monkees"	59
November 25, 1967	15	"Headquarters"	24
	29	"Pisces, Aquarius, Capricorn & Jones Ltd"	1
	31	"More of The Monkees"	43
	95	"The Monkees"	60
December 2, 1967	1	"Pisces, Aquarius, Capricorn & Jones Ltd"	2
	18	"Headquarters"	25
	39	"More of The Monkees"	44
	96	"The Monkees"	61
December 9, 1967	1	"Pisces, Aquarius, Capricorn & Jones Ltd"	3
	24	"Headquarters"	26
	54	"More of The Monkees"	45
	98	"The Monkees"	62

WEEK OF	CHART POSITION	ALBUM	WEEKS ON CHART
December 16, 1967	1	"Pisces, Aquarius, Capricorn & Jones Ltd"	4
	27	"Headquarters"	27
	51	"More of The Monkees"	46
	91	"The Monkees"	63
December 23, 1967	1	"Pisces, Aquarius, Capricorn & Jones Ltd"	5
	28	"Headquarters"	28
	47	"More of The Monkees"	47
	88	"The Monkees"	64
December 30, 1967	1	"Pisces, Aquarius, Capricorn & Jones Ltd"	6
	28	"Headquarters"	29
	44	"More of The Monkees"	48
	86	"The Monkees"	65
January 6, 1968	3	"Pisces, Aquarius, Capricorn & Jones Ltd"	7
	27	"Headquarters"	30
	42	"More of The Monkees"	49
	85	"The Monkees"	66
January 13, 1968	3	"Pisces, Aquarius, Capricorn & Jones Ltd	8
	25	"Headquarters"	31
	38	"More of The Monkees"	50
	53	"The Monkees"	67
January 20, 1968	3	"Pisces, Aquarius, Capricorn & Jones Ltd"	9
	24	"Headquarters"	32
	33	"More of The Monkees"	51
	76	"The Monkees"	68
January 27, 1968	3	"Pisces, Aquarius, Capricorn & Jones Ltd"	10
	29	"Headquarters"	33
	49	"More of The Monkees"	52
	75	"The Monkees"	69
February 3, 1968	4	"Pisces, Aquarius, Capricorn & Jones Ltd"	11
	29	"Headquarters"	34
	50	"More of The Monkees"	53
	69	"The Monkees"	70
February 10, 1968	6	"Pisces, Aquarius, Capricorn & Jones Ltd"	12
	32	"Headquarters"	35
	48	"More of The Monkees"	54
	66	"The Monkees"	71

WEEK OF	CHART POSITION	ALBUM	WEEKS ON CHART
February 17, 1968	6	"Pisces, Aquarius, Capricorn & Jones Ltd"	13
	34	"Headquarters"	36
	45	"More of The Monkees"	55
	62	"The Monkees"	72
February 24, 1968	18	"Pisces, Aquarius, Capricorn & Jones Ltd"	14
	35	"Headquarters"	37
	47	"More of The Monkees"	56
	58	"The Monkees"	73
March 2, 1968	23	"Pisces, Aquarius, Capricorn & Jones Ltd"	15
	35	"Headquarters"	38
	51	"More of The Monkees"	57
	61	"The Monkees"	74
March 9, 1968	34	"Pisces, Aquarius, Capricorn & Jones Ltd"	16
	37	"Headquarters"	39
	53	"More of The Monkees"	58
	63	"The Monkees"	75
March 16, 1968	33	"Pisces, Aquarius, Capricorn & Jones Ltd"	17
	40	"Headquarters"	40
	63	"The Monkees"	76
	75	"More of The Monkees"	59
March 23, 1968	32	"Pisces, Aquarius, Capricorn & Jones Ltd"	18
	40	"Headquarters"	41
	79	"More of The Monkees"	60
	102	"The Monkees"	77
March 30, 1968	34	"Pisces, Aquarius, Capricorn & Jones Ltd"	19
	41	"Headquarters"	42
	92	"More of The Monkees"	61
	108	"The Monkees"	78
April 6, 1968	41	"Headquarters"	43
	45	"Pisces, Aquarius, Capricorn & Jones Ltd"	20
	106	"More of The Monkees"	62
April 13, 1968	50	"Headquarters"	44
	53	"Pisces, Aquarius, Capricorn & Jones Ltd"	21
	127	"More of The Monkees"	63

WEEK OF	CHART POSITION	ALBUM	WEEKS ON CHART
April 20, 1968	53	"Pisces, Aquarius, Capricorn & Jones Ltd"	22
	57	"Headquarters"	45
	151	"More of The Monkees"	64
April 27, 1968	56	"Pisces, Aquarius, Capricorn & Jones Ltd"	23
	85	"Headquarters"	46
	156	"More of The Monkees"	65
May 4, 1968	58	"Pisces, Aquarius, Capricorn & Jones Ltd"	24
	133	"Headquarters"	47
	157	"More of The Monkees"	66
May 11, 1968	65	"Pisces, Aquarius, Capricorn & Jones Ltd"	25
	80	"The Birds, The Bees, & The Monkees"	1
	134	"Headquarters"	48
	191	"More of The Monkees"	67
May 18, 1968	3	"The Birds, The Bees, & The Monkees"	2
	67	"Pisces, Aquarius, Capricorn & Jones Ltd"	26
	134	"Headquarters"	49
	191	"More of The Monkees"	68
May 25, 1968	3	"The Birds, The Bees & The Monkees"	3
	66	"Pisces, Aquarius, Capricorn & Jones Ltd"	27
	132	"Headquarters"	50
	193	"More of The Monkees"	69
June 1, 1968	3	"The Birds, The Bees & The Monkees"	4
	91	"Pisces, Aquarius, Capricorn & Jones Ltd"	28
	193	"More of The Monkees"	70
June 8, 1968	3	"The Birds, The Bees, & The Monkees"	5
	106	"Pisces, Aquarius, Capricorn & Jones Ltd"	29
June 15, 1968	4	"The Birds, The Bees, & The Monkees"	6
	109	"Pisces, Aquarius, Capricorn & Jones Ltd"	30

WEEK OF	CHART POSITION	ALBUM	WEEKS ON CHART
June 22, 1968	4	"The Birds, The Bees, & The Monkees"	7
	110	"Pisces, Aquarius, Capricorn & Jones Ltd"	31
June 29, 1968	7	"The Birds, The Bees, & The Monkees"	8
	114	"Pisces, Aquarius, Capricorn & Jones Ltd"	32
July 6, 1968	7	"The Birds, The Bees, & The Monkees"	9
	115	"Pisces, Aquarius, Capricorn & Jones Ltd"	33
July 13, 1968	10	"The Birds, The Bees, & The Monkees"	10
	117	"Pisces, Aquarius, Capricorn & Jones Ltd"	34
July 20, 1968	15	"The Birds, The Bees, & The Monkees"	11
	112	"Pisces, Aquarius, Capricorn & Jones Ltd"	35
July 27, 1968	16	"The Birds, The Bees, & The Monkees"	12
	112	"Pisces, Aquarius, Capricorn & Jones Ltd"	36
August 3, 1968	31	"The Birds, The Bees, & The Monkees"	13
	110	"Pisces, Aquarius, Capricorn & Jones Ltd"	37
August 10, 1968	29	"The Birds, The Bees, & The Monkees"	14
	109	"Pisces, Aquarius, Capricorn & Jones Ltd"	38
August 17, 1968	33	"The Birds, The Bees, & The Monkees"	15
	118	"Pisces, Aquarius, Capricorn & Jones Ltd"	39
August 24, 1968	33	"The Birds, The Bees, & The Monkees"	16
	124	"Pisces, Aquarius, Capricorn & Jones Ltd"	40
August 31, 1968	43	"The Birds, The Bees, & The Monkees"	17
	154	"Pisces, Aquarius,	

WEEK OF	CHART POSITION	ALBUM	WEEKS ON CHART
		Capricorn & Jones Ltd"	41
September 7, 1968	46	"The Birds, The Bees, & The Monkees"	18
	163	"Pisces, Aquarius, Capricorn & Jones Ltd"	42
September 14, 1968	46	"The Birds, The Bees, & The Monkees"	19
	160	"Pisces, Aquarius, Capricorn & Jones Ltd"	43
September 21, 1968	64	"The Birds, The Bees, & The Monkees"	20
	150	"Pisces, Aquarius, Capricorn & Jones Ltd	44
September 28, 1968	67	"The Birds, The Bees, & The Monkees"	21
	166	"Pisces, Aquarius, Capricorn & Jones Ltd"	45
October 5, 1968	67	"The Birds, The Bees, & The Monkees"	22
	181	"Pisces, Aquarius, Capricorn & Jones Ltd"	46
October 12, 1968	80	"The Birds, The Bees, & The Monkees"	23
	192	"Pisces, Aquarius, Capricorn & Jones Ltd"	47
October 19, 1968	80	"The Birds, The Bees, & The Monkees"	24
October 26, 1968	88	"The Birds, The Bees, & The Monkees"	25
November 2, 1968	101	"The Birds, The Bees, & The Monkees"	26
November 9, 1968	105	"The Birds, The Bees, & The Monkees"	27
November 16, 1968	105	"The Birds, The Bees, & The Monkees"	28
November 23, 1968	106	"The Birds, The Bees, & The Monkees"	29
November 30, 1968	106	"The Birds, The Bees, & The Monkees"	30

WEEK OF	CHART POSITION	ALBUM	WEEKS ON CHART
December 7, 1968	113	"The Birds, The Bees, & The Monkees"	31
December 14, 1968	132	"The Birds, The Bees, & The Monkees"	32
December 28, 1968	132	"The Birds, The Bees, & The Monkees"	33
	158	"Head"	1
January 4, 1969	127	"The Birds, The Bees, & The Monkees"	34
	132	"Head"	2
January 11, 1969	127	"Head"	3
	132	"The Birds, The Bees, & The Monkees"	35
January 18, 1969	116	"Head"	4
	136	"The Birds, The Bees, & The Monkees"	36
January 25, 1969	98	"Head"	5
	136	"The Birds, The Bees, & The Monkees"	37
February 1, 1969	46	"Head"	6
	151	"The Birds, The Bees, & The Monkees"	38
February 8, 1969	45	"Head"	7
February 15, 1969	45	"Head"	8
February 22, 1969	55	"Head"	9
March 1, 1969	104	"Head"	10
	111	"Instant Replay"	1
March 8, 1969	70	"Instant Replay"	2
	108	"Head"	11
March 15, 1969	67	"Instant Replay"	3
	114	"Head"	12
March 22, 1969	36	"Instant Replay"	4
	114	"Head"	13
March 29, 1969	33	"Instant Replay"	5
	129	"Head"	14
April 5, 1969	33	"Instant Replay"	6

WEEK OF	CHART POSITION	ALBUM	WEEKS ON CHART
April 12, 1969	32	"Instant Replay"	7
April 19, 1969	38	"Instant Replay"	8
April 26, 1969	44	"Instant Replay"	9
May 3, 1969	54	"Instant Replay"	10
May 10, 1969	90	"Instant Replay"	11
May 17, 1969	114	"Instant Replay"	12
May 24, 1969	113	"Instant Replay"	13
May 31, 1969	148	"Instant Replay"	14
June 7, 1969	166	"Instant Replay"	15
June 28, 1969	163	"The Monkees Greatest Hits"	1
July 7, 1969	99	"The Monkees Greatest Hits"	2
July 12, 1969	97	"The Monkees Greatest Hits"	3
July 19, 1969	95	"The Monkees Greatest Hits"	4
July 26, 1969	89	"The Monkees Greatest Hits"	5
August 2, 1969	94	"The Monkees Greatest Hits"	6
August 9, 1969	95	"The Monkees Greatest Hits"	7
August 16, 1969	93	"The Monkees Greatest Hits"	8
August 23, 1969	128	"The Monkees Greatest Hits"	9
August 30, 1969	155	"The Monkees Greatest Hits"	10
September 6, 1969	155	"The Monkees Greatest Hits"	11
September 13, 1969	162	"The Monkees Greatest Hits"	12

WEEK OF	CHART POSITION	ALBUM	WEEKS ON CHART
November 1, 1969	187	"Present"	1
November 8, 1969	116	"Present"	2
November 15, 1969	108	"Present"	3
November 22, 1969	108	"Present"	4
November 29, 1969	103	"Present"	5
December 6, 1969	100	"Present"	6
December 13, 1969	147	"Present"	7
December 20, 1969	123	"Present"	8
December 27, 1969	131	"Present"	9
January 3, 1970	155	"Present"	10
January 10, 1970	154	"Present"	11
January 17, 1970	157	"Present"	12
January 24, 1970	157	"Present"	13
January 31, 1970	160	"Present"	14
August 7, 1976	125	"The Monkees Greatest Hits" (Arista)	New Entry
August 14, 1976	112	"The Monkees Greatest Hits" (Arista)	2
August 21, 1976	102	"The Monkees Greatest Hits" (Arista)	3
August 28, 1976	92	"The Monkees Greatest Hits" (Arista)	4
September 4, 1976	80	"The Monkees Greatest Hits" (Arista)	5
September 11, 1976	80	"The Monkees Greatest Hits" (Arista)	6
September 18, 1976	69	"The Monkees Greatest Hits" (Arista)	7
September 25, 1976	59	"The Monkees Greatest Hits" (Arista)	8
October 2, 1976	58	"The Monkees Greatest	

WEEK OF	CHART POSITION	ALBUM	WEEKS ON CHART
		Hits" (Arista)	9
October 9, 1976	63	"The Monkees Greatest Hits" (Arista)	10
October 16, 1976	62	"The Monkees Greatest Hits" (Arista)	11
October 23, 1976	136	"The Monkees Greatest Hits" (Arista)	12
October 30, 1976	156	"The Monkees Greatest Hits" (Arista)	13
November 6, 1976	156	"The Monkees Greatest Hits" (Arista)	14
November 13, 1976	148	"The Monkees Greatest Hits" (Arista)	15
November 20, 1976	149	"The Monkees Greatest Hits" (Arista)	16
May 3, 1986	180	"The Monkees Greatest Hits" (Arista)	Re-debut
May 10, 1986	160	"The Monkees Greatest Hits" (Arista)	1
May 17, 1986	121	"The Monkees Greatest Hits" (Arista)	2
May 24, 1986	107	"The Monkees Greatest Hits" (Arista)	3
May 31, 1986	89	"The Monkees Greatest Hits" (Arista)	4
June 7, 1986	80	"The Monkees Greatest Hits" (Arista)	5
June 14, 1986	71	"The Monkees Greatest Hits" (Arista)	6
June 21, 1986	70	"The Monkees Greatest Hits" (Arista)	7
June 28, 1986	70	"The Monkees Greatest Hits" (Arista)	8
July 5, 1986	69	"The Monkees Greatest Hits" (Arista)	9

WEEK OF	CHART POSITION	ALBUM	WEEKS ON CHART
July 12, 1986	82	"The Monkees Greatest Hits" (Arista)	10
July 19, 1986	77	"The Monkees Greatest Hits" (Arista)	11
July 26, 1986	136	"The Monkees Greatest Hits" (Arista)	12
	71	"Then & Now . . . The Best of The Monkees"	Debut
August 2, 1986	45	"Then & Now . . . The Best of The Monkees"	1
	165	"The Monkees Greatest Hits" (Arista)	13
August 9, 1986	42	"Then & Now . . . The Best of The Monkees"	2
August 16, 1986	31	"Then & Now . . . The Best of The Monkees"	3
	139	"The Monkees"*	Debut
	143	"More of The Monkees"*	Debut
	160	"Headquarters"*	Debut
	177	"Pisces, Aquarius, Capricorn & Jones Ltd"*	Debut
August 23, 1986	27	"Then & Now . . . The Best of The Monkees"	4
	126	"The Monkees"*	1
	134	"More of The Monkees"*	1
	157	"Headquarters"*	1
	154	"Pisces, Aquarius, Capricorn & Jones Ltd"	1
August 30, 1986	24	"Then & Now . . . The Best of The Monkees"	5
	109	"The Monkees"*	2
	110	"More of The Monkees"*	2
	127	"Headquarters"*	2
	140	"Pisces, Aquarius, Capricorn & Jones Ltd"	2
September 6, 1986	22	"Then & Now . . . The Best of The Monkees"	6
	101	"The Monkees"*	3
	108	"More of The Monkees"*	3
	121	"Headquarters"*	3
	124	"Pisces, Aquarius, Capricorn & Jones Ltd"*	3
September 13, 1986	21	"Then & Now . . . The	

*Rhino Records reissue

WEEK OF	CHART POSITION	ALBUM	WEEKS ON CHART
		Best of The Monkees"	7
	101	"The Monkees"*	4
	120	"More of The Monkees"*	4
	121	"Headquarters"*	4
	124	"Pisces, Aquarius, Capricorn, & Jones Ltd"*	4
	185	"The Birds, The Bees & The Monkees"*	Debut
September 20, 1986	21	"Then & Now . . . The Best of The Monkees"	8
	117	"The Monkees"*	5
	121	"More of The Monkees"*	5
	134	"Headquarters"*	5
	141	"Pisces, Aquarius, Capricorn & Jones Ltd"*	5
	165	"The Birds, The Bees & The Monkees"*	2
September 27, 1986	22	"Then & Now . . . The Best of The Monkees"	9
	107	"The Monkees"*	6
	115	"More of The Monkees"*	6
	134	"Headquarters"*	6
	135	"Pisces, Aquarius, Capricorn & Jones Ltd"*	6
	149	"The Birds, The Bees & The Monkees"*	4
October 4, 1986	25	"Then & Now . . . The Best of The Monkees"	10
	107	"The Monkees"*	7
	115	"More of The Monkees"*	7
	135	"Pisces, Aquarius, Capricorn & Jones Ltd"*	7
	142	"Headquarters"*	7
	149	"The Birds, The Bees & The Monkees"*	4
October 11, 1986	28	"Then & Now . . . The Best of The Monkees"	11
	104	"The Monkees"*	8
	111	"More of The Monkees"*	8
	132	"Pisces, Aquarius, Capricorn & Jones Ltd"*	8
	134	"Headquarters"*	8
	145	"The Birds, The Bees & The Monkees"*	5
October 18, 1986	31	"Then & Now . . . The Best of The Monkees"	12
	99	"The Monkees"*	9

*Rhino Records reissue

WEEK OF	CHART POSITION	ALBUM	WEEKS ON CHART
	104	"More of The Monkees"*	9
	134	"Headquarters"*	9
	137	"Pisces, Aquarius, Capricorn & Jones Ltd"*	9
	151	"The Birds, The Bees & The Monkees"*	6
October 25, 1986	33	"Then & Now . . . The Best of The Monkees"	13
	92	"The Monkees"*	10
	96	"More of The Monkees"*	10
	131	"Headquarters"*	10
	145	"Pisces, Aquarius, Capricorn & Jones Ltd"*	10
	148	"The Birds, The Bees & The Monkees"	7
November 1, 1986	41	"Then & Now . . . The Best of The Monkees"	14
	92	"The Monkees"*	11
	96	"More of The Monkees"*	11
	142	"Headquarters"*	11
	145	"Pisces, Aquarius, Capricorn & Jones Ltd"*	11
	148	"The Birds, The Bees & The Monkees"	8
November 8, 1986	41	"Then & Now . . . The Best of The Monkees"	15
	97	"The Monkees"*	12
	105	"More of The Monkees"*	12
	143	"Headquarters"*	12
	147	"Pisces, Aquarius, Capricorn & Jones Ltd"*	12
	158	"The Birds, The Bees & The Monkees"*	9
	174	"Changes"	Debut
November 15, 1986	38	"Then & Now . . . The Best of The Monkees"	16
	99	"The Monkees"*	13
	110	"More of The Monkees"*	13
	151	"Headquarters"*	13
	154	"Changes"*	1
	160	"The Birds, The Bees & The Monkees"*	10
	163	"Pisces, Aquarius, Capricorn & Jones Ltd"*	13
November 22, 1986	48	"Then & Now . . . The of The Monkees"	17
	113	"The Monkees"*	14

*Rhino Records reissue

WEEK OF	CHART POSITION	ALBUM	WEEKS ON CHART
	126	"More of The Monkees"*	14
	152	"Changes"*	2
	183	"Pisces, Aquarius, Capricorn & Jones Ltd"*	14
	184	"Headquarters"*	14
	189	"The Birds, The Bees & The Monkees"*	11
November 29, 1986	55	"Then & Now . . . The Best of The Monkees"	18
	122	"The Monkees"*	15
	134	"More of The Monkees"*	15
	193	"Pisces, Aquarius, Capricorn & Jones Ltd"*	15
	195	"Headquarters"*	15
	199	"Changes"*	3
December 6, 1986	60	"Then & Now . . . The Best of The Monkees"	19
	132	"The Monkees"*	16
	158	"More of The Monkees"*	16
	197	"Headquarters"*	16
	200	"Pisces, Aquarius, Capricorn & Jones Ltd"*	16
December 13, 1986	61	"Then & Now . . . The Best of The Monkees"	20
	151	"The Monkees"*	17
	154	"More of The Monkees"*	17
December 20, 1986	69	"Then & Now . . . The Best of The Monkees"	21
	163	"The Monkees"*	18
	165	"More of The Monkees"*	18
December 27, 1986	74	"Then & Now . . . The Best of The Monkees"	22
	179	"The Monkees"*	19
	183	"More of The Monkees"*	19

*Rhino Records reissue

Foreign Record Releases

JAPAN
1966
"Last Train To Clarksville"
b/w
"Take A Giant Step"

JAPAN
1966
"I Wanna Be Free"
b/w
"(Theme From) The Monkees"

AUSTRALIA
1967
"I Wanna Be Free"
b/w
"You Just May Be The One"

SPAIN
1966
"I'm A Believer"
b/w
"(I'm Not Your) Steppin' Stone"

JAPAN
1967
"I'm A Believer"
b/w
"(I'm Not Your) Steppin' Stone"

GERMANY
1967?
"I'm A Believer"
b/w
"A Little Bit Me, A Little Bit You"

ITALY
1967
"A Little Bit Me, A Little Bit You"
b/w
"The Girl I Knew Somewhere"

JAPAN
1967
"A Little Bit Me, A Little Bit You"
b/w
"The Girl I Knew Somewhere"

GERMANY
1967
"A Little Bit Me, A Little Bit You"
b/w
"The Girl I Knew Somewhere"

GERMANY
1967
"(Theme From) The Monkees"
b/w
"Mary, Mary"

SPAIN?
1967
"No Time"
b/w
"Alternate Title"

JAPAN
1967
"Star Collector"
b/w
"No Time"

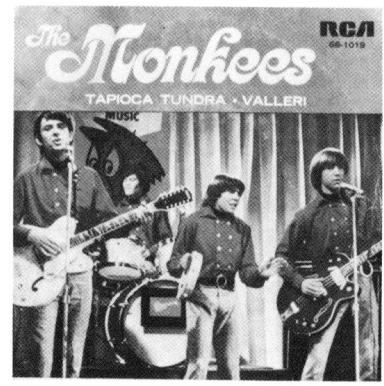

JAPAN
1967
"Daydream Believer"
b/w
"Goin' Down"

JAPAN
1968
"Valleri"
b/w
"Tapioca Tundra"

AUSTRALIA
1968
"Valleri"
b/w
"Tapioca Tundra"

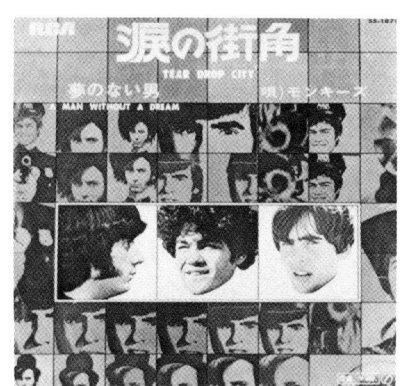

JAPAN
1969
"Tear Drop City"
b/w
"A Man Without A Dream"

JAPAN
1969
"Good Clean Fun"
b/w
"Mommy And Daddy"

SPAIN
1967
"(Theme From) The Monkees"
b/w
"Last Train To Clarksville"

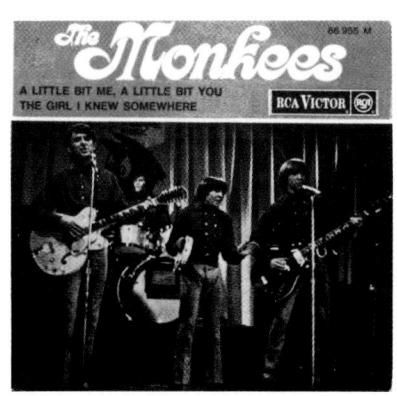

FRANCE
1967
RCA Victor Records
"Words"
"Forget That Girl"
b/w
"Alternate Title (Randy Scouse Git)"
"Pleasant Valley Sunday"

FRANCE
1967
RCA Victor Records
"A Little Bit Me, A Little Bit You"
"Mary, Mary"
b/w
"The Girl I Knew Somewhere"
"She"

AUSTRALIA
1966
RCA Victor Records
"(Theme From) The Monkees"
"Saturday's Child"
b/w
"Tomorrow's Gonna Be Another Day"
"Take A Giant Step"

AUSTRALIA
1966
RCA Victor Records
"I'm A Believer"
"Papa Gene's Blues"
b/w
"This Just Doesn't Seem To Be My Day"
"Let's Dance On"

AUSTRALIA
1967
RCA Victor Records
"She"
"Sunny Girl Friend"
b/w
"Look Out (Here Comes Tomorrow)"
"Gonna Buy Me A Dog"

AUSTRALIA
1967
RCA Victor Records
"Cuddly Toy"
"Laugh"
b/w
"You Told Me"
"No Time"

ENGLAND
1980
Arista Records
"I'm A Believer"
"Last Train To Clarksville"
b/w
"Daydream Believer"
"A Little Bit Me, A Little Bit You"

ENGLAND
1981
Arista Records
"(I'm Not Your) Steppin' Stone)
"Pleasant Valley Sunday"
b/w
"Alternate Title (Randy Scouse Git)"
"What Am I Doin' Hangin' 'Round"

JAPAN
1966
RCA Victor Records
"(Theme From) The Monkees"
"Sweet Young Thing"
b/w
"I Wanna Be Free"
"Gonna Buy Me A Dog"

JAPAN
1966
RCA Victor Records
"The Kind Of Girl I Could Love"
"Your Auntie Grizelda"
b/w
"She"
"The Day We Fall In Love"

JAPAN
1967
RCA Victor Records
"Words"
"Pleasant Valley Sunday"
b/w
"A Little Bit Me, A Little Bit You"
"The Girl I Knew Somewhere"

JAPAN
1967
RCA Victor Records
"Daydream Believer"
"Goin' Down"
b/w
"Star Collector"
"No Time"

JAPAN
1967
RCA Victor Records
"Shades Of Gray"
"Forget That Girl"
b/w
"Randy Scouse Git"
"You Just May Be The One"

JAPAN
1968
RCA Victor Records
"D. W. Washburn"
"It's Nice To Be With You"
b/w
"Valleri"
"Tapioca Tundra"

SPAIN
1966
RCA Victor Records
"Last Train To Clarksville"
"Take A Giant Step"
b/w
"(Theme From) The Monkees"
"Tomorrow's Gonna Be Another Day"

MEXICO
1967
RCA Victor Records
"Forget That Girl"
"I'll Spend My Life With You"
b/w
"You Just May Be The One"
"For Pete's Sake"

JAPAN
1981
Arista Records
"The Monkees"

CHILE
1967
RCA Victor Records
"Headquarters"

BRAZIL
1967
RCA Victor Records
"Headquarters"

ARGENTINA
1967
RCA Victor Records
"Pisces, Aquarius, Capricorn & Jones, Ltd"

MEXICO
1967
RCA Victor Records
"Pisces, Aquarius, Capricorn & Jones, Ltd"

JAPAN
1967
RCA Victor Records
"Pisces, Aquarius, Capricorn & Jones, Ltd"

JAPAN
1968
RCA Victor Records
"The Monkees' Golden Story"

JAPAN
1981
Arista Records
"The Monkees Golden Story"

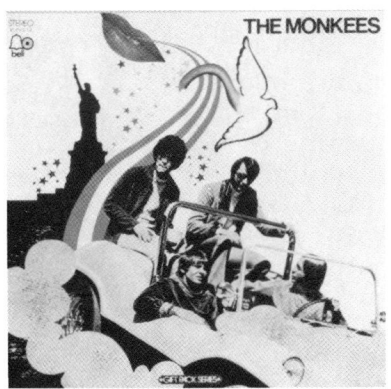

JAPAN
1972
Bell Records
"The Monkees"
(2 LP Greatest Hits Set)

JAPAN
1980
Arista Records
"Monkees The Best"

ENGLAND
1973
Sounds Superb Records
"The Best Of The Monkees"
(Reissue of U.S. 'Refocus')

GERMANY
1973
Crystal Records
"The Best Of The Monkees"
(Reissue of U.S. 'Refocus')

ARGENTINA
1968
RCA Victor Records
"The Birds, The Bees & The Monkees"

JAPAN
1981
Arista Records
"Head"

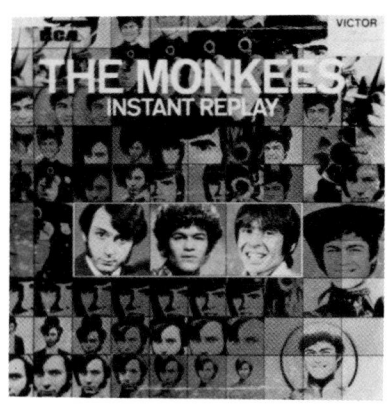

PUERTO RICO
1969
RCA Victor Records
"Instant Replay"

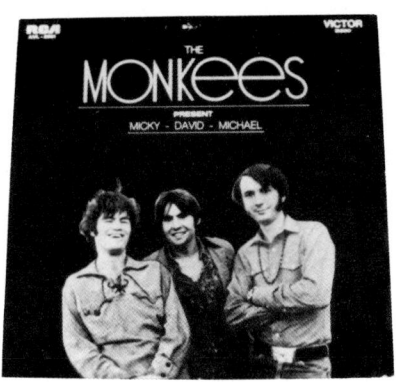

ARGENTINA
1969
RCA Victor Records
"The Monkees Present"

JAPAN
1967
RCA Victor Records
"Monkees Golden Album"

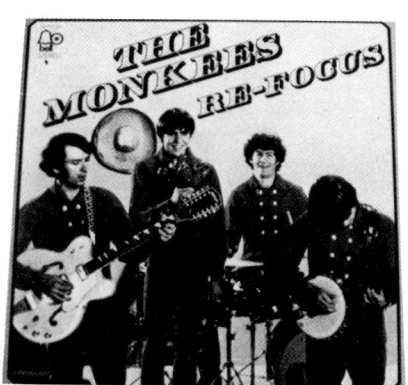

JAPAN
1972
RCA Victor Records
"Refocus"

JAPAN
1972
Bell Records
"The Monkees Greatest Hits"

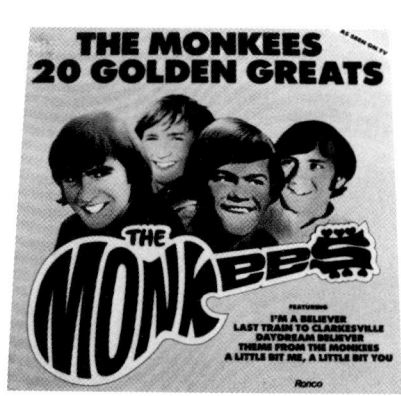

ENGLAND
1982
Ronco
"20 Golden Greats"

      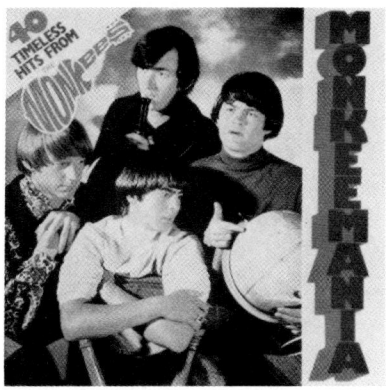

ENGLAND
1983
Reader's Digest
"Here Come The Monkees"

ENGLAND
1982
MFB Records
"The Best Of The Monkees"
(Reissue of U.K. Sounds Superb recording)

AUSTRALIA
1979
Arista Records
"40 Timeless Hits From The Monkees"

▶ Photo courtesy Edmag Archives.

The International Singles Charts, 1966-1968

In the heyday of Monkeemania during the 1960's, the group's standings in the music charts were reported here in the U.S. on a weekly basis. Because of this, information on how well a particular single or album did in this country was readily available; less accessible were the facts and figures on how their releases fared in other parts of the world. The following pages, reflecting data from various foreign trade publications, detail the chart performances of standard Monkee hits, but also of songs appearing on singles overseas which were never issued on domestic singles. From all the charts that were available to us, we have assembled an international Monkees singles chart history as complete as possible from December 1966 to October 1968.

DATE	POSITION	SONG	COUNTRY
December 3, 1966	10	"Last Train To Clarksville"	Eire
	6	"Last Train To Clarksville"	New Zealand
December 10, 1966	5	"Last Train To Clarksville"	Eire
	8	"Last Train To Clarksville"	New Zealand
January 21, 1967	4	"I'm A Believer"	England
	3	"I'm A Believer"	Holland
January 28, 1967	1	"I'm A Believer"	England
	1	"I'm A Believer"	Holland
February 4, 1967	1	"I'm A Believer"	England
	45	"Last Train To Clarksville" (Debut)	England
	1	"I'm A Believer"	Erie
	1	"I'm A Believer"	Holland
February 11, 1967	1	"I'm A Believer"	England
	33	"Last Train To Clarksville"	England
	1	"I'm A Believer"	Erie
	1	"I'm A Believer"	Holland
February 18, 1967	1	"I'm A Believer"	Erie
	27	"Last Train To Clarksville"	England
	1	"I'm A Believer"	England
	1	"I'm A Believer"	Holland
	9	"I'm A Believer"	Philippines
February 25, 1967	8	"I'm A Believer"	Denmark
	1	"I'm A Believer"	Eire
	1	"I'm A Believer"	England
	23	"Last Train To Clarksville"	England
	8	"I'm A Believer"	Mexico
	8	"I'm A Believer"	New Zealand
	1	"I'm A Believer"	Norway
	7	"I'm A Believer"	Philippines

DATE	POSITION	SONG	COUNTRY
	1	"I'm A Believer"	South Africa
March 4, 1967	1	"I'm A Believer"	Australia
	1	"I'm A Believer"	Eire
	26	"Last Train To Clarksville"	England
	3	"I'm A Believer"	England
	1	"I'm A Believer"	Finland
	2	"I'm A Believer"	Mexico
	1	"I'm A Believer"	New Zealand
	6	"I'm A Believer"	Philippines
	9	"I'm A Believer"	Singapore
	1	"I'm A Believer"	South Africa
March 11, 1967	2	"I'm A Believer"	Australia
	8	"I'm A Believer"	Denmark
	2	"I'm A Believer"	Eire
	5	"I'm A Believer"	England
	30	"Last Train To Clarksville"	England
	1	"I'm A Believer"	Finland
	8	"Last Train To Clarksville"	Finland
	2	"I'm A Believer"	Mexico
	1	"I'm A Believer"	New Zealand
	5	"I'm A Believer"	Philippines
March 18, 1967	2	"I'm A Believer"	Australia
	4	"I'm A Believer"	Eire
	36	"Last Train To Clarksville"	England
	7	"I'm A Believer"	England
	2	"I'm A Believer"	Holland
	1	"I'm A Believer"	Norway
	4	"I'm A Believer"	Philippines
	1	"I'm A Believer"	South Africa
March 25, 1967	3	"I'm A Believer"	Australia
	1	"I'm A Believer"	Denmark
	7	"I'm A Believer"	Eire
	14	"I'm A Believer"	England
	4	"I'm A Believer"	Holland
	2	"I'm A Believer"	Mexico
	1	"I'm A Believer"	New Zealand
	2	"I'm A Believer"	Norway
	4	"I'm A Believer"	Philippines
	2	"I'm A Believer"	Singapore
	1	"I'm A Believer"	South Africa
April 1, 1967	5	"I'm A Believer"	Australia
	1	"I'm A Believer"	Denmark
	9	"I'm A Believer"	Eire
	17	"I'm A Believer"	England
	1	"I'm A Believer"	Germany
	9	"I'm A Believer"	Holland
	2	"I'm A Believer"	Mexico

DATE	POSITION	SONG	COUNTRY
	1	"I'm A Believer"	New Zealand
	3	"I'm A Believer"	Philippines
	10	"Last Train To Clarksville"	Rio De Janiero
April 8, 1967	7	"I'm A Believer"	Australia
	1	"I'm A Believer"	Denmark
	24	"I'm A Believer"	England
	1	"I'm A Believer"	Germany
	3	"I'm A Believer"	Mexico
	1	"I'm A Believer"	New Zealand
	2	"I'm A Believer"	Philippines
	3	"I'm A Believer"	South Africa
April 15, 1967	9	"I'm A Believer"	Australia
	28	"I'm A Believer"	England
	14	"A Little Bit Me, A Little Bit You"	England
	3	"I'm A Believer"	Mexico
	3	"I'm A Believer"	New Zealand
	2	"I'm A Believer"	Philippines
April 22, 1967	10	"I'm A Believer"	Australia
	6	"I'm A Believer"	Denmark
	4	"A Little Bit Me, A Little Bit You"	England
	32	"I'm A Believer"	England
	2	"I'm A Believer"	Mexico
	3	"I'm A Believer"	New Zealand
	3	"I'm A Believer"	Philippines
	6	"I'm A Believer"	South Africa
April 29, 1967	9	"I'm A Believer"	Australia
	3	"A Little Bit Me, A Little Bit You"	England
	40	"I'm A Believer"	England
	9	"A Little Bit Me, A Little Bit You"	Holland
	3	"I'm A Believer"	Malaysia
	6	"I'm A Believer"	Mexico
	3	"I'm A Believer"	New Zealand
	1	"I'm A Believer"	Philippines
May 6, 1967	10	"I'm A Believer"	Australia
	9	"A Little Bit Me, A Little Bit You"	Eire
	47	"I'm A Believer"	England
	3	"A Little Bit Me, A Little Bit You"	England
	6	"A Little Bit Me, A Little Bit You"	Holland
	5	"I'm A Believer"	Mexico
	6	"I'm A Believer"	New Zealand
	5	"I'm A Believer"	Norway
	10	"I'm A Believer"	Puerto Rico
May 13, 1967	10	"I'm A Believer"	Argentina
	7	"A Little Bit Me, A Little Bit You"	Eire
	4	"A Little Bit Me, A Little Bit You"	England
	4	"I'm A Believer"	Finland

DATE	POSITION	SONG	COUNTRY
	6	"A Little Bit Me, A Little Bit You"	Holland
	14	"I'm A Believer"	Italy
	5	"I'm A Believer"	Malaysia
	3	"I'm A Believer"	Mexico
	1	"I'm A Believer"	Philippines
	8	"A Little Bit Me, A Little Bit You"	Puerto Rico
May 20, 1967	5	"I'm A Believer"	Argentina
	10	"A Little Bit Me, A Little Bit You"	England
	5	"I'm A Believer"	Malaysia
	3	"I'm A Believer"	Mexico
	9	"(Theme from) The Monkees"	Mexico
	6	"A Little Bit Me, A Little Bit You"	Norway
	9	"I'm A Believer"	Norway
	1	"I'm A Believer"	Philippines
May 27, 1967	5	"I'm A Believer"	Argentina
	7	"A Little Bit Me, A Little Bit You"	Eire
	11	"A Little Bit Me, A Little Bit You"	England
	8	"A Little Bit Me, A Little Bit You"	Holland
	6	"I'm A Believer"	Malaysia
	5	"I'm A Believer"	Mexico
	6	"(Theme from) The Monkees"	Mexico
	1	"I'm A Believer"	Philippines
	1	"A Little Bit Me, A Little Bit You"	Puerto Rico
June 3, 1967	6	"I'm A Believer"	Argentina
	10	"A Little Bit Me, A Little Bit You"	Eire
	18	"A Little Bit Me, A Little Bit You"	England
	9	"A Little Bit Me, A Little Bit You"	Holland
	3	"I'm A Believer"	Malaysia
	1	"I'm A Believer"	Philippines
	10	"A Little Bit Me, A Little Bit You"	Philippines
	10	"A Little Bit Me, A Little Bit You"	South Africa
June 10, 1967	6	"I'm A Believer"	Argentina
	2	"Poco Puedo Darte"	Argentina
	21	"A Little Bit Me, A Little Bit You"	England
	4	"(Theme from) The Monkees"	Mexico
	9	"I'm A Believer"	Mexico
	1	"A Little Bit Me, A Little Bit You"	New Zealand
	1	"I'm A Believer"	Philippines
	10	"A Little Bit Me, A Little Bit You"	Philippines
June 17, 1967	10	"A Little Bit Me, A Little Bit You"	Australia
	9	"A Little Bit Me, A Little Bit You"	Denmark
	32	"A Little Bit Me, A Little Bit You"	England
	10	"A Little Bit Me, A Little Bit You"	Germany
	5	"I'm A Believer"	Malaysia
	2	"(Theme from) The Monkees"	Mexico
	3	"I'm A Believer"	Mexico
	1	"A Little Bit Me, A Little Bit You"	New Zealand

DATE	POSITION	SONG	COUNTRY
	1	"I'm A Believer"	Philippines
	9	"A Little Bit Me, A Little Bit You"	Philippines
	1	"A Little Bit Me, A Little Bit You"	Puerto Rico
	9	"She"	Puerto Rico
June 24, 1967	2	"Poco Puedo Darte"	Argentina
	9	"I'm A Beliver"	Argentina
	9	"A Little Bit Me, A Little Bit You"	Australia
	50	"A Little Bit Me, A Little Bit You"	England
	10	"I'm A Believer"	Malaysia
	2	"(Theme from) The Monkees"	Mexico
	3	"I'm A Believer"	Mexico
	1	"A Little Bit Me, A Little Bit You"	New Zealand
	4	"(Theme from) The Monkees"	Norway
	1	"I'm A Believer"	Philippines
	8	"A Little Bit Me, A Little Bit You"	Philippines
	8	"A Little Bit Me, A Little Bit You"	South Africa
	4	"(Theme from) The Monkees"	Sweden
July 1, 1967	9	"A Little Bit Me, A Little Bit You"	Australia
	49	"A Little Bit Me, A Little Bit You"	England
	30	"Alternate Title"	England
	2	"I'm A Believer"	Mexico
	5	"(Theme from) The Monkees"	Mexico
	1	"A Little Bit Me, A Little Bit You"	New Zealand
	2	"(Theme from) The Monkees"	Norway
	1	"I'm A Believer"	Philippines
	7	"A Little Bit Me, A Little Bit You"	Philippines
	1	"A Little Bit Me, A Little Bit You"	Puerto Rico
	9	"She"	Puerto Rico
	10	"A Little Bit Me, A Little Bit You"	South Africa
	3	"(Theme from) The Monkees"	Sweden
	2	"A Little Bit Me, A Little Bit You"	Switzerland
July 8, 1967	7	"Alternate Title"	England
	34	"A Little Bit Me, A Little Bit You"	England
	2	"(Theme from) The Monkees"	Mexico
	6	"I'm A Believer"	Mexico
	3	"A Little Bit Me, A Little Bit You"	New Zealand
	1	"I'm A Believer"	Philippines
	7	"A Little Bit Me, A Little Bit You"	Philippines
	1	"She"	Puerto Rico
	3	"A Little Bit Me, A Little Bit You"	Puerto Rico
	10	"A Little Bit Me, A Little Bit You"	South Africa
	4	"A Little Bit Me, A Little Bit You"	Spain
	4	"A Little Bit Me, A Little Bit You"	Switzerland
July 15, 1967	3	"Alternate Title"	England
	2	"(Theme from) The Monkees"	Mexico
	3	"She"	Mexico
	5	"I'm A Believer"	Mexico
	3	"A Little Bit Me, A Little Bit You"	New Zealand

DATE	POSITION	SONG	COUNTRY
	1	"(Theme from) The Monkees"	Norway
	2	"I'm A Believer"	Philippines
	6	"A Little Bit Me, A Little Bit You"	Philippines
	4	"A Little Bit Me, A Little Bit You"	Spain
	6	"(Theme from) The Monkees"	Sweden
July 22, 1967	3	"Alternate Title"	England
	2	"She"	Mexico
	4	"I'm A Believer"	Mexico
	5	"(Theme from) The Monkees"	Mexico
	5	"A Little Bit Me, A Little Bit You"	New Zealand
	1	"(Theme from) The Monkees"	Norway
	2	"I'm A Believer"	Philippines
	5	"A Little Bit Me, A Little Bit You"	Philippines
	5	"A Little Bit Me, A Little Bit You"	Spain
	8	"(Theme from) The Monkees"	Sweden
July 29, 1967	2	"Alternate Title"	England
	2	"She"	Mexico
	3	"(Theme from) The Monkees"	Mexico
	4	"I'm A Believer"	Mexico
	7	"A Little Bit Me, A Little Bit You"	New Zealand
	3	"I'm A Believer"	Philippines
	5	"A Little Bit Me, A Little Bit You"	Philippines
	4	"A Little Bit Me, A Little Bit You"	Spain
August 5, 1967	6	"Alternate Title"	Eire
	2	"She"	Mexico
	3	"(Theme from) The Monkees"	Mexico
	5	"I'm A Believer"	Mexico
	3	"I'm A Believer"	Philippines
	5	"A Little Bit Me, A Little Bit You"	Philippines
	4	"She"	Puerto Rico
	7	"A Little Bit Me, A Little Bit You"	Puerto Rico
	9	"A Little Bit Me, A Little Bit You"	Singapore
	4	"A Little Bit Me, A Little Bit You"	Spain
August 12, 1967	6	"Alternate Title"	Eire
	2	"She"	Mexico
	3	"(Theme from) The Monkees"	Mexico
	5	"I'm A Believer"	Mexico
	1	"A Little Bit Me, A Little Bit You"	Philippines
	5	"I'm A Believer"	Philippines
	5	"She"	Puerto Rico
	8	"A Little Bit Me, A Little Bit You"	Puerto Rico
	5	"A Little Bit Me, A Little Bit You"	Singapore
August 19, 1967	8	"Alternate Title"	Denmark
	5	"Alternate Title"	Eire
	9	"Alternate Title"	England
	3	"(Theme from) The Monkees"	Mexico
	7	"She"	Mexico

DATE	POSITION	SONG	COUNTRY
	5	"I'm A Believer"	Mexico
	6	"(Theme from) The Monkees"	Norway
	1	"A Little Bit Me, A Little Bit You"	Philippines
	5	"I'm A Believer"	Philippines
	9	"She"	Puerto Rico
	10	"A Little Bit Me, A Little Bit You"	Puerto Rico
	2	"A Little Bit Me, A Little Bit You"	Singapore
	9	"A Little Bit Me, A Little Bit You"	Spain
August 26, 1967	4	"Alternate Title"	Eire
	22	"Pleasant Valley Sunday"	England
	14	"Alternate Title"	England
	4	"(Theme from) The Monkees"	Mexico
	6	"I'm A Believer"	Mexico
	9	"She"	Mexico
	9	"(Theme from) The Monkees"	Norway
	1	"A Little Bit Me, A Little Bit You"	Philippines
	5	"A Little Bit Me, A Little Bit You"	Philippines
	9	"She"	Puerto Rico
	2	"A Little Bit Me, A Little Bit You"	Singapore
	5	"Alternate Title"	Sweden
September 2, 1967	6	"The Monkees EP Vol. 1"	Australia
	6	"Alternate Title"	Denmark
	6	"Alternate Title"	Eire
	11	"Pleasant Valley Sunday"	England
	22	"Alternate Title"	England
	4	"(Theme from) The Monkees"	Mexico
	5	"She"	Mexico
	8	"I'm A Believer"	Mexico
	1	"A Little Bit Me, A Little Bit You"	Philippines
	7	"I'm A Believer"	Philippines
	5	"Alternate Title"	Poland
	9	"She"	Puerto Rico
	2	"A Little Bit Me, A Little Bit You"	Singapore
	5	"Alternate Title"	Sweden
September 9, 1967	6	"The Monkees EP Vol. 1"	Australia
	9	"Alternate Title"	Denmark
	6	"Alternate Title"	Eire
	11	"Pleasant Valley Sunday"	England
	27	"Alternate Title"	England
	5	"(Theme from) The Monkees"	Mexico
	6	"She"	Mexico
	8	"I'm A Believer"	Mexico
	2	"A Little Bit Me, A Little Bit You"	Philippines
	9	"I'm A Believer"	Philippines
	10	"She"	Puerto Rico
	3	"A Little Bit Me, A Little Bit You"	Singapore
	7	"Alternate Title"	Switzerland
	10	"I'm A Believer"	Venezula

DATE	POSITION	SONG	COUNTRY
September 16, 1967	3	"The Monkees EP Vol. 1"	Australia
	8	"I Wanna Be Free"	Australia
	4	"Tema de los Monkees"	Chile
	8	"Alternate Title"	Eire
	34	"Alternate Title"	England
	11	"Pleasant Valley Sunday"	England
	5	"(Theme from) The Monkees"	Mexico
	6	"She"	Mexico
	8	"I'm A Believer"	Mexico
	3	"Alternate Title"	Norway
	2	"A Little Bit Me, A Little Bit You"	Philippines
	9	"I'm A Believer"	Philippines
	9	"Pleasant Valley Sunday"	Puerto Rico
	10	"She"	Puerto Rico
	4	"A Little Bit Me, A Little Bit You"	Singapore
September 23, 1967	2	"The Monkees EP Vol. 1"	Australia
	5	"Tema de los Monkees"	Chile
	17	"Pleasant Valley Sunday"	England
	2	"(Theme from) The Monkees"	Mexico
	5	"She"	Mexico
	9	"I'm A Believer"	Mexico
	10	"Pleasant Valley Sunday"	New Zealand
	3	"Alternate Title"	Norway
	2	"A Little Bit Me, A Little Bit You"	Philippines
	10	"I'm A Believer"	Philippines
	7	"Pleasant Valley Sunday"	Puerto Rico
	10	"She"	Puerto Rico
	6	"A Little Bit Me, A Little Bit You"	Singapore
September 30, 1967	1	"The Monkees EP Vol. 1"	Australia
	10	"Pleasant Valley Sunday"	Denmark
	22	"Pleasant Valley Sunday"	England
	7	"Pleasant Valley Sunday"	New Zealand
	5	"A Little Bit Me, A Little Bit You"	Philippines
	7	"Pleasant Valley Sunday"	Puerto Rico
	7	"A Little Bit Me, A Little Bit You"	Singapore
October 7, 1967	1	"(Theme from) The Monkees"	Australia
	28	"Pleasant Valley Sunday"	England
	3	"(Theme from) The Monkees"	Mexico
	5	"She"	Mexico
	9	"I'm A Believer"	Mexico
	2	"Pleasant Valley Sunday"	New Zealand
	7	"A Little Bit Me, A Little Bit You"	Philippines
	10	"Shades Of Gray"	Philippines
	6	"Pleasant Valley Sunday"	Puerto Rico
	10	"A Little Bit Me, A Little Bit You"	Singapore
October 14, 1967			
	2	"(Theme from) The Monkees"	Australia
	9	"Pleasant Valley Sunday"	Australia

DATE	POSITION	SONG	COUNTRY
	41	"Pleasant Valley Sunday"	England
	3	"(Theme from) The Monkees"	Mexico
	4	"She"	Mexico
	9	"I'm A Believer"	Mexico
	3	"Pleasant Valley Sunday"	New Zealand
	8	"A Little Bit Me, A Little Bit You"	Philippines
	9	"Shades Of Gray"	Philippines
	6	"Pleasant Valley Sunday"	Puerto Rico
October 21, 1967			
	1	"(Theme from) The Monkees"	Australia
	10	"Pleasant Valley Sunday"	Australia
	4	"(Theme from) The Monkees"	Mexico
	5	"She"	Mexico
	3	"Pleasant Valley Sunday"	New Zealand
	5	"Pleasant Valley Sunday"	Norway
	8	"Shades Of Gray"	Philippines
	9	"A Little Bit Me, A Little Bit You"	Philippines
October 28, 1967	4	"(Theme from) The Monkees"	Mexico
	6	"She"	Mexico
	4	"Pleasant Valley Sunday"	New Zealand
	7	"Pleasant Valley Sunday"	Norway
	7	"Shades Of Gray"	Philippines
	9	"A Little Bit Me, A Little Bit You"	Philippines
	10	"Pleasant Valley Sunday"	Poland
November 4, 1967	4	"Gonna Buy Me A Dog"	Mexico
	5	"She"	Mexico
	6	"(Theme from) The Monkees"	Mexico
	5	"Alternate Title"	New Zealand
November 11, 1967	4	"Gonna Buy Me A Dog"	Mexico
	5	"She"	Mexico
	8	"(Theme from) The Monkees"	Mexico
	7	"Shades Of Gray"	Philippines
November 18, 1967	4	"Pleasant Valley Sunday"	Malaysia
	3	"Gonna Buy Me A Dog"	Mexico
	5	"She"	Mexico
	6	"(Theme from) The Monkees"	Mexico
November 25, 1967	42	"Daydream Believer"	England
	3	"Gonna Buy Me A Dog"	Mexico
	5	"She"	Mexico
	6	"(Theme from) The Monkees"	Mexico
	8	"Shades Of Gray"	Philippines
December 2, 1967	25	"Daydream Believer"	England
	5	"Pleasant Valley Sunday"	Malaysia
	4	"Gonna Buy Me A Dog"	Mexico
	5	"She"	Mexico

DATE	POSITION	SONG	COUNTRY
	8	"(Theme from) The Monkees"	Mexico
	8	"Shades Of Gray"	Philippines
December 9, 1967	19	"Daydream Beleiver"	England
	10	"Daydream Believer"	Israel
	4	"Gonna Buy Me A Dog"	Mexico
	6	"She"	Mexico
	7	"(Theme from) The Monkees"	Mexico
December 16, 1967	7	"Alternate Title"	Australia
	15	"Daydream Believer"	England
	9	"Daydream Believer"	Israel
	15	"(Theme from) The Monkees"	Japan
	10	"Pleasant Valley Sunday"	Malaysia
	3	"Gonna Buy Me A Dog"	Mexico
	6	"She"	Mexico
	9	"(Theme from) The Monkees"	Mexico
	9	"Shades Of Gray"	Philippines
December 23, 1967	8	"Alternate Title"	Australia
	13	"Daydream Believer"	England
	12	"(Theme from) The Monkees"	Japan
	3	"Look Out (Here Comes Tomorrow)"	Mexico
	7	"She"	Mexico
	9	"(Theme from) The Monkees"	Mexico
December 30, 1967	8	"Alternate Title"	Australia
	5	"Daydream Believer"	Eire
	8	"Daydream Believer"	England
	7	"(Theme from) The Monkees"	Japan
	3	"Look Out (Here Comes Tomorrow)"	Mexico
	8	"(Theme from) The Monkees"	Mexico
	5	"Daydream Believer"	Puerto Rico
	7	"Words"	Venezuela
January 6, 1968	6	"Alternate Title"	Australia
	4	"Daydream Believer"	Eire
	7	"Daydream Believer"	England
	9	"Daydream Believer"	Holland
	10	"(Theme from) The Monkees"	Japan
	3	"Look Out (Here Comes Tomorrow)"	Mexico
	8	"(Theme from) The Monkees"	Mexico
	10	"Forget That Girl"	Philippines
	4	"Daydream Believer"	Puerto Rico
	7	"Words"	Venezuela
January 13, 1968	6	"Daydream Believer"	England
	5	"(Theme from) The Monkees"	Japan
	2	"Look Out (Here Comes Tomorrow)"	Mexico
	7	"(Theme from) The Monkees"	Mexico
	9	"Forget That Girl"	Philippines

DATE	POSITION	SONG	COUNTRY
January 20, 1968	4	"Daydream Believer"	Denmark
	5	"Daydream Beliver"	England
	10	"Daydream Believer"	Germany
	6	"Daydream Believer"	Holland
	4	"(Theme from) The Monkees"	Japan
	2	"Look Out (Here Comes Tomorrow)"	Mexico
	8	"(Theme from) The Monkees"	Mexico
	10	"Daydream Believer"	New Zealand
	3	"Daydream Believer"	Norway
	8	"Forget That Girl"	Philippines
	10	"Daydream Believer"	South Africa
January 27, 1968	10	"Daydream Believer"	Australia
	5	"Daydream Believer"	Denmark
	1	"Daydream Believer"	Eire
	6	"Daydream Believer"	England
	8	"Daydream Believer"	Germany
	4	"Daydream Believer"	Holland
	6	"Daydream Believer"	Israel
	4	"(Theme from) The Monkees"	Japan
	2	"Look Out (Here Comes Tomorrow)"	Mexico
	6	"(Theme from) The Monkees"	Mexico
	8	"Daydream Believer"	New Zealand
	2	"Daydream Believer"	Norway
	8	"Forget That Girl"	Philippines
	4	"Daydream Believer"	Puerto Rico
	9	"Daydream Believer"	South Africa
February 3, 1968	9	"Daydream Believer"	Australia
	1	"Daydream Believer"	Eire
	6	"Daydream Believer"	England
	5	"Daydream Believer"	Holland
	4	"Daydream Believer"	Israel
	5	"(Theme from) The Monkees"	Japan
	2	"Look Out (Here Comes Tomorrow)"	Mexico
	8	"(Theme from) The Monkees"	Mexico
	8	"Daydream Believer"	New Zealand
	10	"Forget That Girl"	Philippines
	6	"Daydream Believer"	Puerto Rico
	6	"Daydream Believer"	South Africa
February 10, 1968	11	"Daydream Believer"	England
	8	"Daydream Believer"	Germany
	6	"Daydream Believer"	Holland
	9	"(Theme from) The Monkees"	Japan
	1	"Look Out (Here Comes Tomorrow)"	Mexico
	6	"(Theme from) The Monkees"	Mexico
	3	"Daydream Believer"	New Zealand
	3	"Daydream Believer"	South Africa
February 17, 1968	3	"Daydream Believer"	Australia
	6	"She"	Australia

DATE	POSITION	SONG	COUNTRY
	16	"Daydream Believer"	England
	4	"Daydream Believer"	Germany
	8	"Daydream Believer"	Holland
	10	"(Theme from) The Monkees"	Japan
	17	"Daydream Believer"	Japan
	3	"Look Out (Here Comes Tomorrow)"	Mexico
	8	"(Theme from) The Monkees"	Mexico
	2	"Daydream Believer"	New Zealand
	10	"Daydream Believer"	Philippines
	1	"Daydream Believer"	South Africa
February 24, 1968	17	"Daydream Believer"	England
	4	"Daydream Believer"	Germany
	9	"(Theme from) The Monkees"	Japan
	19	"Daydream Believer"	Japan
	5	"Daydream Believer"	Malaysia
	3	"Look Out (Here Comes Tomorrow)"	Mexico
	8	"(Theme from) The Monkees"	Mexico
	1	"Daydream Believer"	New Zealand
	9	"Daydream Believer"	Philippines
	2	"Daydream Believer"	South Africa
March 2, 1968	3	"Daydream Believer"	Australia
	5	"She"	Australia
	22	"Daydream Believer"	England
	5	"Daydream Believer"	Germany
	14	"Daydream Believer"	Japan
	17	"(Theme from) The Monkees"	Japan
	3	"Daydream Believer"	Malaysia
	6	"Look Out (Here Comes Tomorrow)"	Mexico
	8	"(Theme from) The Monkees"	Mexico
	1	"Daydream Believer"	New Zealand
	8	"Daydream Believer"	Philippines
	3	"Daydream Believer"	South Africa
March 9, 1968	29	"Daydream Believer"	England
	16	"(Theme from) The Monkees"	Japan
	2	"Daydream Believer"	Malaysia
	2	"Look Out (Here Comes Tomorrow)"	Mexico
	7	"(Theme from) The Monkees"	Mexico
	1	"Daydream Believer"	New Zealand
	4	"Daydream Believer"	Philippines
	10	"Daydream Believer"	Spain
	3	"Daydream Believer"	South Africa
March 16, 1968	34	"Daydream Believer"	England
	18	"Daydream Believer"	Japan
	20	"(Theme from) The Monkees"	Japan
	2	"Daydream Believer"	Malaysia
	6	"(Theme from) The Monkees"	Mexico
	1	"Daydream Believer"	New Zealand

DATE	POSITION	SONG	COUNTRY
	4	"Daydream Believer"	Philippines
	9	"Daydream Believer"	Poland
	4	"Daydream Believer"	South Africa
March 23, 1968	6	"Daydream Believer"	Belgium
	11	"Daydream Believer"	Japan
	18	"(Theme from) The Monkees"	Japan
	5	"Daydream Believer"	Malaysia
	2	"Look Out (Here Comes Tomorrow)"	Mexico
	4	"(Theme from) The Monkees"	Mexico
	2	"Daydream Believer"	New Zealand
	4	"Daydream Believer"	Philippines
	10	"Hard To Believe"	Philippines
	8	"Daydream Believer"	South Africa
March 30, 1968	5	"Daydream Believer"	Japan
	6	"Daydream Believer"	Malaysia
	4	"Look Out (Here Comes Tomorrow)"	Mexico
	6	"(Theme from) The Monkees"	Mexico
	5	"Daydream Believer"	Philippines
	8	"Hard To Believe"	Philippines
April 6, 1968	41	"Valleri"	England
	5	"Daydream Believer"	Japan
	7	"Daydream Believer"	Malaysia
	5	"Hard To Believe"	Philippines
	6	"Daydream Believer"	Philippines
April 13, 1968	19	"Valleri"	England
	4	"Daydream Believer"	Japan
	4	"Hard To Believe"	Philippines
	6	"Daydream Believer"	Philippines
April 20, 1968	12	"Valleri"	England
	5	"Daydream Believer"	Japan
	3	"Hard To Believe"	Philippines
	8	"Daydream Believer"	Philippines
April 27, 1968	12	"Valleri"	England
	6	"Daydream Believer"	Japan
	10	"Valleri"	New Zealand
	2	"Hard To Believe"	Philippines
	9	"Daydream Believer"	Philippines
May 4, 1968	16	"Valleri"	England
	7	"Daydream Believer"	Japan
	7	"Valleri"	New Zealand
	1	"Hard To Believe"	Philippines
	9	"Daydream Believer"	Philippines
May 11, 1968	9	"Valleri"	Australia
	18	"Valleri"	England

DATE	POSITION	SONG	COUNTRY
	8	"Daydream Believer"	Japan
	9	"Valleri"	Norway
	1	"Hard To Believe"	Philippines
	9	"Daydream Believer"	Philippines
May 18, 1968	27	"Valleri"	England
	9	"Daydream Believer"	Japan
	9	"Valleri"	Norway
	1	"Hard To Believe"	Philippines
May 25, 1968	7	"Valleri"	Australia
	30	"Valleri"	England
	6	"Valleri"	Israel
	16	"Valleri"	Japan
	19	"Daydream Believer"	Japan
	9	"Valleri"	Malaysia
	6	"Valleri"	New Zealand
	1	"Hard To Believe"	Philippines
	8	"Valleri"	Singapore
June 1, 1968	9	"Valleri"	Israel
	4	"Valleri"	Japan
	4	"Valleri"	New Zealand
	2	"Hard To Believe"	Philippines
	10	"Valleri"	Philippines
	6	"Valleri"	Singapore
June 8, 1968	7	"Valleri"	Australia
	6	"Valleri"	Japan
	7	"Valleri"	New Zealand
	2	"Hard To Believe"	Philippines
	9	"Valleri"	Philippines
	5	"Valleri"	Singapore
June 15, 1968	4	"Valleri"	Japan
	6	"Valleri"	Malaysia
	9	"Valleri"	New Zealand
	4	"Hard To Believe"	Philippines
	7	"Valleri"	Philippines
	5	"Valleri"	Singapore
June 22, 1968	9	"Valleri"	Japan
	4	"Valleri"	Malaysia
	5	"Valleri"	Philippines
	7	"Hard To Believe"	Philippines
	7	"Valleri"	Singapore
	4	"Valleri"	Venezuela
June 29, 1968	6	"Valleri"	Japan
	1	"Valleri"	Malaysia
	3	"Valleri"	Philippines
	10	"Hard To Believe"	Philippines

DATE	POSITION	SONG	COUNTRY
July 6, 1968	37	"D. W. Washburn"	England
	7	"Valleri"	Japan
	1	"Valleri"	Malaysia
	3	"Valleri"	Philippines
July 13, 1968	20	"D. W. Washburn"	England
	13	"Valleri"	Japan
	3	"Valleri"	Malaysia
July 20, 1968	17	"D. W. Washburn"	England
	14	"Valleri"	Japan
	5	"Valleri"	Malaysia
July 27, 1968	21	"D. W. Washburn"	England
	17	"Valleri"	Japan
	6	"Valleri"	Malaysia
August 3, 1968	27	"D. W. Washburn"	England
	8	"Valleri"	Malaysia
August 10, 1968	32	"D. W. Washburn"	England
August 17, 1968	3	"We Were Made For Each Other"	Philippines
	6	"It's Nice To Be With You"	Philippines
August 24, 1968	2	"We Were Made For Each Other"	Philippines
	7	"It's Nice To Be With You"	Philippines
August 31, 1968	4	"It's Nice To Be With You"	Philippines
	6	"We Were Made For Each Other"	Philippines
September 7, 1968	3	"It's Nice To Be With You"	Philippines
	4	"We Were Made For Each Other"	Philippines
September 14, 1968	3	"It's Nice To Be With You"	Philippines
September 21, 1968	5	"D. W. Washburn"	New Zealand
	2	"It's Nice To Be With You"	Philippines
September 28, 1968	20	"D. W. Washburn"	Japan
	7	"D. W. Washburn"	New Zealand
	1	"It's Nice To Be With You"	Philippines
October 12, 1968	3	"It's Nice To Be With You"	Philippines
October 19, 1968	4	"It's Nice To Be With You"	Philippines
October 26, 1968	6	"It's Nice To Be With You"	Philippines

▶ Photo courtesy Edmag Archives.

Monkee Solo Recordings

On the next few pages are displayed, in chronological order of release, the solo releases of David, Micky, Peter, and Michael in their pre- and post-Monkees careers. The catalog is complete, with the following exceptions, which were unavailable for reproduction at press time:

1963   "How Can You Kiss Me" - (Mike [Nesmith], John & Bill)
1966   "I Told You I Love You" - The Missing Links (Micky Dolenz)
1972   "You're A Lady" - (Davy Jones)
1978   "I'm Your Man" - (Micky Dolenz)

SEPTEMBER 1965
Edan Records 1001
"Just A Little Love"
b/w
"Curson Terrace"

1965
Colpix Records CP 764
"Dream Girl"
b/w
"Take Me To Paradise"

1965
Colpix Records CP-784
"This Bouquet"
b/w
"What Are We Going To Do?"

OCTOBER 1965
Colpix Records CP-787
"The New Recruit"
b/w
"A Journey With Michael Blessing"

1965
Colpix Records CP-789
"The Girl From Chelsea"
b/w
"Theme For A New Love"

1965
Colpix Records CP 493
"David Jones"

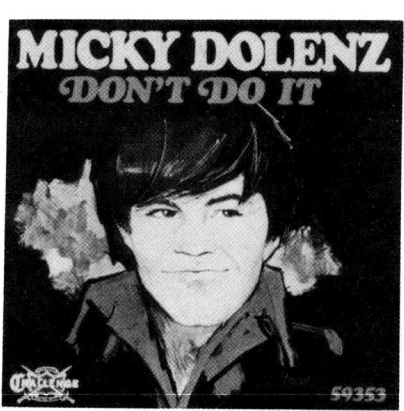
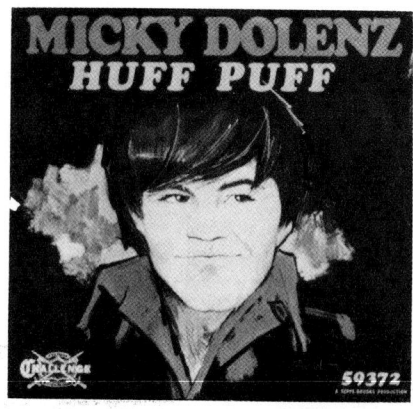

JANUARY 1966
Colpix Records CP-792
"Until It's Time For You To Go"
b/w
"What Seems To Be The Trouble, Officer"

FEBRUARY 1967
Challenge Records 59353
"Don't Do It"
b/w
"Plastic Symphony III" (Instrumental)

FEBRUARY 1967
Challenge Records 59372
"Huff Puff"
b/w
"Fate" (Instrumental)

JULY 1968
Dot Records DLP 25861
"The Wichita Train Whistle Sings"

JULY 1968
Dot Records 45-17152
"Don't Cry Now"
b/w
"Tapioca Tundra"

JULY 1970
RCA Records 47-9853
"Little Red Rider"
b/w
"Rose City Chimes"

JULY 1970
RCA Records LSP-4371
"Magnetic South"

AUGUST 1970
RCA Records 74-0368
"Joanne"
b/w
"One Rose"

NOVEMBER 1970
RCA Records 74-0399
"Silver Moon"
b/w
"Lady Of The Valley"

NOVEMBER 1970
RCA Records LSP-4415
"Loose Salute"

APRIL 1971
Bell Records 986
"Do It In The Name Of Love"
b/w
"Lady Jane"

JUNE 1971
Bell Records 45-111
"Rainy Jane"
b/w
"Welcome To My Love"

JUNE 1971
Bell Records 6067
"Davy Jones"

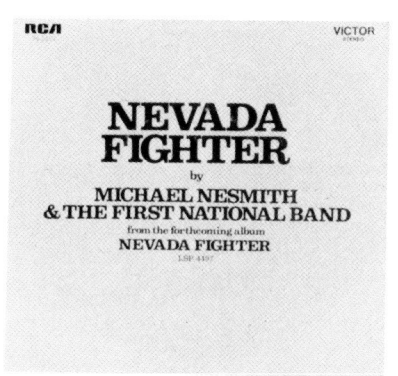

APRIL 1971
RCA Records 74-0453
"Nevada Fighter"
b/w
"Here I Am"

MAY 1971
RCA Records LSP 4497
"Nevada Fighter"

JUNE 1971
RCA Records 74-0540
"I've Just Begun To Care (Propinquity)"
b/w
"Only Bound"

JUNE 1971
RCA Records SPS-45-263
"Texas Morning"
b/w
"Tumbling Tumbleweeds"

OCTOBER 1971
Bell Records 45-136
"I Really Love You"
b/w
"Sitting In The Apple Tree"

OCTOBER 1971
MGM Records K14309
"Easy On You"
b/w
"Oh Someone"

NOVEMBER 1971
Bell Records 45-159
"Girl"
b/w
"Take My Love"

JANUARY 1972
RCA Records 74-0629
"Mama Rocker"
b/w
"Lazy Lady"

FEBRUARY 1972
RCA Records LSP-4563
"Tantamount To Treason - Volume 1"

JANUARY 1972
Bell Records 45-178
"I'll Believe In You"
b/w
"The Road To Love"

JUNE 1972
MGM Records K-14395
"Unattended In The Dungeon"
b/w
"A Lover's Prayer"

AUGUST 1972
RCA Records 74-0804
"Roll With The Flow"
b/w
"Keep On"

AUGUST 1972
RCA Records LSP 4695
"And The Hits Just Keep On Comin'"

1972
MGM Records K-14458
"Who Was It"
b/w
"Lady Jane"

OCTOBER 1972
Lion Records 132
"Johnny B. Goode"
b/w
"It's Amazin' To Me"

JANUARY 1973
MGM Records K-14524
"Rubberene"
b/w
"Rubberene"

1973
Romar Records RO-710
"Daybreak"
b/w
"Love War"

OCTOBER 1973
RCA Records ALPI 0164
"Pretty Much Your Standard Ranch Stash"

1974
Romar Records RO-715
"Buddy Holly Tribute"
b/w
"Ooh She's Young"

MARCH 1975
Pacific Arts Records PAC-101
"The Prison"

1975
Capitol Records 4180
"I Remember The Feeling"
b/w
"You & I"

1975
Capitol Records 4271
"I Love You (And I'm Glad That I Said It)"
b/w
"Savin' My Love For You"

MAY 1976
Capitol Records ST-11513
"Dolenz, Jones, Boyce & Hart"

DECEMBER 1976
Christmas Records CDS-700
"Christmas Is My Time Of Year"
b/w
"White Christmas"

FEBRUARY 1977
Pacific Arts Records PAC 7-106
"Compilation"

MARCH 1977
Pacific Arts Records PAC 7-107
"From A Radio Engine To A Photon Wing"

MARCH 1977
Pacific Arts Records IP084
"Rio"
b/w
"Life, The Unsuspecting Captive"

JANUARY 1978
MCA Records MCF 2826
"The Point"

1978
MCA Records MCA 348
"Lifeline"
b/w
"It's A Jungle Out There"
"Gotta Get Up"

250

MAY 1978
Warner Brothers Records 17161
(England)
"Hey Ra, Ra, Happy Birthday Mickey
Mouse"
b/w
"You Don't Have To Be A Country Boy To
Sing A Country Song"

1978
Pacific Arts Records PAC 7-113
"The Wichita Train Whistle Sings"

JUNE 1978
Pacific Arts Records PAC 45-101
"Roll With The Flow"
b/w
"I've Just Begun To Care"

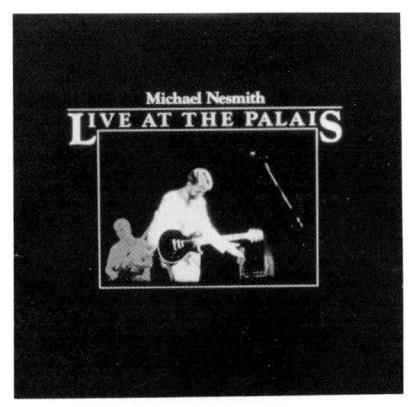

AUGUST 1978
Pacific Arts Records PAC 7-118
"Live At The Palais"

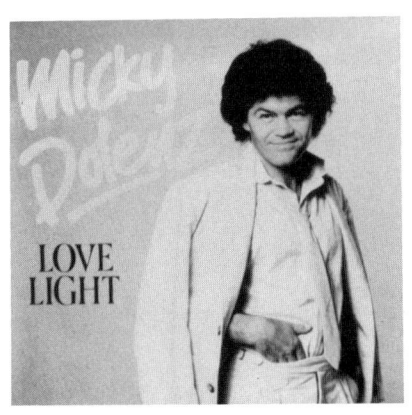

MARCH 1979
Chrysalis Records CHS 2297
"Love Light"
b/w
"Alicia"

MAY 1979
Pacific Arts Records PAC 7-130
"Infinite Rider On The Big Dogma"

JUNE 1979
Pacific Arts Records PAC 45-106
"Magic (This Night Is Magic)"
b/w
"Dance (Dance & Have A Good Time)"

AUGUST 1979
Pacific Arts Records PAC 45-108
"Cruisin'"
b/w
"Horserace"

JUNE 1979
Pacific Arts Records PAC 7-1300
"The Michael Nesmith Radio Special"

FEBRUARY 1981
Claude's Music Works MW 1001
"Higher & Higher"
b/w
"(I'm Not Your) Steppin' Stone"

MAY 1981
Japan Record JAS-2007
(Japan)
"It's Now"
b/w
"How Do You Know"

JUNE 1981
Japan Record JAL-1003
(Japan)
"Davy Jones Live"

JUNE 1981
Japan Record JAS-2010
(Japan)
"Dance Gypsy"
b/w
"Can She Do It (Like She Dances)"

AUGUST 1981
Capitol Records ECS-91018
(Japan)
"Dolenz, Jones, Boyce & Hart Concert In Japan"

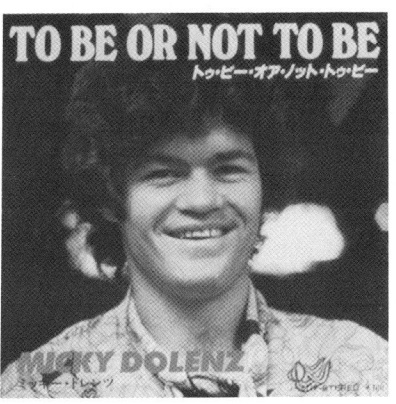

JANUARY 1982
Jam Record J-8112B
(Japan)
"To Be Or Not To Be"
b/w
"Beverly Hills"

MARCH 1982
Pioneer Records K-10025
(Japan)
"Hello Davy"

MARCH 1982
Pioneer Records K-1517
(Japan)
"Baby, You'll Soon Be Sixteen"
b/w
"Baby, Holdout"

JUNE 1982
Coop Record SE 105
"I Truly Understand"
(Peter Tork Cut)

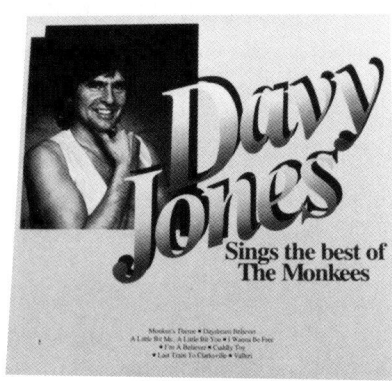

1983
K-Tel Records NA587
(Australia)
"Davy Jones Sings The Best Of The Monkees"

MAY 1983
A&M Records Bugsy 1-AA
(England)
"Tomorrow"
b/w
"Fat Sam's Grand Slam"

DECEMBER 1984
(Limited Edition) JJ 2001
(England)
"I'll Love You Forever"
b/w
"When I Look Back On Christmas"

Part four
Monkee Memorabilia

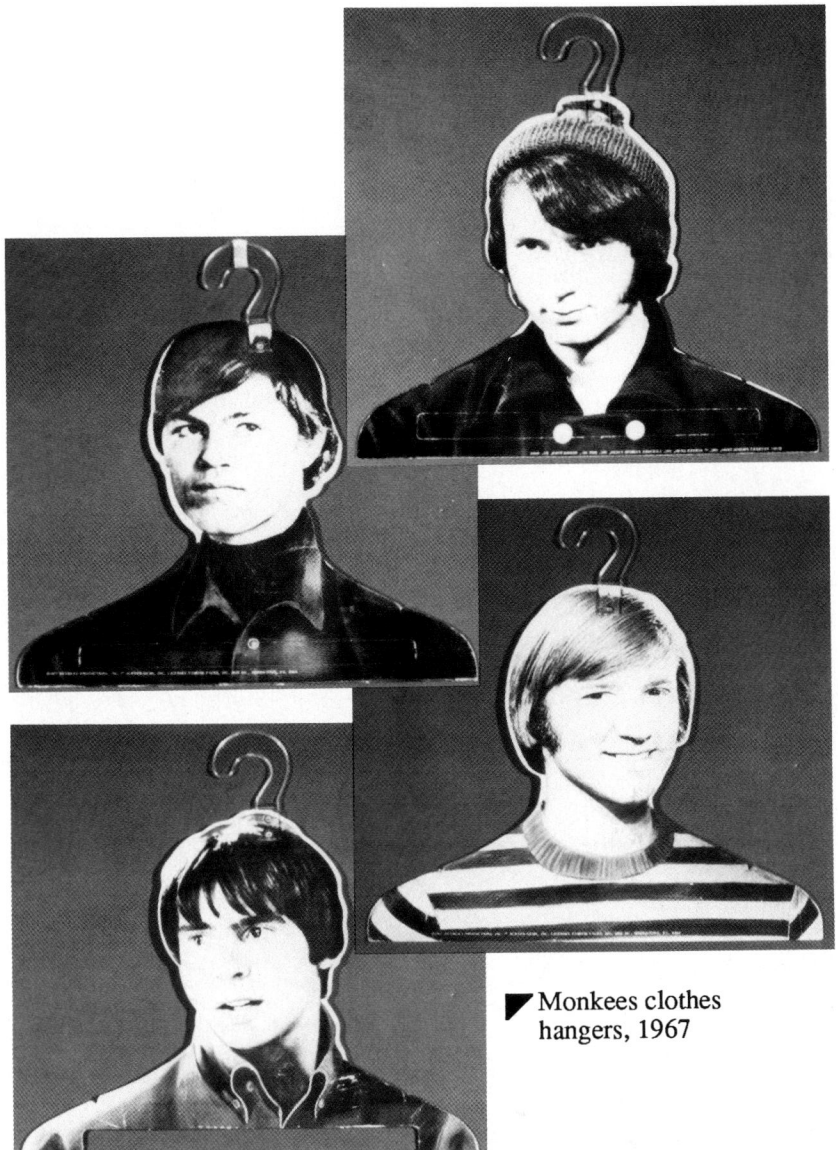

Monkees clothes hangers, 1967

▲ Monkees cereal box records, 1969
Three series were available, four songs each, cut from the backs of Post cereals boxes, to make a complete series of twelve.

▶ GAF Viewmaster Reel Set, 1967

◀ Photo courtesy Edmag Archives.

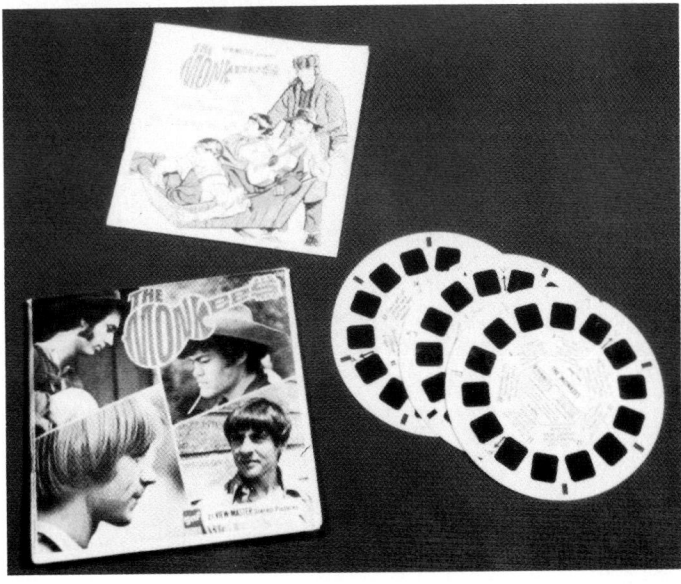

257

◀ Monkees comic books, Dell Comics, 1967-1969 #1 - #16 were issued, with #17 a reprint of #1.

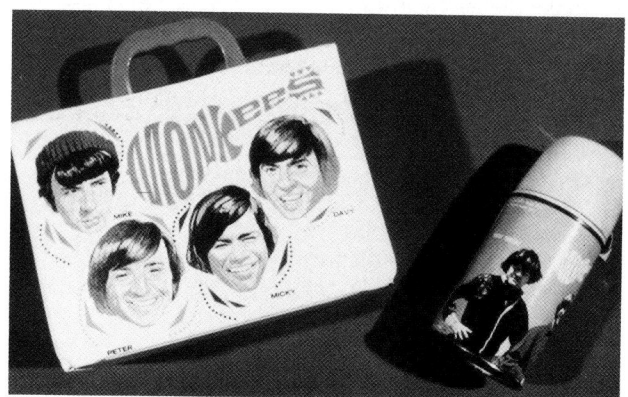

◀ Monkees lunchbox and thermos, 1967

▲ Monkees buttons, 1966, available from gum machines.

◀ Monkees Game, 1967 Two versions were available, the other used a toy xylophone in place of the plastic guitar.

▶ The Official 1967 Monkees Fan Club Kit

▲ Radio disc jockey's press release kit, 1967

▼ David Jones Fan Club membership application and button, 1965

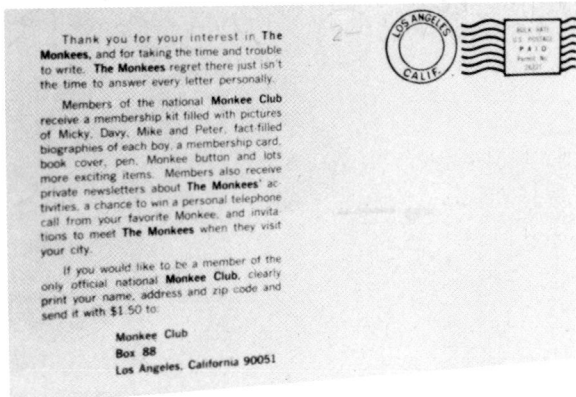

▲ Fans who wrote to the Monkees in 1967 received in reply a picture postcard of the group, with an invitation to join the fan club on the reverse.

▼ Monkees toy tamborine, 1967

▲ Monkees toy guitar, Mattel, 1966

▼ Monkees music in its various forms: the now-defunct 8-track and reel-to-reel tapes.

▶ 1967 Monkees sweatshirts

▼ Monkees bandana, 1967

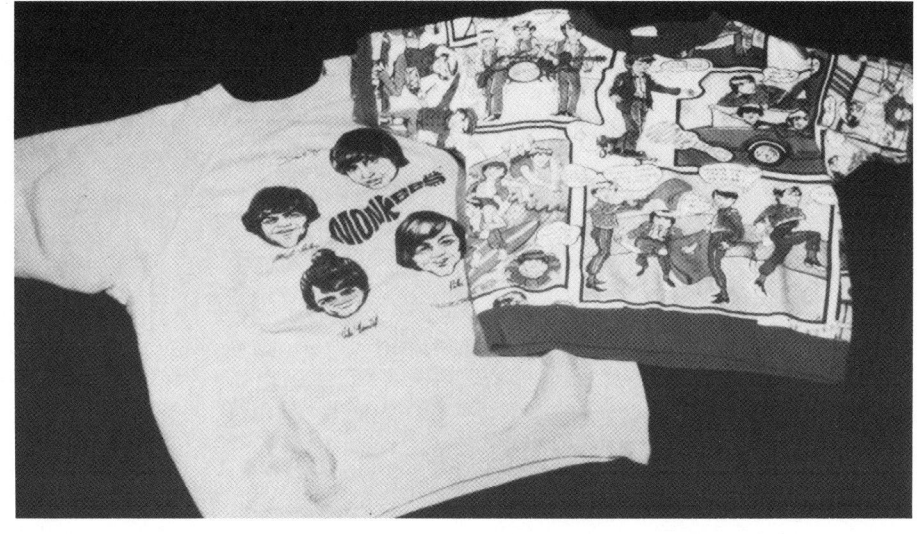

▶ 1967 Monkee jewelry: pendant, bracelets, and earrings (not pictured).

▼ Halloween costumes, available in styles for boys and girls, each packed with an autographed photo of the group.

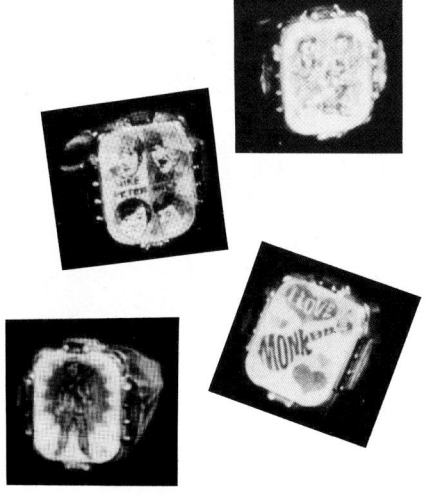

▲ Flasher rings, available in gumball machines and later in cereal boxes.

◀ Tiger Beat's "Monkee Spectacular" magazine. Sixteen issues published, April 1967 - August 1968.

◀ Monkees books published by and available by mail order from Tiger Beat publications, 1967.

◀ Monkees books published by and available by mail order from 16 Magazine Inc., 1967.

▲ Monkees hardback fiction novel, 1968 (Whitman)

▲ "Monkees Monthly" magazines, published in Great Britain. Thirty-two issues, February 1967 - September 1969.

◀ Paperback books.

▶ 1967 American tour book

◀ Monkees storybooks for children published in Great Britain.

▶ 1969 American tour book. Two versions were published, one with an ad for the "Instant Replay" LP.

263

▲ First series, issued in black and white in 1966 by Donruss Co.

▲ Series A (second series), issued in color with black border, 1967 by Donruss Co.

◀ Backs of gum cards were fragments of a larger Monkees picture puzzle. Each series formed a different puzzle. The one at left is from the first series.

◀ Series B (third series) issued in color with yellow border, 1967, by Donruss Co. Some cards featured Monkees questions on the reverse instead of a puzzle piece.

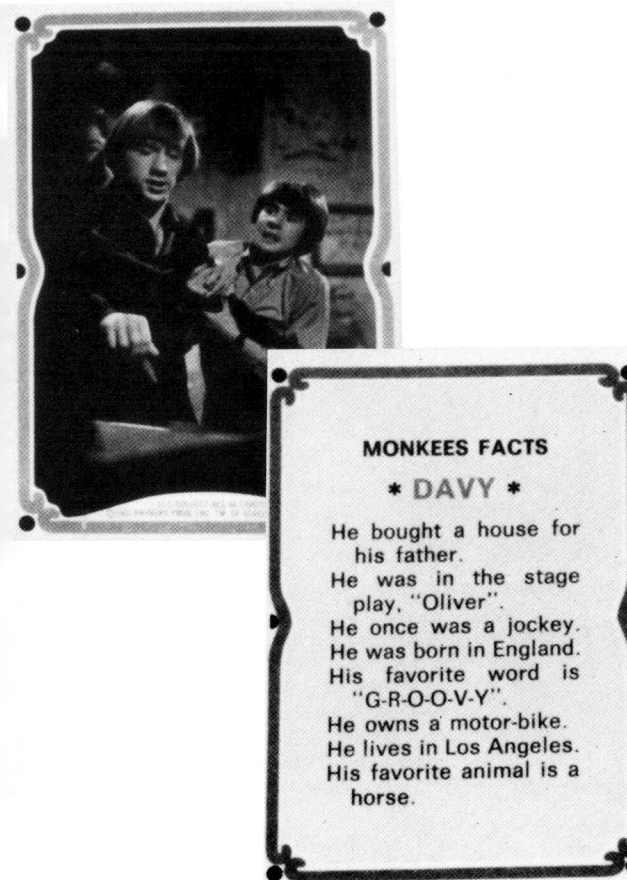

◀ Series C (fourth series) issued in color with blue and pink borders, 1967, by Donruss Co. Backs of cards included puzzle pieces, Monkees facts, and Monkees tour dates.

▶ Flip movies issued in series of sixteen books, 1967, by Topps.

▲ Various display cartons for Monkee bubblegum items.

▶ Monkee badges: unnumbered, punch-out, stick-on badges issued in color in set of forty-four, 1967, Donruss Co.

◀ Set of twenty-five miniature Monkee cards from England, 1967.

▶ Front and back views of Monkees Hit Songs Cards, 1967, from England. Set of thirty in color.

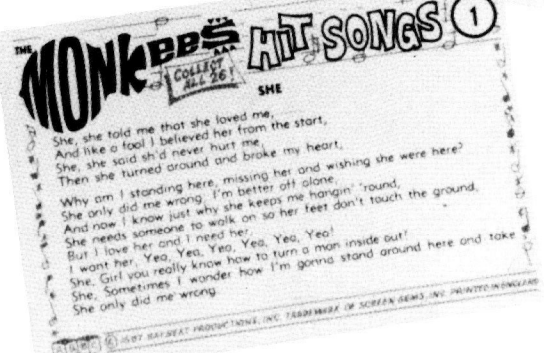

◀ Black and white gum cards, 1967, from England. Series of fifty-five cards.

▶ Monkees coins, distributed in Kellogg's cereals in Canada. Series of twelve.

▼ Gum cards, 1967, from England. Series of fifty-five in color.

267

▲ Monkees Songbooks

▲ Monkees Sheet Music

◀ Monkees looseleaf binder and toy wallet, 1966, Mattel.

◀ Monkees playing cards, 1966, by Educards. Fifty-two-card deck with jokers, featuring photos on all but the face cards.

▲ Monkees record tote, 1966, for 45 rpm singles (Mattel).

◀ "The Monkees" mini-LP for jukeboxes, six songs. Included mini album covers and title cards. "More of the Monkees" was also released.

▲ Punch-out model book with pages for coloring, 1967, from Holland.

▲ Jigsaw puzzles, four available, 1967, by Fairchild.

◀ 1966 Monkees hand puppet, talked when string was pulled. By Mattel.

▲ Paint-by-number set, four different sets available, two pictures per set, 1967.

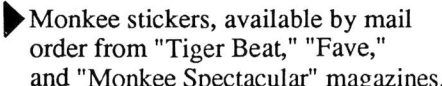

▶ Monkee stickers, available by mail order from "Tiger Beat," "Fave," and "Monkee Spectacular" magazines.

▲1967 Monkees Annual from England. Collage of photos, comics, jokes, gags, involving the group. Released in various countries such as Australia, Sweden and Denmark.

◄Monkees souvenir booklet published after the guys toured England in July, 1967

▼Australian special publicatio dedicated entirely on the grou

▶1968 Monkees Annual from England.

▶1982 Japanese publication cashing in on the renewed Monkeemania that hit this country.

▲1969 Monkees Annual from England.

▲ Monkees poster calendar, sold in Japan, 1982.

▲ Monkees caricature wall poster, 1967, available in two styles.

◀ Large chain convenience store souvenir cup commemorting the Dolenz, Jones, Boyce and Hart tour of 1976.

▼ Vest from the J.C. Penney line of Monkee sportswear, 1966.

▶ Flexidisc released through Davy Jones Fan Club in Japan, 1968, containing Davy's spoken message to the fans about the upcoming concert tour and the movie "Head."

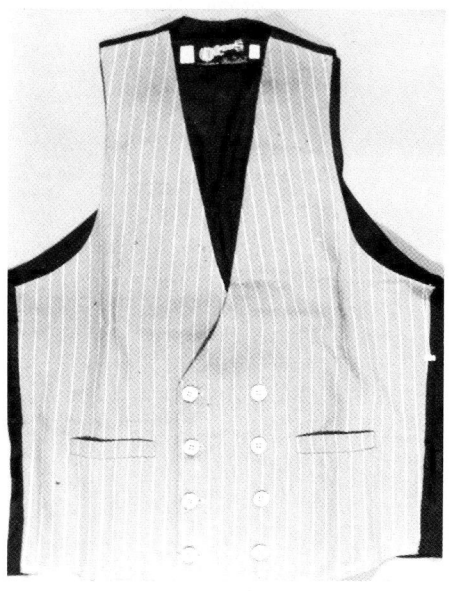

◀ Monkeemobile models (clockwise from left): Matchbox, 1967; Corgi (made in Great Britain), 1967; Plastic model kit by MPC, 1967; and musical Monkeemobile from Japan, 1967.

▲ Show Biz Babies: four-inch tall Monkee dolls, each complete with a plexidisc record of narration about each Monkee, 1967, Hasbro.

▶ Monkee fingerdolls: five-inch tall dolls, issued by Remco in 1970 after Peter had exited the group.

▲ Monkees' 1986 tour merchandise featured t-shirts, sweatshirts, hat, button, and tour program. Sales of these items broke all records for tour merchandising in the summer of 1986, over $15 per capita.

▶ A second edition of the tour program was issued which replaced a photo of David and Jessica Jones with a photo of David Fishof and the three Monkees.

▲ Could this be the ultimate Monkees collectible? Their tour plane sported a large Monkees logo on the side and came complete with official Monkees stewardess. (Monkees not included, of course.)

Photo by Henry Diltz

Part five
Indexes

Song and Album Title Index

Acapulco

Acapulco Sun (song)
183, 194
Alicia (song)
251
All Alone In The Dark (song)
183, 194
All Night Long (song)
107
All The Gray Haired Men (song)
181
All The King's Horses (song)
133, 134, 177
Alternate Title (song)
42, 217, 219, 220,
231, 232, 233, 234,
235, 236
Alvin (song)
181
And The Hits Just Keep On Comin'
(LP)
91, 99, 248
Angel Band (song)
182
Anytime, Anyplace, Anywhere (song)
198
Apples, Peaches, Bananas & Pears
(song)
178
As We Go Along (song)
159, 182, 185, 189,
192
At The Hop (song)
157
Auntie & The Municipal Court (song)
180
Auntie's Municipal Court (song)
180, 192
Baby, Holdout (song)
253
Baby, You'll Soon Be Sixteen (song)
105, 253
Band 6 (song)
179, 191
Barrel Full Of Monkees (LP)
86, 194
The Best Of The Monkees (LP)
198
The Best Of The Monkees
(LP-England)
223, 225
The Best Of The Monkees
(LP-Germany)
223
Beverly Hills (song)
105, 253
The Birds, The Bees & The Monkees
(LP)
65, 74, 192, 205,
206, 207, 208
The Birds, The Bees & The Monkees
(LP-Argentina)
223
The Birds, The Bees & The Monkees
(LP-Arista)
102
The Birds, The Bees & The Monkees
(LP-reissue)
213, 214
The Birds, The Bees & The Monkees
(LP-Rhino)
110
Black And Blue (song)
179
Blue Monday (song)
157
Blues (song)
179
Buddy Holly Tribute (song)
93, 249
The Bus That Never Comes (song)
182
Bye Bye Baby Bye Bye (song)
183, 193
Calico Girlfriend (song)
84
Calico Sombra Girlfriend (song)
182
California Here I Come (song)
157
Can She Do It (Like She Dances) (song)
253
Can You Dig It (song)
159, 180, 192, 197
Carlisle Wheeling Effervescent Popsicle
(song)
180
Ceiling In My Room (song)
180
Changes (LP)
83, 194
Changes (LP-reissue)
214, 215
Changes (song)
181
Christmas Is My Time Of Year (song)
96, 250
Circle Sky (song)
65, 159, 180, 192,
197
Come On In (song)
181
Compilation (LP)
97, 250
Consider Yourself (song)
30, 76
The Coop: The Fast Folk Musical
Magazine (LP)
253
Cripple Creek (song)
145
The Crippled Lion (song)
181
Cruisin' (song)
100, 101, 252
Cuddly Toy (song)
44, 146, 151, 179,
192, 193, 194, 195,
196, 219

Don't

Curson Terrace (song)
243
Daddy's Song (song)
65, 159, 180, 192
Daily Nightly (song)
53, 152, 156, 179,
192, 197
Dance (song)
100
Dance (Dance & Have A Good Time)
(song)
252
Dance, Gypsy (song)
104, 253
Dandruff (song)
182, 192
Darwin (song)
182
David Jones (LP)
200, 201, 243
Davy Jones (LP)
246
Davy Jones Live (LP)
104
Davy Jones Live (LP-Japan)
252
Davy Jones Sings The Best Of The
Monkees (LP-Australia)
254
Daybreak (song)
248
Daydream Believer (song)
44, 51, 52, 58, 86,
96, 101, 102, 104,
147, 148, 150, 179,
184, 188, 192, 193,
195, 196, 198, 218,
220, 235, 236, 237,
238, 239, 240
Daydream Believer (Remix) (song)
190
The Day We Fall In Love (song)
178, 191, 194, 220
Ditty Diego (song)
182, 192
Do I Have To Do This All Over Again
(song)
159, 180, 181, 192
Do It In The Name Of Love (song)
183, 245
Dolenz, Jones, Boyce & Hart (LP)
95, 249
Dolenz, Jones, Boyce & Hart Concert
In Japan (LP-Japan)
253
Do Not Ask For Love (Prithee) (song)
178
Don't Call On Me (song)
154, 179, 192
Don't Cry Now (song)
244
Don't Do It (song)
29, 244

Photo courtesy Edmag Archives.

SONG & ALBUM TITLE INDEX

Don't

Don't Listen To Linda (song)
178, 180, 193
Don't Say Nothing Bad (song)
181
Don't Wait For Me (song)
181, 193
The Door Into Summer (song)
151, 156, 179, 192
Down The Highway (song)
182
Down The Line (song)
157
Do You Feel It Too (song)
183, 194
Dream Girl (song)
243
Dream World (song)
181, 192, 197
D.W. Washburn (song)
66, 181, 185, 189,
196, 197, 198, 221,
241
Early Morning Blues And Greens (song)
179, 191
Easy On You (song)
88, 247
Empire (song)
180
Eve Of My Sorrow (song)
179
Everybody Loves A Nut (song)
80
The Fast Folk Musical Magazine (LP)
253
Fate (Instrumental) (song)
244
Fat Sam's Grand Slam (song)
107, 254
Floyd Cramer Plays The Monkees (LP)
31
Forget That Girl (song)
45, 179, 191, 194,
197, 219, 221, 236,
237
For Pete's Sake (song)
45, 179, 191, 196,
198, 221
40 Timeless Hits From The Monkees
(LP-Australia)
225
French Song (song)
182, 193
From A Radio Engine To A Photon
Wing (LP)
97, 250
Girl (song)
86, 247
The Girl From Chelsea (song)
243
The Girl I Knew Somewhere (song)
6, 32, 45, 115, 143,
144, 184, 195, 196,
198, 217, 219, 220
The Girl I Left Behind Me (song)
178, 180, 193
Go Away Little Girl (song)
181
Goin' Down (song)
52, 115, 149, 150,
151, 153, 154, 179,
184, 188, 196, 198,
218, 220
Gonna Buy Me A Dog (song)
137, 177, 191, 194,
197, 219, 220, 235,
236, 237
Good Afternoon (song)
182
Good Clean Fun (song)
81, 181, 185, 190,
193, 195, 197, 198,
218
The Good Earth (song)
183
Good Time (song)
180
Gotta Get Up (song)
250
Gotta Give It Time (song)
178
Gravy (song)
182, 192
Happy Birthday (song)
182
Hard To Believe (song)
180, 192, 239, 240
Head (LP)
74, 192, 208
Head (LP-Japan)
223
Head (LP-Rhino)
110
Headquarters (LP)
30, 34, 36, 38, 40,
42, 47, 58, 74, 191,
200, 201, 202, 203,
204, 205
Headquarters (LP-Arista)
103
Headquarters (LP-Brazil)
222
Headquarters (LP-Chile)
221
Headquarters (LP-reissue)
212, 213, 214, 215
Headquarters (LP-Rhino)
113
Hello Davy (LP)
104, 105
Hello Davy (LP-Japan)
253
Here Come The Monkees
(LP-England)
225
Here I Am (song)
246
Hey Ra Ra, Happy Birthday, Mickey
Mouse (song)
99, 251
Higher & Higher (song)
103, 252
Hold Me (song)
181
Hold On Girl (song)
178, 191
Hollywood (song)
181
Horserace (song)
100, 252
How Can I Tell You (song)
183
How Can You Kiss Me (song)
6, 243
How Do You Know (song)
252
How Insensitive (song)
181
Huff Puff (song)
244
I Can't Get Her Off My Mind (song)
191
I Can't Get Her Out Of My Mind
(song)
179
I Didn't Know You Had It In You,
Sally (song)
178
I Don't Think You Know Me (song)
177, 178
I Feel Good (song)
47
If I Ever Get To Saginaw Again (song)
181
If I Knew (song)
183, 193
If I Learned To Play The Violin (song)
179
If You Have The Time (song)
65, 182
I Go Ape (song)
182
I Got A Woman (song)
145
I Had A Dream Last Night (song)
179
I'll Be Back Up On My Feet (song)
138, 140, 181, 192,
197
I'll Believe In You (song)
90, 247
I'll Be True To You (song)
177, 191, 197
I'll Love You Forever (song)
109, 254
I'll Spend My Life With You (song)
178, 179, 191, 221,
I Love You (And I'm Glad That I Said
It) (song)
95, 249
I Love You Better (song)
183, 185, 194, 197,
I'm A Believer (song)
22, 23, 27, 29, 58,
62, 66, 83, 96, 103,
138, 139, 157, 178,
184, 187, 191, 193,
194, 195, 196, 198,
216, 219, 220, 227,
228, 229, 230, 231,
232, 233, 234, 235,
I'm A Man (song)
180
I'm A Wind Up Man (song)
157

SONG & ALBUM TITLE INDEX

I'm Gonna Try (song)
 180
(I'm Not Your) Steppin' Stone (song)
 103, 132, 133, 137,
 139, 145, 177, 184,
 187, 191, 193, 194,
 195, 196, 198, 216,
 220, 252
Impact (song)
 181
I'm Ready (song)
 157
I'm Your Man (song)
 99, 243
I Never Thought It Peculiar (song)
 178, 194
Infinite Rider On The Big Dogma (LP)
 100, 251
Instant Replay (LP)
 76, 103, 193, 208,
 209
Instant Replay (LP-Puerto Rico)
 224
Instant Replay (LP-Rhino)
 110
I Really Love You (song)
 246
I Remember The Feeling (song)
 95, 249
I Think It's Gonna Rain (song)
 181
I Told You I Love You (song)
 243
I Truly Understand (song)
 105, 253
It's A Jungle Out There (song)
 250
It's Amazing To Me (song)
 91, 248
It's Got To Be Love (song)
 183, 194
It's Nice To Be With You (song)
 66, 181, 185, 189,
 195, 196, 221, 241,
It's Now (song)
 104, 252
I've Just Begun To Care (Propinquity) (song)
 86, 181, 246, 251,
I Wanna Be Free (song)
 103, 134, 136, 145,
 177, 191, 193, 194,
 195, 196, 216, 220,
 234, 235
I Wanna Be Your Puppy Dog (song)
 178
I Was Not Born To Follow (song)
 181
I Won't Be The Same Without Her (song)
 177, 193
Joanne (song)
 84, 85, 86, 245
Johnny B. Goode (song)
 91, 248
A Journey With Michael Blessing (song)
 243

Just A Game (song)
 181, 193
Just A Little Love (song)
 243
Keep On (song)
 248
Kicks (song)
 198
The Kind Of Girl I Could Love (song)
 133, 142, 177, 191,
 220
Kitty Hawk (song)
 182
L.A. Turnaround (LP)
 93
Ladies Aid Society (song)
 82, 178, 193
Lady Jane (song)
 183, 245, 248
Lady Of The Valley (song)
 245
Lady's Baby (song)
 180
Large As Life (song)
 181
Last Train To Clarksville (song)
 6, 16, 18, 19, 23,
 30, 32, 75, 96, 103,
 114, 131, 132, 133,
 144, 145, 177, 184,
 187, 191, 193, 194,
 195, 196, 197, 198,
 216, 218, 220, 221,
 227, 228, 229
Laugh (song)
 140, 142, 191, 219
Lazy Lady (song)
 247
Let's Dance On (song)
 136, 177, 191, 219
Lifeline (song)
 250
Life, The Unsuspecting Captive (song)
 250
Listen To The Band (song)
 66, 78, 116, 157,
 182, 185, 190, 193,
 194, 195, 196, 198,
A Little Bit Me, A Little Bit You (song)
 32, 45, 66, 83, 178,
 184, 187, 193, 195,
 196, 198, 216, 217,
 219, 220, 229, 230,
 231, 232, 233, 234,
 235
Little Darlin' (song)
 157
Little Girl (song)
 183, 193, 197
Little Red Rider (song)
 84, 182, 244
Little Tommy Blue (song)
 182
Live At The Palais (LP)
 99, 251
Living Strings Play 'I'm A Believer' And Other Monkees Hits (LP)
 31

London Bridge (song)
 182
Long Tall Sally (song)
 157
Long Title: Do I Have To Do This All Over Again (song)
 159, 180, 181, 192
Look Down (song)
 181
Looking For The Good Times (song)
 82, 178, 193, 197,
Look Out (Here Comes Tomorrow) (song)
 143, 144, 178, 191,
 196, 219, 236, 237,
 238, 239
Loose Salute (LP)
 85, 86, 245
Love Is Only Sleeping (song)
 51, 146, 147, 154,
 179, 192, 197
Love Is On The Way (song)
 178, 179
Love Light (song)
 100, 251
A Lover's Prayer (song)
 90, 247
Love Song - Tippy Taylor (song)
 179
Love To Love (song)
 178, 196
Love War (song)
 248
The Love You Got Inside (song)
 179
Lynn Harper (song)
 182
Magic (song)
 100, 252
Magnetic South (LP)
 66, 84, 85, 86, 245
Magnolia Simms (song)
 192
Mama Rocker (song)
 90, 247
The Manhattan Strings Play Instrumental Versions Of Hits Made Famous By The Monkees (LP)
 31
A Man Without A Dream (song)
 179, 182, 185, 193,
 218
Mary, Mary (song)
 137, 141, 142, 145,
 177, 191, 193, 194,
 195, 196, 198, 217,
 219
Masking Tape (song)
 179
Merry Go Round (song)
 180
Me Without You (song)
 180, 182, 193
The Michael Nesmith Radio Special (LP)
 252

281

SONG & ALBUM TITLE INDEX

Michigan

Michigan Blackhawk (song)
182
Midnight Train (song)
183, 194
Mr. Richland's Favorite Song (song)
180
Mr. Webster (song)
178, 179, 191
Mommy And Daddy (song)
81, 181, 182, 185, 190, 193, 218
Monday, Monday (song)
32
Monkee Business (LP)
105, 196
Monkee Flips (LP)
108, 197
The Monkees (LP)
18, 19, 29, 36, 58, 96, 191, 195, 199, 200, 201, 202, 203, 204
The Monkees (LP-Arista)
102
The Monkees (LP-Japan)
221
The Monkees (LP-reissue)
212, 213, 214, 215
The Monkees (LP-Rhino)
114
The Monkees (2 LPs-Japan)
223
The Monkees EP Vol. 1 (EP)
233, 234
Monkees Golden Album (LP-Japan)
224
The Monkees Golden Hits (LP)
194
Monkees Golden Story (LP)
103, 104
The Monkees' Golden Story (LP-Japan)
222
The Monkees Greatest Hits (LP)
79, 193, 209
The Monkees Greatest Hits (LP-Arista)
96, 196, 210, 211, 212
The Monkees Greatest Hits (LP-Japan)
224
The Monkees/Hit Factory (LP)
197
The Monkees Present Micky, David & Michael (LP)
82, 193, 210
The Monkees Present Micky, David & Michael (LP-Argentina)
224
The Monkees Present Micky, David & Michael (LP-Rhino)
110
The Monkees Song Book Played By The Golden Gate Strings (LP)
31, 200
Monkees The Best (LP-Japan)
223
Monkey Business (LP)
31
Monkeys A-Go-Go (LP)
31
More Greatest Hits Of The Monkees (LP)
105, 196
More Of The Monkees (LP)
27, 29, 58, 96, 191, 199, 200, 201, 202, 203, 204, 205
More Of The Monkees (LP-Arista)
102
More Of The Monkees (LP-reissue)
212, 213, 214, 215
More Of The Monkees (LP-Rhino)
113
Music Of The World A-Turnin' (song)
181
My Head (song)
180
My Share Of The Sidewalk (song)
180, 182
My Song In 7 (song)
180
Nevada Fighter (LP)
85, 86, 246
Nevada Fighter (song)
86, 246
Never Tell A Woman Yes (song)
182, 193
The New Recruit (song)
243
Nine Times Blue (song)
80, 181
99 lbs. Of Dynamite (song)
178
99 Pounds (song)
194
No Time (song)
147, 154, 179, 191, 197, 217, 219, 220,
Octopus's Garden (song)
82
Of You (song)
177
Oh My My (song)
83, 183, 185, 190, 194, 195, 197
Oh Someone (song)
88, 247
Oklahoma Backroom Dancer (song)
182, 193
Omega (song)
182
One Rose (song)
245
Only Bound (song)
246
The Only Thing I Believe Is True (song)
157
Ooh She's Young (song)
249
Opening Ceremony (song)
182, 192
Opening Night (song)
183
Papa Gene's Blues (song)
18, 19, 134, 139, 148, 177, 191, 194, 219
Party (song)
181
Penny Music (song)
182
Peter Percival Patterson's Pet Pig Porky (song)
179, 192
Pillow Time (song)
183, 193
Pisces, Aquarius, Capricorn & Jones Ltd (LP)
53, 74, 192, 202, 203, 204, 205, 206, 207, 213, 214, 215,
Pisces, Aquarius, Capricorn & Jones Ltd (LP-Argentina)
222
Pisces, Aquarius, Capricorn & Jones Ltd (LP-Arista)
103
Pisces, Aquarius, Capricorn & Jones Ltd (LP-Japan)
222
Pisces, Aquarius, Capricorn & Jones Ltd (LP-Mexico)
222
Pisces, Aquarius, Capricorn & Jones Ltd (LP-reissue)
212
Pisces, Aquarius, Capricorn & Jones Ltd (LP-Rhino)
114
Plastic Symphony III (Instrumental) (song)
244
Pleasant Valley Sunday (song)
44, 45, 51, 58, 116, 146, 147, 179, 184, 188, 192, 193, 194, 195, 196, 198, 219, 220, 233, 234, 235, 236, 237
P.O. Box 9847 (song)
180, 192
Poco Puedo Darte (song)
230, 231
The Point (LP)
98, 250
Poll (song)
182, 192
Poor Little Me (song)
178
Porpoise Song (song)
72, 181, 185, 189, 192, 195, 196, 197, 198
The Poster (song)
181, 192
Pretty Little Princess (song)
6
Pretty Much Your Standard Ranch Stash (LP)
92, 99, 249
The Prison (LP)
249

Prison

SONG & ALBUM TITLE INDEX

Prithee

Prithee (Thou Makest Demands On Me) (song)
157
Propinquity (song)
86, 181, 246, 251
Rainy Jane (song)
86, 89, 90, 245
Randy Scouse Git (song)
42, 45, 145, 146, 147, 179, 191, 193, 194, 196, 198, 219, 220, 221
Refocus (LP)
91, 96, 195
Refocus (LP-Japan)
224
Ride Baby Ride (song)
183
Rio (song)
97, 100, 250
Riu Chiu (song)
44, 152, 180
The Road To Love (song)
90, 247
Rock & Roll Music (song)
179
Roll With The Flow (song)
91, 99, 248, 251
Rose City Chimes (song)
244
Rose Marie (song)
181
Rubberene (song)
90, 248
Saint Matthew (song)
181
Salesman (song)
44, 154, 179, 192
Saturday's Child (song)
132, 177, 191, 196, 219
Savin' My Love For You (song)
249
Scarborough Fair (song)
82
Seasons (song)
181
Seeger's Theme (song)
180
Sgt. Pepper's Lonely Hearts Club Band (LP)
29, 40
Shades Of Gray (song)
45, 47, 179, 191, 193, 195, 196, 221, 234, 235, 236, 237,
Shadow Of A Man (song)
181
Shake A Tail Feather (song)
157
Shake 'Em Up (song)
181
She Calls Herself St. Matthew (song)
181
She (song)
137, 141, 178, 191, 193, 194, 195, 196, 198, 219, 220, 231, 232, 233, 234, 235, 236, 237, 238
She Hangs Out (song)
28, 32, 44, 149, 156, 178, 179, 192, 194, 196
She'll Be There (song)
179
Shorty Blackwell (song)
180, 193, 197
Silver Moon (song)
85, 245
Sitting In The Apple Tree (song)
246
Sixteen (song)
105, 253
Smile (song)
181
So Goes Love (song)
177
Someday Man (song)
78, 82, 182, 185, 189, 195, 196
Some Of Shelley's Blues (song)
181
Sometime In The Morning (song)
141, 143, 178, 191, 196, 198
Sound Of The Sunset, Sound Of The Sea (song)
180
Star Collector (song)
53, 149, 150, 153, 154, 155, 179, 192, 194, 196, 217, 220,
Steam Engine (song)
182, 183, 196
Storybook Of You (song)
182
String For My Kite (song)
157, 182
Sugar Man (song)
178
Sunny Girlfriend (song)
147, 179, 191, 219
Superstitious (song)
182, 192
Supplicio (song)
182, 192
The Surprise (song)
180
Susanna Sometime (song)
182
Swami: Plus Strings (song)
182, 192
Sweet Young Thing (song)
134, 139, 145, 177, 191, 197, 220
Symphony Is Over (song)
179
Take A Giant Step (song)
131, 135, 177, 184, 191, 196, 198, 216, 219, 221
Take Me To Paradise (song)
243
Take My Love (song)
247

To

Tantamount To Treason, Volume I (LP)
90, 247
Tapioca Tundra (song)
180, 184, 189, 192, 195, 197, 218, 221, 244
Tear Drop City (song)
75, 178, 185, 189, 193, 194, 195, 197, 198, 218
Tears Of Joy (song)
180
Tear To Top Off My Head (song)
181
Teeny Tiny Gnome (song)
178
Tell Me Love (song)
183, 194
Tell Your Mommy (Mommy & Daddy) (song)
181
Tema Dei Monkees (song)
196
Tema De Los Monkees (song)
234
Texas Morning (song)
86, 246
Thank You My Friend (song)
182
That's What It's Like Lovin You (song)
181
That Was Then, This Is Now (song)
114, 115, 190, 198
Theme For A New Love (song)
243
(Theme From) The Monkees (song)
102, 134, 177, 191, 194, 195, 196, 197, 198, 216, 217, 218, 219, 220, 221, 230, 231, 232, 233, 234, 235, 236, 237, 238, 239
Then & Now...The Best Of The Monkees (LP)
114, 115, 198, 212, 213, 214, 215
Thirteen Is Not Our Lucky Number (song)
182
This Bouquet (song)
243
This Just Doesn't Seem To Be My Day (song)
131, 135, 177, 191, 219
Through The Looking Glass (song)
178, 180, 193, 197
Ticket On A Ferry Ride (song)
183, 194
Till Then (song)
182
Time & Time Again (song)
183
Title Unknown (song)
181
To Be Or Not To Be (song)

283

SONG & ALBUM TITLE INDEX

Today
105, 253
Today (song)
182
Tomorrow (song)
107, 254
Tomorrow's Gonna Be Another Day (song)
132, 134, 177, 191, 197, 219, 221
Tumbling Tumbleweeds (song)
246
Tutti Frutti (song)
157
20 Golden Greats (LP-England)
224
Unattended In The Dungeon (song)
90, 247
Until It's Time For You To Go (song)
244
Up, Up & Away (song)
62
Valleri (song)
6, 64, 103, 141, 144, 156, 178, 184, 188, 192, 193, 194, 195, 196, 198, 218, 221, 239, 240, 241
Valley Hi (LP)
92
War Games (song)
180
Welcome To My Love (song)
245
We Were Made For Each Other (song)
180, 192, 241
What Am I Doing Hangin' 'Round (song)
145, 148, 154, 179, 192, 194, 196, 198, 220

What Are We Going To Do (song)
243
Whatever's Right (song)
177
What Seems To Be The Trouble, Officer (song)
244
When I Look Back On Christmas (song)
109, 254
When Love Comes Knockin' (At Your Door) (song)
144, 178, 191, 197
Where Has It All Gone (song)
179
Where Time Won't Fly (song)
157
Which Way (Do You Want It) (song)
183
While I Cried (song)
180
While I Cry (song)
193
"White Album" (LP)
66
White Christmas (song)
250
Whole Lotta Shakin' (song)
157
Who Was It (song)
90, 248
Who Will Buy (song)
180
The Wichita Train Whistle Sings (LP)
68, 99, 244, 251
Winchester Cathedral (song)
32
Wind Up Man (song)
182
Words (song)
45, 144, 145, 151, 153, 179, 184, 188, 192, 195, 196, 198, 219, 220, 236
Writing Wrongs (song)
180, 192
You And I (song)
193
You Can't Judge A Book By It's Cover (song)
145
You Can't Tie A Mustang Down (song)
178
You Don't Have To Be A Country Boy To Sing A Country Song (song)
251
You & I (song)
181, 249
You Just May Be The One (song)
45, 47, 138, 142, 177, 191, 196, 198, 216, 221
Your Auntie Grizelda (song)
139, 141, 142, 178, 191, 195, 220
You're A Lady (song)
90, 243
You're So Good (To Me) (song)
182, 183, 194
Yours Until Tomorrow (song)
179
You Told Me (song)
45, 179, 191, 197, 219
Zilch (song)
179, 191
Zor And Zam (song)
156, 180, 192, 193, 197

Index to People, Places and Things

ABC

ABC Records
  6
ABC-TV
  50, 80, 82, 86, 88,
  91, 92, 93, 95, 104,
  108
"A.M. Chicago" (TV show)
  105, 106
AVA Hall Of Fame Awards
  106
Aberdeen, SD
  126
Academy Awards
  78
Ace, Mr. & Mrs.
  159
"Adam 12" (TV show)
  91
Adelaide, Australia
  123
Adelaide Centennial Hall
  123
Adler, Toby
  152
Albany Civic Center
  125
Albany, GA
  125
Alberoni, Sherry
  135
Albuquerque Civic Auditorium
  123
Albuquerque, NM
  123
"Alias Micky Dolenz" (episode)
  142
Allison, Keith
  3
"All Night Long" (video)
  107
Ambrosio, Arthur
  145
"American Bandstand" (TV show)
  86, 95, 100
American Video Association
  108
American Video Awards
  106, 108
Anderson, Jon
  149, 152, 156, 159
Andrews, Dick
  144
Angel, Jack
  33
Angelita
  145
Ann
  149
Antonio, Lou
  148
April
  143
Archerd, Army
  23

Area Code 615
  66
The Arena
  121
Arista Records
  96, 102, 103, 105,
  110, 114, 115, 116,
Arlington Stadium
  125
Arlington, TX
  125
Arnold
  143
Arnold, Jeanne
  138
Arnold, Paul
  157
"Art, For Monkees' Sake" (episode)
  147
Artful Dodger
  4
Arthur
  143
Arthur, Maureen
  142
Artist
  147
Ashley, Merri
  153
Ashman, Gene
  159
Askin, Leon
  149
Assembly Center Arena
  121, 123
The Assistant
  153
Assistant #1
  142
Assistant #2
  142
Astor, David
  151
Athletic Center, Notre Dame Univ.
  127
Atlanta, GA
  127
Atlantic City, NJ
  86, 112, 125, 127,
Attila the Hun
  154
Aubuchon, Jacques
  133
Audience Studies, Inc.
  5
"The Audition (Find The Monkees)"
    (episode)
  139
Auditorium
  123
Audubon Zoo
  125
Auger, Brian
  78

Beatles

Augusta, GA
  123
Aunt Kate
  151
Austin, TX
  125
Australia
  112, 70
"Aware" (magazine)
  61
Babbit
  132, 134, 135, 143
Baccala, Donna
  141
Badderly, Mrs.
  138
Bagdad, William
  146, 159
Bail, Chuck
  134
Baio, Joey
  141
Baker, Mackinley
  144
Ballantine, Carl
  139
Ballard, Ray
  134
Baltimore Civic Center
  127
Baltimore, MD
  121, 126, 127
Bandit
  145
Bangor Auditorium
  128
Bangor, ME
  128
The Baron
  154
Barris, George
  107
Barry, Davy
  142
Barry, Jeff
  83
Barton Coliseum
  127
Basil, Toni
  65, 159
Basile, Vinnie
  33
Batmobile
  107
Battle Creek, MI
  127
Bayfront Arena
  125
Bean, Roy, Judge
  154
The Beatles
  5, 14, 16, 27, 29,
  40, 58, 66, 96

INDEX TO PEOPLE, PLACES & THINGS

Beaumont

Beaumont Civic Center
 125
Beaumont, TX
 125
Beaver, Paul
 53
Beck, Billy
 154
Beck, Jeff
 40
Beck, Vincent
 131, 138, 149
Beckman, Henry
 146, 153
Bel Air, CA
 83
Bell, Michael
 147
Bell Auditorium
 123
Bellin, Tom
 143
Bell Records
 86, 89, 91, 96
Benedict, William (Bill)
 147, 155
Benny
 137
Benson, Hubbell
 139
Beregal, Oscar
 141
Bernie
 137
Bethlehem, PA
 109, 128
Beverly Hills, CA
 28
Beverly Hills Hotel
 28
Big Butch
 149
Biggy
 151
The Big Victor
 159
"Billboard" (magazine)
 16, 23, 29, 36, 40,
 44, 47, 53, 58, 66,
 68, 72, 74, 76, 78,
 79, 81, 83, 84, 96,
 97, 106, 114
Billy the Kid
 154
Bilson, Bruce
 65
Binghampton, NY
 127
Birmingham, AL
 123
Blackbeard
 154
Black Sheik
 159
Blauner
 149
Blavat, Jerry
 156

Blindfolded Man
 149
"Blitz" (magazine)
 73
Bloomington, MN
 126
Bloomsburg Fair
 126
Bloomsburg, PA
 126
Blossom Music Festival
 125
Blound, Inspector
 142
"The Bluegrass Special" (TV special)
 97
Bogert, Dick
 38
Boles, Jim
 134, 148
Bonar, Ivan
 139
Bordon, David
 17
Boris
 133, 150
Boston Garden
 121
Boston, MA
 73, 121
Boyce, Tommy
 12, 21, 64, 94, 95,
 97
Boyd, Pattie
 40
"The Brady Bunch" (TV show)
 86
Bramley, William
 143
"Breakfast Television" (TV show)
 106
"Break The Bank" (TV show)
 95
Breakthrough Influence Company
 74
Brenda
 147
Brendan Byrne Arena, Meadowlands
 127
Brian Auger & Trinity
 78
Bride
 144
Brinco
 74
Brisbane, Australia
 123
Broadway Theatre
 17
Brocco, Peter
 147
Brodman, Jon
 73
Bronson Canyon
 62
Bronson, Harold
 76, 113
Brooks, Foster

Camp

 144
Broome City Arena
 127
Brown, James
 76
Brown, Nyles
 5, 148, 156
Brown County Arena
 127
Brown County Fair
 126
Browning, Susan
 143
Bruno
 139
Buckingham Suite Ballroom
 40
Buckley, Tim
 156
The Buddy Miles Express
 78, 157
Budokan Hall
 123
Buffalo, NY
 121, 126
Buffalo Springfield
 40
"Bugsy Malone" (musical)
 106, 107
Bulk
 147
Bully
 140
Buntwell, Miss
 138
Burlington, IA
 125
Burstyn, Neil
 147, 152, 153
Burton, Charlie
 85
"Butch Cassidy And The Sundance
 Kids" (TV show)
 92
Butler
 144, 152, 154, 155
Butler-Glouner
 159
Buzzi, Ruth
 150
The Byrds
 5
CBGB's
 98
CBS-TV
 50, 73, 75, 78, 81,
 91
Cabot, Ceil
 131, 134
Callas, Charlie
 134
Camberley Civic Theatre
 109
Cambria War Memorial Coliseum
 127
Cambridge, Godfrey
 145
Camp, Elisabeth

INDEX TO PEOPLE, PLACES & THINGS

Camp
138
Camp, Hamilton
144
Campbell, Glen
75
The Candy Store Prophets
12, 24
"Cannon" (TV show)
91
Canon, Peter
140, 154
Cape Cod Melody Tent
126
Capitol Records
11, 94, 95, 96, 104
Captain
132, 142, 150, 153,
Captain Crocodile
141
"Captain Crocodile" (episode)
45, 141
"Card Carrying Red Shoes" (episode)
149
Cardinal
141
Carey, Timothy
159
Carlson, Violet
147
Carlsson, Carl
141
Carlton Celebrity Theatre
126
Carnes, Kim
97
Carson, Johnny
79
Cartwheel, Bart/Ben
151
Caruso, Dee
133, 134, 135, 137,
138, 139, 140, 141,
142, 143, 144, 147,
"The Case Of The Missing Monkee" (episode)
45, 139
Cash, Johnny
80
"Cashbox" (magazine)
58, 65, 74, 81, 82
Cashier
146
Catalina, Frankie
144
Catskill Mountains
112
Cedar Rapids, IA
127
Centennial Hall
127
Centrum
127
Chadwick, Bill
3, 39, 44, 47, 78,
108, 154
Challenge Records
29
Chambermaid
131
The Champ
140
Chaney, Lon, Jr.
134
Chang
142
Chapel Hill, NC
127
"The Chaperone" (episode)
45, 135
Chapman, Leigh
137
Chapman, William
141
Charles, Arlene
133
Charleston, WV
123, 128
Charlotte Coliseum
128
Charlotte, NC
121, 128
Charone, Irwin
137, 147
Chasen's
54
Chattanooga Arena, Univ. of Tenn.
127
Chattanooga, TN
127
Chautauqua Institute
125
Chautauqua, NY
125
Chemist
141
Cherry, Stanley Z.
156
Chesney, Diana
135
Chicago, IL
44, 83, 105, 121,
123
"Chicago Tribune TV Week" (newspaper)
32
Chief
153
The Chief
133
Cholis, Neko
44
Chomsky, Miss
139
"The Christmas Show" (episode)
152
Chrysalis Records
100
Chubber, Ella Mae
148
Chubber, Paw
148
Chuce
147
Churchill, Winston
40
Cicalo, Hank
30, 38, 52
Cincinnati Gardens
121
Cincinnati, OH
121, 126
"Cinderella" (pantomime)
109
Cintron, Sharon
156
"Circus Boy" (TV show)
5
Cisar, George
140
Civic Arena
121
Civic Center
121
Civic Center Arena
123, 128
Civic Coliseum
127
Civic Stadium
126
The Clara Ward Singers
78
Clarisse
143
Clark, Dick
24, 93
Clark, Dort
137, 146, 151
Clarkston, MI
126
Claude's Music Works Records
103
Clearwater, FL
125
Cleveland, OH
121, 125, 127
Club Casino
126
"A Coffin Too Frequent" (episode)
150
Cohasset, MA
125
Coit, Stephen
138
Coleman, Booth
133
Colette
146
Colgems Records
11, 28, 33, 36, 47,
81, 86
The Coliseum
121, 123
Coliseum, Eastern States Exposition
123
Colonna, Jerry
134
Colorado State Fair
123
Columbia Pictures
73, 112
Columbia Records
11, 28, 81, 116
Columbus, OH
125

INDEX TO PEOPLE, PLACES & THINGS

Compton
144
Compton Terrace
100
Concord Hotel
125
Cone, Hal
33, 54, 61
Conreid, Hans
153
Contest Manager
132
Conventioneer
144
Convention Hall
123
"The Co-op" (record magazine)
105
Cooper, Jackie
5
Corden, Henry
132, 134, 135, 143, 149
Cordic, Rege
152
Corell, Dr.
144
Cornthwaite, Robert
149
"Coronation Street" (TV show)
105, 109
Corpus Christi, TX
125
Costa Mesa, CA
126
Cotillion Ballroom
125
Cottonmouth
101
Count Dracula
153
Count Myron
141
Countryside Records
91, 92, 93
The Count's Kid
98
Courtier
141
"Cowboy In Africa" (TV show)
50
Cow Palace
121
Cox, Wally
143
Cramer, Floyd
31
The Creeps
5
The Critic
159
Crosse, Rupert
148
Crumpets, T.N.
154
Cumberland County Civic Center
127
Curad

146
Curator
147
Curtis, Billy
133
Curtis Hixon Hall
123
Customs Man
155
Cuyahoga Falls, OH
125
Cynthia
135
The Cyrkle
5
D.A.
146
Daggert
132
"Daily Variety" (newspaper)
3
Dallas, TX
121
Dallimore, Maurice
154
"Dance, Monkee, Dance" (episode)
138
Dancer
149
Dane County Arena
126
Daphne
156
Darden, Severn
132, 153
Daughter
153
Davis, Elias
154
Davis, Pepper
151
Davis, Spencer
40
Davy Jones Records
33, 39, 54
Day, Arlan
100
Dayton, OH
127
Dean Dome, Univ. of North Carolina
127
Dear, Bill
92
De Benning, Jeff
138
De Corsia, Ted
150, 154
"Dee Time" (TV show)
66
DeGroot, Myra
155
Del Conte, Ken
132
Della
151
Del Mar, CA
17
Dennis, Al

143
Dennis, Alfred
144
Denver, CO
121, 123, 126
Denver Coliseum
121, 123
Des Moines Civic Center
125
Des Moines, IA
121, 125
Detroit, MI
44, 121
Deuel, Geoffrey
144
"The Devil And Peter Tork" (episode)
65, 154
Deville, Paul
137
Devil/Mr. Zero
154
"Devlin" (TV show)
93
Devon, PA
126
Devon, Richard
141
Dewberry, Bonnie J.
151
DeWit, Jacqueline
151
El Diablo
145
Dick Clark Productions
24
"Dick Whittington" (pantomime)
107
"Dinah!" (TV show)
88, 95
Director
137, 143
Disneyland
95
District Attorney
146
Doda, Carol
159
Dodger Stadium
16
Dolenz, Coco
97, 98
Dolenz Jones Boyce & Hart
94, 95
Domino, Fats
78, 157
"Don Kirshner's Rock Concert" (TV show)
95, 100, 101
"The Donna Reed Show" (TV show)
3
Donner, Jack
143
Donovan
12
"Don't Look A Gift Horse In The Mouth" (episode)
134
"Don't Walk On My Grass" (film)

INDEX TO PEOPLE, PLACES & THINGS

Dot
88
Dot Records
54
Douglas, Chip
30, 34, 52, 53, 96
Douglas, Mike
95
Douglas County Fair
126
Doyle, Peter
100
Dragonman
142
Draper, Dave
147
Drehdal
143
Driscoll, Julie
78, 157
Duce
147
Duke, Patty
4
Duluth Arena
127
Duluth, MN
127
Dynarski, Gene
138, 142
"Easy Rider" (film)
75
"Echoes Of The Sixties" (TV special)
100
Edmiston, Walker
147
"Ed Stewart's Christmas Request Show" (TV show)
56
Electra Records
91
"Elephant Parts" (video)
104, 105, 108
Ellen
143
Ellie
132
Elliot, Mike
5, 13, 136
Elmira, NY
125
El Paso, Texas
125
Emerson, Allen
148
Emmy Awards
38, 65, 101
Empire Pool
40
Empire Theatre
100
Entertainment International
33
"Entertainment Tonight" (TV show)
110
Epstein, Brian
14
Erie, PA
125

Esformes, Nate
145
Evans, Dave
132, 134, 138, 139,
142, 152, 154, 156,
Evansville, IN
127
"Everywhere A Shiek, Shiek" (episode)
146
Extra
159
"Fabulous 208" (magazine)
27, 29
Fairchild, June
159
Fairfax, VA
127
Fairy Of The Locket
152
"Fairy Tale" (episode)
152
Farrell, Mike
142
Fax, Jesslyn
134
Feedback, Major
159
Fern
138
Festival Hall
123
Field House-State Univ.
121
Fielding, Elaine
132
Fife, Jack
153
The Fifth Dimension
62
Filchok, Mrs.
147
Fingerhead, Rob Roy
142
Fingerlakes Performing Arts Center
125
Finn, Huck
98
First Announcer
140
First Annual Pops Festival
123
First Cop
134
The First National Band
78, 82, 83, 84, 85,
86, 92
Fish, Nancy
139
Fisher, Art
78, 157
Fisher, Farmer
134
Fishof, David
112
Five Seasons Center
127
Flagler Greyhound Track
125

Flora
137
Flower Eater
154
Fonzie
92
Foran, Mary
137
"Forbes" (magazine)
83
Ford, Tennessee Ernie
82
Forest Hills Music Festival
79
Forest Hills Tennis Stadium
44, 121
Forman, Joey
141, 142
Fort Bliss Army Base
125
Fortune Theatre
111
Fort Wayne Coliseum
127
Fort Wayne, IN
127
Foster, Donald
134, 141, 146
Foster, Patricia
143
Foulger, Byron
139
4-H Dane County Junior Fair
123
Fox, Bernard
155
Foxboro, MA
127
Frady, Garland
91
Frank
150
Frank, David
144
Frank Erwin Center
125
Fraser, Elisabeth
146
Frawley, James
38, 65, 10, 131, 132,
134, 137, 138, 140,
141, 142, 143, 145,
146, 148, 149, 150,
151, 152, 153, 154,
156
Freberg, Stan
132
Freedom Hall
121
Fresholtz, Les
159
Friar, Mary
155
Friar, Mr.
155
"The Frodis Caper" (episode)
54, 156
Frome, Milton

289

INDEX TO PEOPLE, PLACES & THINGS

Fromholtz
143, 156
Fromholtz, Steve
91
Frosted Flakes
81
Funicello, Annette
159
"The Funky Phantom" (TV show)
88
Furth, George
137, 150
Fuselli
137
Gainesville, FL
127
Gan, Ginny
149
Gardenia, Vincent
139
Garden State Arts Center
126
Gardiner, Reginald
155
Gardner, Gerald
133, 134, 135, 136,
137, 138, 139, 140,
141, 142, 143, 144,
147, 154
Garner, Mousy
137
Garr, Terri
159
Garrett, Snuff
12
Gaspar, Chuck
159
Gelman, Larry
137, 141, 152
Gendarme
154
Genie
133
George
132, 134
Gershfield, Burton
159
"Get Smart!" (TV show)
65
Giorgio, Tony
156
Girl
143
Glass, Ned
140
"The Glen Campbell Goodtime Hour" (TV show)
75
Glick
156
Gloria
141
Glover, William
154
"Godspell" (musical)
110, 111, 112
Goffin, Gerry
12
The Golden Gate Strings
31
"Goldmine" (magazine)
115
Gold Records
18, 23, 24, 27, 32,
36, 52, 53, 58, 64,
65
Gonzalez, Pedro
145
Good, Jack
78, 155, 157
Gordon, Clark
153
Gorilla
148
Grabowski, Norman
149
Graham, John
144
Grammy Awards
30, 32, 62, 105
Grandfather
134
Grand Haven, MI
126
Grand Island, NE
126
Great Adventure Amusement Park
115, 125, 126
"The Great Golden Hits Of The Monkees By The Guys Who Sang 'Em And The Guys Who Wrote 'Em" (stage act)
94
Greek Theatre
116, 126
Green, Alan
100
Green Bay, WI
127
Greensboro, NC
121
Greenwich Village, New York City
51, 98
Griffin, Merv
92
Griffith, James J.
151
Groom
144
Groot
139
Guard
136
Guggins
132
"Gunsmoke" (TV show)
50
Hack
138
Hall County Fair
126
Hampton Beach, NH
126
Hanna-Barbera
92
Hannibal, MO
125

Hillbilly
"Happening '69" (TV show)
76
"Happy Days" (TV show)
92
Happy Together (concert tours)
112
Hard Rock Cafe
112
Harmon, Joy
146, 151
Harold
152
Harper, Jonathan
146
Harper, Pop
132
Harrison, George
40, 60
Harry
137, 150
Hart, Bobby
12, 15, 18, 21, 24,
34, 64, 82, 94, 95,
97
Hartford Civic Center
127
Hartford, CT
127
Harvey
146
Hausner, Jerry
140
Hay, Alexandra
142, 143
Hayes, Billy
148
Hayn, Claude
103
"Head" (film)
68, 72, 73, 158
"Head" (video)
116
Heathrow Airport
40
Helton, Percy
159
Henchman
156
Hendrix, Jimi
44
Henry
150
Heraldic Messenger
159
"Here Come The Monkees - The Pilot" (episode)
45, 136
Herman's Hermits
105
Hershey Arena
128
Hershey, PA
128
Higgins, Joe
136, 139, 141
Hilda
137
"Hillbilly Honeymoon" (episode)

INDEX TO PEOPLE, PLACES & THINGS

Hillyer

Hillyer
148
Hillyer, Sharyn
151
Hilton Hotel
126
"Hit Parader" (magazine)
76
"Hitting The High Seas" (episode)
150
Hoffman Estates, IL
126
Hollbrook, Tim
91
Hollywood Bowl
121
Hollywood, CA
73, 121
"Hollywood Reporter" (magazine)
3
"Hollywood Squares" (TV show)
74
Holman, Rex
151
Holmdel, NJ
126
Holt, John
139
Homer, Mrs.
147
Honeywell
133
Honolulu, HI
23, 121, 123
Honolulu International Center Arena
121, 123
Horace
132
"Horse In The House" (TV show)
100
Horseman #1
152
Hoss
151
"Hot City Disco" (TV show)
100
Hotel George V
40
Houston, TX
121, 123, 125
Howard
141
Howard, Judy
141
Howard, Susan
144
Howard, Vince
132
Howco Pictures
92
Howe, Bones
72
Hoyt, Clegg
141
Hugo, Michael
159
Hull, Cynthia
145
Hull, David
132
Hurst, David
154
Hutton, Danny
3
Hyannis, MA
126
Ice Cream Man
134
The Ice House
83
Indianapolis, IN
126
The Inevitables
5
Inspector
137, 139
International Center Arena
23
Irving, Charles
159
Irving Plaza, New York City
106
Irwin, Wayne
12
"It's A Nice Place To Visit" (episode)
145
"It's Rock 'N' Roll" (TV show)
105
Ivan
149
"I've Got A Little Song Here" (episode)
45, 137
"I Was A 99 Pound Weakling" (episode)
147
"I Was A Teenage Monkee" (MTV segment)
113
"I Was A Teenage Monster" (episode)
139
J.C. Penney
22
J.L.
146
"Jack & The Beanstalk" (pantomime)
100
Jackson Coliseum
127
Jackson, MS
123, 127
Jackson, NJ
125, 126
Jacksonville, FL
121
Jagger, Mick
27, 40
Jailer
141
James, Karen
138
James, Lisa
137
Jan
149
Jane
148
Janitor
156

Kennedy

Janowitz, Walter
132
Jansch, Bert
93
Japan
70, 103, 104, 105,
Japan Music Festival
99
Jarvis, Felton
66
Jefferson, I.J.
159
Jefferson Airplane
34
Jenkins
134
Jill
136
Joannie
137
"The Johnny Cash Show" (TV show)
80
Johnson, Arch
135
Johnson, Bobby
137
Johnson, Coslough
143, 147, 151, 153, 155
Johnstown, PA
127
Jonathan
134
Jones, Brian
40
Jones, T.C.
159
Jones Beach Theater
125, 126
Jools
157
Jose
145
Judge
146
Judy
143
The Jumper
159
"Junior Point Of View" (TV show)
30
Juste, Samantha
40, 65, 68
Kalamazoo, MI
127
Kane, Joel
156
Kansas City, MO
125
Kaufman, Robert
154
Kaye, Stubby
154
Kellogg's
9
Kelly, Claire
143
Kennedy, Don

INDEX TO PEOPLE, PLACES & THINGS

Kensington
 137, 154
Kensington, London, England
 40
Kessler, Bruce
 135, 137, 141, 142
Kiamesha Lake, NY
 125
Kibee, Lance, The Sot
 155
Kiel, Richard
 139
Kiel Auditorium
 121, 127
Kiko
 138
Kimba
 148
King
 146
King, Carole
 12
Kirk, Linda
 141
Kirshner, Don
 11, 12, 27, 28, 30,
 33, 36, 40, 64, 95,
 100, 101
Klein, Richard (Rick)
 44, 152, 154, 156
Knoxville, TN
 127
Kodak
 101, 102
Kolima, Lee
 133, 154
Komack, James
 141
Konrad, Dorothy
 132
Kool-Aid
 76, 81
Kowal, Jon
 137
Kramm
 144
Kyoto, Japan
 123
Kyoto Kaikan Hall
 123
L., J.
 146
La Crosse Center
 127
La Crosse, WI
 127
Lady
 134
Lady Pleasure
 159
The Lagoon
 126
Laine, Frankie
 6
Lake Canadaigua, NY
 125
Lake Geneva, WI
 123
The Lakeside Country Club
 108
Landis, Monte
 113, 146, 147, 148,
 154, 156
Landmark Theatre
 127
Lane, Bruce
 159
Lapid, Faye, Officer
 159
Larry
 143
Las Vegas, NV
 126
"Late Night With David Letterman" (TV show)
 105, 106
Latham
 156
Latimer, Cherie
 146
The Laughing Dogs
 97
"Laugh-In" (TV show)
 76, 81, 82
Lawrence, John
 152
Lawyer
 146
Leeds, Phil
 137
Lefcowitz, Eric
 82, 113
Lembeck, Harvey
 137
Lennon, Jimmy
 140
Lenny
 134
Leslie
 135
Lesser, Len
 134, 151
Lester, Jerry
 144
Letterman, David
 106
Lewis, Art
 139, 146
Lewis, Billy
 12
Lewis, Bobo
 139
Lewis, Buddy
 137
Lewis, Derrik
 138
Lewis, Forrest
 141
Lewis, Gary
 12
Lewis, Jerry Lee
 78, 157
The Lewis & Clarke Expedition
 47
Liberace
 147
"Linda Lovelace For President" (film)
 93
Linden, Stella
 150
Lindsay, Mark
 76, 105
Lion Records
 91
Liquid Paper
 93
Liston, Sonny
 159
Little Richard
 78, 157
Little Rock, AR
 127
Litwack, Sydney Z.
 159
Liverpool, England
 100
Living Strings
 31
Lloyd, Michael
 91
London, John
 148, 3, 78, 86
London, England
 40, 51, 98, 99, 106,
 111, 121
Lord High 'n' Low
 159
Lorelei
 153
Loren, Donna
 146
Los Angeles, CA
 16, 116, 126
Louisiana Tech
 127
Louisville, KY
 121
"Love American Style" (TV show)
 84, 92
"Love Letters To Laugh-In" (TV show)
 82
Lovin' Spoonful
 3
Lucy
 151
Lukas, Karl
 137
Lulu
 40
"Luna" (TV show)
 107
Lupe
 145
Lyons, Robert
 140
MTV
 112, 113, 114, 115,
McCartney, Paul
 29, 106
Macaulay, Charles
 159
McDonald's
 94
McGee, Gerry

292

INDEX TO PEOPLE, PLACES & THINGS

McGiveney
12
McGiveney, Owen
137
McGowan, Oliver
132, 141
McKinney, Bill
156
MacLane, Barton
151
MacLane, Kerry
134
MacMurray, Fred
90
McQuinney
132
Madame Roselle
132
Madison, WI
123, 126
Maiden #1
146
Maiden #2
146
Maiden #3
146
Main, Laurie
155
"Make Room For Granddaddy" (TV show)
84
Malet, Arthur
147
The Mamas & The Papas
32, 36
Manager
151, 153
The Manhattan Strings
31
Mann, Dr.
134
Mann Music Center
126
Manny
143
Man with Paper
143
Maple Leaf Gardens
34, 121
March, Hal
138
March, Judy
143
Marco
138
Marcovich, Dr.
139
Marcuse, Theo
131
Margolin, Stuart
153
Maria
138
Marie, Rose
134, 143
Marketplace Arena
126
Marmer, Lea
132, 143

Marriott's Great America
126
Marshall
151
Martel, Arlene
133, 153
Martin, Deana
156
Martin, D'Urville
140
Masak, Ron
153
Masseur
139
Matthews, Ian
92
Mature, Victor
159
Max
141
Maxine
156
"Maxwell Smart, Private Eye" (episode)
65
Maxwell, Stacey
132
Mayberry
150
Mayberry, Russell
144
Mayor
147
Mazursky, Paul
4, 136
"Meet The Kids" (TV show)
58
Melbourne, Australia
98, 123
Mell, Joseph
137
Melvin
152
Memorabilia: badges
266
Memorabilia: bandana
261
Memorabilia: binders
270
Memorabilia: booklet
272
Memorabilia: books
262, 263, 266, 272,
Memorabilia: bracelets
261
Memorabilia: bubblegum displays
266
Memorabilia: buttons
258, 275
Memorabilia: calendar
273
Memorabilia: cards
267
Memorabilia: cereal box records
257
Memorabilia: children's books
263
Memorabilia: clothes hangers

Memorabilia
257
Memorabilia: coins
267
Memorabilia: comic books
258
Memorabilia: costumes
261
Memorabilia: cup
273
Memorabilia: dolls
274
Memorabilia: earrings
261
Memorabilia: 8-track tapes
260
Memorabilia: fan club application
259
Memorabilia: fan club button
259
Memorabilia: fan club kit
259
Memorabilia: fingerdolls
274
Memorabilia: flexidisc
273
Memorabilia: flip movies
266
Memorabilia: game
258
Memorabilia: guitar
260
Memorabilia: gum cards
264, 265, 267
Memorabilia: Halloween costumes
261
Memorabilia: hand puppet
271
Memorabilia: hats
275
Memorabilia: jewelry
261
Memorabilia: jigsaw puzzle
271
Memorabilia: looseleaf binder
270
Memorabilia: lunchbox
258
Memorabilia: models
274
Memorabilia: Monkeemobile models
274
Memorabilia: "Monkees Annual"
272
Memorabilia: "Monkees Monthly" issues
263
Memorabilia: "Monkee Spectacular" issues
262
Memorabilia: paint-by-number set
271
Memorabilia: pendants
261
Memorabilia: playing cards
270
Memorabilia: postcard
259
Memorabilia: poster

INDEX TO PEOPLE, PLACES & THINGS

Memorabilia

Memorabilia
 273
Memorabilia: poster calendar
 273
Memorabilia: press release kit
 259
Memorabilia: programs
 275
Memorabilia: punch-out model book
 271
Memorabilia: puppet
 271
Memorabilia: puzzles
 264, 265, 271
Memorabilia: record tote
 270
Memorabilia: reel-to-reel tapes
 260
Memorabilia: rings
 261
Memorabilia: sheet music
 268
Memorabilia: songbooks
 268
Memorabilia: stickers
 271
Memorabilia: sweatshirts
 261, 275
Memorabilia: tambourine
 260
Memorabilia: thermos
 258
Memorabilia: tour book
 263
Memorabilia: tour books
 275
Memorabilia: t-shirts
 275
Memorabilia: vest
 273
Memorabilia: Viewmaster
 257
Memorabilia: wallet
 270
Memorabilia: wall poster
 273
Memorial Auditorium
 121
Memorial Coliseum
 123, 126
Memphis, TN
 121, 125
Mendoza, Dr.
 139
Mendrek the Magician
 153
Mermaid Theatre
 98
Messenger
 134
"Metal Micky" (TV show)
 101
Meyerson, Peter
 131, 134, 141, 143, 148, 152, 156
MGM Records
 88, 90, 93
Miami Beach Convention Hall
 121

Miami Beach, FL
 121
Miami, FL
 125
"Michael Nesmith In Elephant Parts" (video)
 104, 105, 108
"Michael Nesmith In Television Parts" (TV special)
 108, 110
"Michael Nesmith In Television Parts Home Companion" (video)
 110
Michaels, Robert (Bob)
 146, 156
Mickey Mouse 50th Birthday Party
 99
Midget
 133, 141
Mid-South Coliseum
 121
"Mijacogeo (The Frodis Caper)" (episode)
 54, 156
"The Mike Douglas Show" (TV show)
 95
Miles, Buddy
 78
Millan, Robyn
 136
Miller, Sidney
 139
Milly
 143
Milwaukee, WI
 47, 123, 126
Minneapolis, MN
 47
Minnie
 159
The Missing Links
 9
Mitchell, Lisa
 146
Mobile, AL
 121, 127
Mobile Municipal Auditorium
 127
Modell, Agent
 142
Moeblis, Herb
 28
"Monkee Business Fanzine" (magazine)
 70
"Monkee Chow Mein" (episode)
 45, 142
"Monkee Mayor" (episode)
 147
Monkeemobile
 17, 107
"Monkee Mother" (episode)
 143
"Monkees A La Carte" (episode)
 137
"Monkees A La Mode" (episode)
 142
"Monkees At The Circus" (episode)
 141

Murdock

"Monkees At The Movies" (episode)
 144
"Monkees Blow Their Minds" (episode)
 156
"Monkee See, Monkee Die" (episode)
 45, 132
"Monkees Get Out More Dirt" (episode)
 143
"Monkees In A Ghost Town" (episode)
 134
"Monkees In Manhattan" (episode)
 144
"Monkees In Paris" (episode)
 40, 154
"Monkees In Texas" (episode)
 151
"Monkees In The Ring" (episode)
 140
"Monkees Marooned" (episode)
 58, 148
"Monkees Mind Their Manor" (episode)
 56, 155
"Monkees On The Line" (episode)
 143
"Monkees On The Wheel" (episode)
 151
"Monkees On Tour" (episode)
 116, 145
"Monkee Spectacular" (magazine)
 33, 53, 68
"Monkees Race Again" (episode)
 154
Monkees Soft Drink Night Clubs
 33
"Monkees Watch Their Feet" (episode)
 153
"Monkee Vs. Machine" (episode)
 45, 132
"The Monkey's Paw" (episode)
 153
Monster
 139
"Monstrous Monkee Mash" (episode)
 153
Monterey, CA
 40, 44
Moon, Keith
 40
The Moon Express
 157
"The Morning Show" (TV show)
 108
Morrison, Hollis
 134
Morton, Mickey
 150
Moss, Arnold
 146
Most, Mickie
 12
Mud Island Amphitheatre
 125
Mulligan's Hollow
 126
Municipal Auditorium
 121, 123
Murdock, Judy

INDEX TO PEOPLE, PLACES & THINGS

Murphy
   135
Murphy, Jimmy
   142
"Music Bag" (TV show)
   82
"Music Scene" (TV show)
   82
Musicvision
   116
Mustin, Burt
   148, 152
"My Three Sons" (TV show)
   90
NBC-TV
   11, 17, 30, 50, 62,
   68, 76, 82, 9, 91,
   92, 97, 100, 105,
   106, 108, 110
Nan
   149
Narrator/Town Cryer
   152
Nashville, TN
   121, 125
Natasha
   149
National Association Of Record
   Merchants
   32
National Cable Television Association
   105
Nebraska Land Days
   125
Nesmith, Kathryn
   93
Nesmith, Phyliss
   36
Newman, Randy
   90
Newmar, Julie
   143
The New Monks
   103, 104, 105
New Orleans, LA
   125, 127
Newport Music Hall
   125
"The New Scooby Doo Movies" (TV show)
   92
"Newsweek" (magazine)
   18
The New Vaudeville Band
   32
New York City, NY
   17, 44, 73, 98, 112
"New York Daily News" (newspaper)
   61
New York, NY
   121, 126
"New York Post" (newspaper)
   62, 68
"New York Times" (newspaper)
   73
New Zealand
   70
Nicholson, Jack
   62, 73, 159

Nicolai
   149
"Night Of The Strangler" (film)
   92
Niles, Fred
   44
Nilsson, Harry
   98
Nitschke, Ray
   159
Noone, Peter
   105
Norfolk, VA
   127
North, Heather
   141
North Carolina State Fair
   123
North Platte, NE
   125
"Northville Cemetary Massacre" (film)
   92
Norton, Cliff
   146
Norwich, England
   110
Nunis, Richard
   139
Nurse
   139
Nyetovich
   149
Oakdale Music Theater
   126
Oakland, CA
   125
Oakland Coliseum
   125
Ober, Philip
   144
Oblio
   98
O'Brien, Richard
   143
O'Connell Center
   127
Official
   154
Official Monkees Convention
   115
"Ohayo Studios" (TV show)
   104, 105
Ojai, CA
   62
Oklahoma City, OK
   123, 126
Oklahoma State Fair
   126
Old Man
   137, 155
Old Woman
   134
Olinsky, Madame
   133
"Oliver!" (stage show)
   4, 30, 76
Olympia Stadium
   121

Omaha Civic Auditorium
   125
Omaha, NE
   125
The Omni
   127
Omnibus Records
   6
"One Man Shy (Peter And The Debutante)" (episode)
   45, 137
Ontario Place
   125
Oraculo
   156
Orenstein, Bernie
   134, 137, 138
Osaka, Japan
   123
Ottawa, Canada
   125
Ottawa Congress Center
   125
Otto
   131, 156
"Owen Marshall, Counselor At Law" (TV show)
   92
Pacific Amphitheatre
   126
The Pacific Arts Corporation
   93, 105
Pacific Arts Records
   97, 99, 106
Pacific Arts Video Corporation
   105
Pacific Hills School
   95
Paddy
   137
Palais Theatre
   98
Panich, David
   132, 141, 153
"Parade" (magazine)
   24
Paris, France
   40, 51
Parking Attendant
   145
Parsons, Milton
   132
Parsons, Ned
   159
Pasadena, CA
   83
Patrick, Butch
   152
Patriot Center
   127
Patrolman
   142
Patterson, Melody
   148
Paul Revere & The Raiders
   3, 76, 105
Paulsen, Pat
   153

INDEX TO PEOPLE, PLACES & THINGS

"Pea Picker In Picadilly" (TV show)
82
Pearl, David
44, 148, 153
Penny, Don
133
"People Now" (TV show)
106
Peoria Civic Center
126, 127
Peoria, IL
126, 127
Perina, George
132
Perry, Joseph
140
Peters, Kelly Jean
138
Petersen, Paul
3
Peter Tork & Release
74
The Peter Tork Project
106, 107, 108
The Pheasant Run Theatre
83
Philadelphia, PA
115, 121, 126
Philbin, Regis
108
Phillippe, Andre
17, 132
Philo
144
Phoenix, AZ
28, 100, 121, 126
Pickwick Records
109
"The Picture Frame (The Bank Robbery)" (episode)
146
Pier 84
126
Pierre
156
Pier Six Pavillion
126
Pine Knob Music Theatre
126
Pintoff
141
Pintoff, Junior
141
Pitlik, Norm
146, 150
Pittsburgh Civic Center
125, 127
Pittsburgh, PA
121, 125, 127
"Playbill" (magazine)
4
"Pleasant Valley Sunday" (Feb. 23, 1986)
112
Poco
97
"The Point" (musical)
98, 99

Policeman
132, 137, 139, 142, 146, 148, 151, 156,
Pollock, David
154
Pontiac, MI
127
Pop
137, 141
Poplar Creek Music Theatre
126
Portland, ME
127
Portland, OR
123, 126
Postman
137
Powell Hall
126
Pozen, Michael
159
Preacher
148
Presley, Elvis
23, 96
Press Photographer #1
148
Press Photographer #2
148
Price, David
44, 88, 141, 154
"The Prince And The Paupers" (episode)
141
Princess Bettina
131
"The Prison" (multimedia project)
93, 96
Private One
159
Producer
137
Providence Civic Center
128
Providence, RI
128
Pshaw, Major
148
Psychiatrist
153
Public Auditorium
121
Publisher
147
Pueblo, CO
123
Purdy, Mrs.
134
"Puss In Boots" (pantomime)
101
"Puzzle Trail" (TV show)
109
Quagmeyer, Madame
142
Queen Elizabeth II (ocean liner)
108, 109
Question Mark & The Mysterians
34

Quick, Eldon
142
Quinn, Louis
132
RCA Records
11, 16, 23, 27, 47, 51, 65, 66, 75, 78, 84, 90, 91, 92, 96, 99, 116
RCA Studios
18, 34
R.I.A.A.
18, 23, 27, 32, 36
RKO Studios
17
Rafelson, Robert (Bob)
3, 5, 9, 12, 28, 58, 62, 75, 107, 113, 132, 133, 134, 139, 145, 154, 159
Rafferty, Chips
150
Raleigh, NC
123
Ralph
132
Ramos, Richard S.
140
Ramsey, Logan
159
Randall, Anne
146
Randall, Leslie
150
Randell, Lynn
44
Rantha, Madame
138
Rawls, Lou
40
Real Prop Man
155
Red
137, 151
Red Rocks Amphitheatre
126
Reed, Rex
73
Release
74
"Remains To Be Seen" (stage play)
83
Renaldo
138
Rensselaer Polytechnic Institute Fieldhouse
127
Reporter
144
Reporter #1
140
Reporter #2
140
Revere, Paul
76
Rhino Records
105, 108, 110, 113, 114

INDEX TO PEOPLE, PLACES & THINGS

Rhodes, Red
 85, 86, 91, 92
Richard
 152
Richards, Keith
 40
Richfield Stadium
 127
Richie, Lionel
 107
Richmond Coliseum
 127
Richmond, VA
 127
Ring Announcer
 140
Riverbend
 126
Riverfront Amphitheatre
 125
Roanoke Civic Center
 128
Roanoke, VA
 128
Robarts Arena
 125
Robertson, Brian
 99
Roberts Stadium
 127
Rob Roy's Assistant
 142
Rocco
 137, 138
Roccuzzo, Mario
 138
Rochester, NY
 121, 128
Rochester War Memorial
 121, 128
Rocket, Charlie
 44, 154
"The Rolf Harris Show" (TV show)
 30
"Rolling Stone" (magazine)
 85
The Rolling Stones
 29, 40, 58
Rolls Owner
 134
Roman, Murray
 152
Romar Records
 93
Ronnie
 137
Ronstadt, Linda
 78
Rooney, Mickey
 3
Rooney, Tim
 3
Rosemont Horizon
 127
Rosemont, IL
 127
Ross, Stanley Ralph
 148, 149

Roth, Phil
 141
"Royal Flush" (episode)
 38, 45, 131
Royal Garden Hotel
 40
Ruby
 142
Rudelson, Rob
 156
Rudi
 156
Rudy
 136
Russell, Bing
 136
Russell, Mr.
 136
Russell, Mrs.
 136
Ruston, LA
 127
Ruth Eckerd Hall
 125
Rutherford, Gene
 141
Sacramento, CA
 98
St. John, Richard
 136
St. John's Wood, London, England
 29
St. Louis, MO
 47, 94, 121, 126, 127
St. Paul, MN
 121
Salesgirl
 152
Salesman
 152
Salt Lake City, UT
 65, 123, 126
Sam And The Goodtimers
 76
Sam Houston Coliseum
 121
Samuel Clemens Center
 125
San Antonio, TX
 125
Sandstone
 125
Sanford, Lee
 149
San Francisco, CA
 73, 96, 121
Santa Clara, CA
 126
Santa Monica, CA
 95
Santa Teresa Country Club
 125
Santa Teresa, NM
 125
Sarasota, FL
 125
Saratoga Performing Arts Center
 126
Saratoga Springs, NY
 126
"Saturday Evening Post" (magazine)
 10, 28
Sawyer, Tom
 98
Scardino, Don
 3
Schiller, Norbert
 139
Schlitt, Robert
 131, 134, 141, 143
Schlossberg, Marilyn
 159
Schmidt, Georgia
 148
Schneider, Bert
 3, 5, 9, 12, 28, 33, 58, 74, 75, 159
Schneider, Harold
 159
Schneider, Mr.
 9, 24
Schnitzler
 139
Scoop 33 Records
 109
Scope Convention Center
 127
Scott, Janelle Dolenz
 6, 14
Scotti, Vito
 139, 159
Scrawny Young Man
 147
Screen Gems
 3, 4, 5, 9, 11, 16, 17, 33, 36, 47, 58, 74, 78, 81
Seattle Center Coliseum
 123
Seattle, WA
 123
Secaucus, NJ
 127
"Secombe & Friends" (TV show)
 38
The Second National Band
 90
Secretary
 132, 141, 147, 153,
Sedaka, Neil
 86
The Seekers
 100
Sergeant
 146
Shah-Ku
 147
Shalet, Diane
 152
Shane, Gene Otis
 149
Shaw, Reta
 138
Shazar
 146

INDEX TO PEOPLE, PLACES & THINGS

Sheldon
148
Shelton, Louis
12
Sheppard, Gerald (Jerry)
143, 151
Sherman, Bobby
144
Sherman, Don
142, 148
Shimatsu, Kay
142
Sholto
140
Shreveport, LA
121
Shrink, Inspector
159
Sigmund
131
Silicone, Sally
159
Sill, Lester
21, 30, 66, 74
Silla, Felix
141
Silverdome
127
Silverman, Treva
132, 137, 138, 145
Simon, Neil
86
Sinatra, Frank
96
Singer, Alex
142, 146, 147, 153
Sioux Empire Fair
126
Sioux Falls, SD
126
Sisters, Dr.
143
Six Flags Over Mid-America
94
Skywriter
147
Smalls, Charlie
156
Smasher
140
Smith, Mr.
143
Smith, Mrs.
143
Smith, Queenie
147
Smoothie
138
Sneak
151
Snyder, Tom
98
Society Of West End Theatres
107
Sofaer, Abraham
159
"Some Like It Lukewarm (The Band Contest)" (episode)
58, 156
"Son Of Gypsy" (episode)
138
Sorenson, Paul
137
Soret, Jeanne
152
Soule, Olan
144
"The Sounds Of The Monkees" (concerts)
112
South Bend, IN
127
Southend-On-Sea, Essex
107
Southern Star Amphitheater
125
South Shore Music Circus
125
Spokane, WA
123
Sports Coliseum
121
"The Spy Who Came In From The Cool" (episode)
45, 133
Stabler Arena
128
The Stadium
121
Stage Manager
141
Stanley Theatre
125
Starship
91
"The Star Spangled Girl" (film)
86
Starwood Amphitheatre
125
State Fair Arena
123
State Fair Coliseum
121
State Theater
125
Steamboat Days
125
"The Steel Pier Show" (TV show)
86
Stevenson, Jerry
149
Stewart, Reine
73
Stills, Stephen
3
Stratton, George
142
Strauss, Robert
142
Strong Man
141
"Success Story" (episode)
45, 134
Sullivan Stadium
127
The Sundowners
44
Sunken Gardens
125
Superdome
127
Surrey, England
108
Susan
141
Swami
159
Swansea, Wales
101
Swezey, Mr.
147
Swine #1
132
Sword Swallower
141
Sydney, Australia
71, 123
Sydney Stadium
123
Sylvester, Ward
4, 34, 58, 75
Syracuse, NY
127
"TV Guide" (magazine)
28, 50
T.V. Interviewer
136
TV Viewer
156
Talbot, Nita
153
Tampa, FL
123
Tartikoff, Brandon
108
Tax Man
153
Tayback, Vic
132, 138, 147
Taylor, Dub
148
Taylor, June Whitley
136
Taylor, Larry
12
Taylor, Rip
151, 156
"Teen" (magazine)
21
"Television Parts" (TV special)
108, 110
"The Tennessee Ernie Ford Show" (TV show)
82
Thailand
95
"That Was Then, This Is Now" (video)
115
Theatre Royal
110
"These Are The Days" (TV show)
93
"33 1/3 Revolutions Per Monkee" (TV special)

INDEX TO PEOPLE, PLACES & THINGS

This
74, 75, 78, 79, 80, 157
"This Is Tom Jones" (TV show)
76
Thomas, Danny
84
Thorkelson, Peter H.
155
Thorne, Ken
159
Three Dog Night
3
Thursday
148
"Tiger Beat" (magazine)
33, 34, 76, 80
"'Til Death Do Us Part" (TV show)
42
"Time" (magazine)
22
"Timerider" (film)
106, 108
Timid Man
138
Toast
100
"Today" (TV show)
105, 108, 110
Tokyo, Japan
71, 101, 123
Tokyo Music Festival
105
Toldeo, OH
127
"The Tomorrow Show" (TV show)
98
"Tom Sawyer" (musical)
98
"The Tonight Show" (TV show)
79
Tony
142
"Too Many Girls (Davy And Fern)" (episode)
138
"The Top Of The Pops" (TV show)
24, 29, 40, 44, 61, 65, 66
Toronto, Canada
34, 121, 125
Toto
142
Townsend, Pete
40
The Trinity
157
Tropicana Hotel
125
Troy, NY
127
True, Testy
159
Trump
132
Trump Plaza
127
Tucker, Larry
4, 136

Tulsa, OK
121, 123
Turner, Dr.
136
Turner, Ike
76
Turner, Tina
76
The Turtles
5
Twiggly
155
U.S. Navy Public Service Radio
91
"The Uncle Floyd Show" (TV show)
101, 104, 105, 108
United Artists
17
Univ. of Dayton Arena
127
"Untitled" (film)
62, 64
Upton, Corey
149
Utica, NY
125, 128
Utica War Memorial
128
Valerie
137
Valley Auditorium
65, 123
Valley Forge Music Fair
126
Vancouver, Canada
123
Vandenburg, General
135
Vandersnoot, Mrs.
152
Vanessa
136
Van Ness, Jill
136
"Variety" (newspaper)
23, 24, 30, 33, 54, 58
Vaughn, Ondine
149
Venice, CA
95
Vernon
140
Veterans Memorial Auditorium
121
Veteran's Stadium
126
Vice President
146
Victor
141
Vidaru
146
Vienna, VA
125, 126
Vince
142
Vitteloni, I.

159
Vogue Theater
73
WTBS-TV
105, 106
Wagner, Mike
142
Waiter
144
Wakefield, Kathy
147
Wallingford, CT
126
Walsh, Ed
142
Walsh, Katherine
131
Walters, Nancy
142
Wantagh, NY
125, 126
Ward, Clara
78
Ware, John
78, 86
War Memorial Arena
126
Warner Brothers Records
99
Warner Theatre
125
Warwick Musical Theatre
125
Warwick, RI
125
Washington, DC
73
Watchman
137
Waterloo, NE
126
Waynesmith, Gary
147
Weatherspoon, Mrs.
150
Weatherwax
144
Weaver, Doodles
144
Weifers, Mrs.
135
Wembley, London, England
40
Wembley Pool
121
Wendy
141
Weskitt, Judd
148
Weskitt, Maw
148
Westbury Music Fair
127
Westbury, NY
127
Westcliffe Pavilion
107
West Palm Beach, FL

INDEX TO PEOPLE, PLACES & THINGS

West
 123
West Springfield, MA
 123
We Three
 157
"Whatever Became Of...?" (TV special)
 104
Whitney, Peter
 145
Wichita, KS
 121, 123, 125
The Wichita Train Whistle
 54, 66
"The Wild Monkees" (episode)
 149
Wilkes-Barre, PA
 125
Williams, Carole
 142
Williams, Christine
 149
Williams, Jack H.
 155
Williams, Paul
 3, 106
Willis, Toby
 142
Wing Stadium
 127
Winnipeg, Canada
 121
Winston, Helene
 137, 143
Winston-Salem Colisuem
 121
Winston-Salem, NC
 121
Winter, Jack
 146, 147, 150, 151,
Winters, David
 150, 156
Wisconsin State Fair
 126
Wolfe, Digby
 143
Wolfgang
 154
Wolfman
 153
Wolftrap Park
 125, 126
Woman
 138
The Woodlands
 125
Woolf, Venita
 147
Worcester, MA
 127
Worthington, Carol
 149
Wright, Ben
 134
Wyncote Records
 31
Wynmore, Patrice
 142
Yakimoto
 133
Yardley
 9
Yarnell, David
 17
Yester, Jerry
 3
Young, Lee
 33
The Young Rascals
 36
"Your Friendly Neighborhood Kidnappers" (episode)
 45, 132
Zappa, Frank
 156, 159
Zeckenbush
 147
Zelda
 151
Zeppo
 138
Zilch (boutique)
 51
Zukerman, Mrs.
 132

Record Number Index

084				**COS 115**
084	188	1109	14524	66-1031
250	195	197	248	185
0164	263	1300	17152	66-5000
249	246	252	244	185
0188	329	1517	17161	66-5004
195	194	253	251	185
0368	348	2001	25861	66-5005
245	250	254	244	185
0399	368	2007	59353	66-5011
245	245	196, 252	244	185
0453	399	2010	59372	74-0368
246	245	253	244	245
0540	453	2297	91018	74-0399
246	246	251	253	245
0629	493	2826	2-1109	74-0453
247	243	250	197	246
0804	540	4089	7-106	74-0540
248	246	196	250	246
1-AA	587	4180	7-107	74-0629
254	254	249	250	247
84	629	4271	7-113	74-0804
250	247	249	251	248
101	700	4371	7-118	AA
191, 249, 251	250	245	251	254
102	701	4415	7-130	ABM 2007
191	196	245	251	196
103	710	4497	7-1300	AL 4089
191	248	246	252	196
104	715	4563	9-8432	AL9-8432
192	249	247	198	198
105	764	4695	45-101	ALPI 0164
253	243	248	251	249
106	784	5000	45-106	ARPDL2-1109
250, 252	243	185	252	197
107	787	5004	45-108	Bugsy 1-AA
250	243	185	252	254
108	789	5005	45-111	CDS-700
252	243	185	245	250
109	792	5008	45-136	CHS 2297
192	244	192	246	251
111	804	5011	45-159	COM 101
245	248	185	247	191
113	986	6067	45-178	COM 102
193, 197, 251	245	246	247	191
115	1001	6081	45-263	COM 103
193	184, 194, 243, 252	195	246	191
117	1002	8009	45-17152	COM 104
193	184	195	244	192
118	1003	8112B	47-9853	COM 109
251	252	253	244	192
119	1004	8432	66-1001	COS 101
194	184	198	184	191
130	1007	9853	66-1002	COS 102
251	184	244	184	191
132	1012	10025	66-1004	COS 103
248	184	253	184	191
136	1019	11513	66-1007	COS 104
246	184	249	184	192
159	1023	14309	66-1012	COS 109
247	185	247	184	192
164	1031	14395	66-1019	COS 113
249	185	247	184	193
178	1048	14458	66-1023	COS 115
247	198	248	185	193

RECORD NUMBER INDEX

COS 117	ECS-91018	K-14395	MW 1001	PRS 329
193	253	247	252	194
COS 119	IP084	K-14458	NA587	RNLP 113
194	250	248	254	197
COSO 5008	J-8112B	K-14524	PAC-101	RNLP 701
192	253	248	249	196
CP 493	JAL-1003	LH-8009	PAC7-106	RO-710
243	252	195	250	248
CP 764	JAS-2007	LSP-4371	PAC7-107	RO-715
243	252	245	250	249
CP-784	JAS-2010	LSP-4415	PAC7-113	SCOS-1001
243	253	245	251	194
CP-787	JJ 2001	LSP-4497	PAC7-118	SE 105
243	254	246	251	253
CP-789	K-1517	LSP-4563	PAC7-130	SE 1048
243	253	247	251	198
CP-792	K-10025	LSP-4695	PAC7-1300	SPS-45-263
244	253	248	252	246
DLP 25861	K-14309	MCA 348	PAC45-106	ST-11513
244	247	250	252	249
DLP2-0188		MCF 2826	PAC45-108	
195		250	252	

Date Index

September 1965

September 1965
243
September 9, 1965
3
September 10, 1965
3
October 1965
243
October 9, 1965
5
November 13, 1965
6
December 25, 1965
6
January 1966
244
January 17, 1966
9
February 1966
9
March 1966
10
April 1966
11
May 1966
12
May 31, 1966
12
June 1966
14
June 10, 1966
14, 177
June 25, 1966
14, 177
July 1966
15
July 5, 1966
177
July 7, 1966
177
July 9, 1966
177
July 18, 1966
177
July 19, 1966
177
July 23, 1966
177
July 25, 1966
177
July 26, 1966
177
August 1966
16, 53, 184
August 6, 1966
178
August 15, 1966
178
August 16, 1966
16
August 23, 1966
178
August 28, 1966
16

September 1, 1966
17
September 3, 1966
17
September 10, 1966
178
September 11, 1966
17
September 12, 1966
17, 131, 161
September 19, 1966
132, 161
September 26, 1966
132, 161
October 1966
191
October 3, 1966
132, 161
October 10, 1966
18, 133, 161
October 13, 1966
178
October 14, 1966
18
October 15, 1966
178
October 17, 1966
134, 161
October 23, 1966
178
October 24, 1966
18, 134, 162
October 25, 1966
178
October 26, 1966
178
October 28, 1966
178
October 29, 1966
178
October 31, 1966
134, 162
November 1966
22, 184
November 7, 1966
135, 162
November 11, 1966
22
November 12, 1966
22
November 14, 1966
136, 162
November 17, 1966
178
November 21, 1966
137, 162
November 23, 1966
178
November 28, 1966
137, 162
December 3, 1966
23, 121
December 5, 1966
137, 162

December 9, 1966
23, 24
December 10, 1966
23
December 12, 1966
138, 162
December 19, 1966
138, 163
December 24, 1966
23
December 25, 1966
24
December 26, 1966
121, 138, 163
December 27, 1966
121
December 28, 1966
121
December 29, 1966
121
December 30, 1966
121
December 31, 1966
121
January 1967
178, 191
January 1, 1967
27, 121, 139
January 2, 1967
121, 163
January 7, 1967
27
January 9, 1967
163
January 10, 1967
27
January 14, 1967
121
January 15, 1967
121
January 16, 1967
139, 163, 178
January 21, 1967
121, 178
January 22, 1967
121, 178
January 23, 1967
139, 163
January 26, 1967
178, 179
January 27, 1967
179
January 28, 1967
10, 28
January 30, 1967
140, 163
February 1967
29, 179, 244
February 6, 1967
141, 163
February 7, 1967
29
February 9, 1967
29

February 11, 1967
29
February 12, 1967
30
February 13, 1967
141, 163
February 18, 1967
30
February 20, 1967
141, 164
February 23, 1967
30, 179
February 24, 1967
30, 179
February 27, 1967
142, 164
February 28, 1967
30
March 1967
179, 184
March 2, 1967
32, 179
March 3, 1967
179
March 4, 1967
179
March 6, 1967
142, 164
March 7, 1967
179
March 8, 1967
32
March 13, 1967
32, 142, 164
March 15, 1967
33
March 16, 1967
179
March 17, 1967
179
March 18, 1967
179
March 20, 1967
33, 143, 164
March 21, 1967
33
March 22, 1967
179
March 23, 1967
179
March 25, 1967
33
March 27, 1967
143, 164
April 1967
34
April 1, 1967
34, 121
April 2, 1967
34, 121
April 3, 1967
143, 164
April 8, 1967
36

June 26, 1967

April 10, 1967
144, 164
April 17, 1967
144, 164
April 24, 1967
145
April 26, 1967
179
April 29, 1967
36
May 1967
191
May 1, 1967
45, 165
May 5, 1967
179
May 6, 1967
121
May 8, 1967
36, 45, 165
May 15, 1967
45, 165
May 20, 1967
36
May 22, 1967
45, 165
May 23, 1967
38
May 27, 1967
38
May 28, 1967
38
May 29, 1967
45, 165, 179
June 1967
179
June 4, 1967
38
June 5, 1967
165
June 9, 1967
38, 121
June 10, 1967
179
June 12, 1967
165
June 14, 1967
179
June 16, 1967
40
June 18, 1967
40
June 19, 1967
45, 166, 179
June 20, 1967
179
June 21, 1967
179
June 22, 1967
179
June 24, 1967
40
June 26, 1967
45, 166

DATE INDEX

June 28, 1967
40
June 29, 1967
40
June 30, 1967
40, 121
June 31, 1967
40
July 1967
184
July 1, 1967
42, 121
July 2, 1967
121
July 3, 1967
166
July 7, 1967
44
July 8, 1967
121
July 9, 1967
121
July 10, 1967
44, 45, 166
July 11, 1967
121
July 12, 1967
121
July 14, 1967
44, 121
July 15, 1967
121
July 16, 1967
44, 121
July 17, 1967
45, 166
July 20, 1967
121
July 21, 1967
121, 179
July 22, 1967
121
July 23, 1967
121
July 24, 1967
166
July 27, 1967
121
July 28, 1967
121
July 29, 1967
44
July 30, 1967
121
July 31, 1967
45, 166
August 1967
34
August 2, 1967
47
August 4, 1967
47, 121
August 5, 1967
121
August 6, 1967
121
August 7, 1967
45, 166

August 9, 1967
121
August 10, 1967
121
August 11, 1967
121
August 12, 1967
47, 121
August 13, 1967
44, 121
August 14, 1967
45, 167
August 17, 1967
121
August 18, 1967
123
August 19, 1967
123
August 20, 1967
123
August 21, 1967
45, 167, 180
August 25, 1967
47, 123
August 26, 1967
123
August 27, 1967
47, 123
August 28, 1967
167
September 1967
48
September 4, 1967
167
September 6, 1967
180
September 11, 1967
50, 145, 167
September 18, 1967
146, 167
September 25, 1967
146, 167
October 1967
51
October 2, 1967
147, 167
October 9, 1967
147, 167
October 16, 1967
147, 168
October 17, 1967
180
October 20, 1967
51
October 23, 1967
148, 168
October 25, 1967
52
October 30, 1967
148, 168
November 1967
180, 184, 192
November 4, 1967
180
November 6, 1967
149, 168
November 11, 1967
53

November 13, 1967
149, 168
November 14, 1967
53
November 18, 1967
54
November 19, 1967
54
November 20, 1967
150, 168
November 27, 1967
54, 150, 168
November 30, 1967
54
December 3, 1967
180
December 4, 1967
56, 151, 168
December 11, 1967
151, 168
December 12, 1967
56
December 17, 1967
180
December 18, 1967
169
December 22, 1967
58
December 25, 1967
58, 152, 169
December 26, 1967
180
December 29, 1967
58
December 30, 1967
58, 180
December 31, 1967
180
January 1968
61, 180
January 1, 1968
169
January 4, 1968
61
January 6, 1968
180
January 7, 1968
180
January 8, 1968
152, 169
January 9, 1968
180
January 10, 1968
180
January 11, 1968
180
January 14, 1968
180
January 15, 1968
153, 169, 180
January 19, 1968
180
January 20, 1968
180
January 22, 1968
153, 169, 180

January 23, 1968
180
January 24, 1968
180
January 25, 1968
180
January 28, 1968
180
January 29, 1968
153, 169
February 1968
181
February 3, 1968
180
February 4, 1968
181
February 5, 1968
154, 169
February 6, 1968
61, 181
February 7, 1968
181
February 8, 1968
181
February 9, 1968
61, 181
February 11, 1968
62
February 12, 1968
154, 169
February 15, 1968
181
February 17, 1968
62, 181
February 19, 1968
154, 170
February 21, 1968
62
February 24, 1968
181
February 26, 1968
155, 170
February 28, 1968
181
February 29, 1968
62
March 2, 1968
64
March 4, 1968
156, 170
March 9, 1968
181
March 11, 1968
156, 170
March 14, 1968
181
March 18, 1968
170
March 25, 1968
156, 170
March 28, 1968
181
April 1968
65, 184, 192
April 1, 1968
170
April 8, 1968
170

April 9, 1968
181
April 15, 1968
170
April 22, 1968
65, 171
April 29, 1968
171
May 1968
181, 185
May 6, 1968
171
May 13, 1968
171
May 19, 1968
65
May 20, 1968
171
May 21, 1968
65, 123
May 23, 1968
65
May 27, 1968
171, 181
May 29, 1968
181
May 31, 1968
181
June 1, 1968
66, 181
June 3, 1968
171, 181
June 6, 1968
66
June 8, 1968
66
June 10, 1968
171
June 12, 1968
68
June 17, 1968
172
June 22, 1968
66
June 24, 1968
172
July 1968
244
July 1, 1968
172
July 8, 1968
172
July 12, 1968
62, 68
July 15, 1968
172
July 22, 1968
172
July 29, 1968
172
August 1968
182
August 1, 1968
181
August 3, 1968
68, 182
August 5, 1968
172

DATE INDEX

August 12, 1968
172
August 19, 1968
68, 173
August 26, 1968
173
September 1968
70
September 18, 1968
123
September 19, 1968
123
September 21, 1968
123
September 23, 1968
123
September 27, 1968
123
September 28, 1968
123
September 29, 1968
123
October 1968
185
October 3, 1968
123
October 4, 1968
123
October 5, 1968
72, 123
October 7, 1968
123
October 8, 1968
72, 123
October 26, 1968
72
November 6, 1968
73
November 19, 1968
73
December 1968
182, 192
December 2, 1968
74
December 7, 1968
74
December 9, 1968
182
December 23, 1968
182
January 1969
75
January 11, 1969
182
January 14, 1969
182
January 22, 1969
182
February 1969
193
February 5, 1969
75
February 8, 1969
75
February 11, 1969
76
February 15, 1969
76

February 16, 1969
76
March 22, 1969
76
March 29, 1969
76, 123
March 30, 1969
123
April 1969
185
April 11, 1969
123
April 12, 1969
78, 123
April 13, 1969
123
April 14, 1969
78, 157, 173
April 17, 1969
123
April 26, 1969
78, 123
April 28, 1969
78
May 1, 1969
182
May 3, 1969
123
May 4, 1969
123
May 9, 1969
123
May 10, 1969
123
May 12, 1969
182
May 24, 1969
79
May 27, 1969
182
May 28, 1969
182
May 29, 1969
182
May 30, 1969
182
May 31, 1969
182
June 1969
183, 193
June 2, 1969
182
June 5, 1969
182
June 6, 1969
182
June 9, 1969
182
June 10, 1969
182
June 14, 1969
79
June 16, 1969
79
June 17, 1969
182
June 18, 1969
79

June 20, 1969
123
June 21, 1969
79
June 22, 1969
123
June 26, 1969
182
June 27, 1969
182, 183
July 1969
185
July 16, 1969
183
July 18, 1969
123, 183
July 19, 1969
80, 123
July 26, 1969
123
August 1969
80
August 1, 1969
123
August 14, 1969
183
August 28, 1969
123
August 29, 1969
123
August 30, 1969
80
September 1969
185
September 6, 1969
81
September 13, 1969
81
September 17, 1969
81
October 1969
193
October 6, 1969
82
October 11, 1969
82
October 17, 1969
123
November 9, 1969
82
November 24, 1969
82
November 30, 1969
82, 125
December 8, 1969
82
December 22, 1969
82
December 31, 1969
82
1970
83
February 5, 1970
183
March 1970
183
March 1, 1970
73

March 25, 1970
183
March 26, 1970
183
April 1970
185
April 2, 1970
183
May 1970
83, 194
June 1970
83
June 8, 1970
83
July 1970
84, 244, 245
July 27, 1970
83
August 1970
84, 245
November 1970
85, 245
February 1971
86, 194
April 1971
245, 246
May 1971
86, 246
June 1971
245, 246
July 1971
86
September 1971
88
October 1971
88, 246, 247
November 1971
247
1972
90
January 1972
247
February 1972
76, 90, 247
April 1972
90
June 1972
90, 247
July 1972
91
August 1972
91, 248
September 1972
91, 195
September 9, 1972
91
September 13, 1972
91
September 27, 1972
91
October 1972
91, 248
January 1973
248
July 1973
92
September 1973
92

October 1973
92, 249
November 1973
92
1974
93
1975
94
March 1975
249
July 1975
94
July 4, 1975
94
1976
95
April 1976
95
May 1976
95, 249
July 1976
95, 96, 195, 196,
July 4, 1976
95
December 1976
96, 250
February 1977
97, 250
March 1977
250, 97, 250
March 12, 1977
97
May 1977
97
July 1977
98
August 1977
98
August 22, 1977
98
August 28, 1977
98
September 1977
98
November 1977
98
November 3, 1977
98
November 19, 1977
98
November 21, 1977
98
December 1977
98
December 22, 1977
98
January 1978
250
February 1978
99
February 23, 1978
99
May 1978
99, 251
May 12, 1978
99
June 1978
251

DATE INDEX

August 1978
99, 251
November 1978
99
November 6, 1978
99
November 13, 1978
99
March 1979
100, 251
March 30, 1979
100
May 1979
73, 100, 251
May 17, 1979
100
June 1979
252
July 1979
100
July 25, 1979
100
August 1979
100, 252
August 11, 1979
100
September 1979
100
September 1, 1979
100
October 1979
100
October 28, 1979
100
December 1979
100
December 22, 1979
100
1980
101
June 1980
101
June 20, 1980
101
July 1980
101
July 25, 1980
101
September 1980
101
September 6, 1980
101
September 7, 1980
101
September 25, 1980
101
October 1980
101
December 1980
102
December 21, 1980
102
December 22, 1980
102
January 1981
103
January 5, 1981
103

February 1981
103, 252
February 13, 1981
103
April 1981
104
May 1981
104, 252
May 1, 1981
104
June 1981
104, 252, 253
June 17, 1981
104
June 25, 1981
104
August 1981
104, 253
October 1981
104
October 25, 1981
104
November 1981
104
December 1981
104
December 18, 1981
104
December 25, 1981
104
January 1982
105
February 1982
105, 253
February 5, 1982
105
February 24, 1982
105
February 25, 1982
105
March 1982
61, 105, 253
March 27, 1982
105
March 28, 1982
105
April 1982
105
June 1982
105, 253
July 1982
105
October 1982
105, 196
October 9, 1982
105
October 30, 1982
105
November 1982
105, 196
November 15, 1982
105
December 1982
105
December 2, 1982
105
January 1983
106

April 1983
106
May 1983
106, 254
May 25, 1983
106
June 1983
106
July 1983
106
August 1983
107
September 1983
107
October 1983
107
October 22, 1983
107
December 1983
107
December 19, 1983
107
January 1984
108
February 1984
108, 197
April 1984
108
April 4, 1984
108
April 7, 1984
108
April 9, 1984
108
April 28, 1984
108
June 1984
70, 109
June 8, 1984
109
July 1984
109
July 17, 1984
109
September 1984
109
December 1984
109, 254
December 22, 1984
109
January 22, 1985
82
March 1985
110
May 1985
110
May 22, 1985
110
June 1985
110
June 14, 1985
110
June 27, 1985
110
July 1985
110
July 29, 1985
110

November 1985
111
December 1985
111, 197
December 16, 1985
111
1986
112
January 1986
112
February 1986
112
February 23, 1986
112
February 25, 1986
112
March 1986
112
March 19, 1986
112
April 1986
113
May 1986
113
May 3, 1986
113
May 4, 1986
113
May 24, 1986
125
May 25, 1986
113
May 28, 1986
113
May 30, 1986
113, 125
May 31, 1986
125
June 1986
198
June 1, 1986
125
June 3, 1986
125
June 4, 1986
125
June 5, 1986
125
June 6, 1986
125
June 7, 1986
125
June 8, 1986
125
June 10, 1986
125
June 11, 1986
125
June 12, 1986
125
June 13, 1986
125
June 14, 1986
125
June 15, 1986
125
June 17, 1986
125

June 18, 1986
125
June 19, 1986
125
June 20, 1986
125
June 21, 1986
125
June 22, 1986
114, 125
June 24, 1986
125
June 25, 1986
125
June 26, 1986
125
June 27, 1986
114, 125
June 28, 1986
125
June 29, 1986
125
July 1986
114
July 1, 1986
125
July 2, 1986
125
July 3, 1986
125
July 4, 1986
125
July 5, 1986
125
July 6, 1986
125
July 8, 1986
125
July 9, 1986
125
July 10, 1986
125
July 11, 1986
125
July 12, 1986
125
July 13, 1986
114, 125
July 14, 1986
125
July 17, 1986
125
July 18, 1986
125
July 19, 1986
125
July 20, 1986
126
July 21, 1986
126
July 22, 1986
126
July 23, 1986
126
July 25, 1986
115, 126
July 26, 1986
126

DATE INDEX

July 29, 1986 — December 3, 1986

July 29, 1986
126
July 30, 1986
126
July 31, 1986
126
August 1986
115
August 1, 1986
115, 126
August 2, 1986
115, 126
August 3, 1986
115, 126
August 5, 1986
126
August 6, 1986
126
August 7, 1986
126
August 8, 1986
126
August 9, 1986
126
August 10, 1986
126
August 12, 1986
126
August 13, 1986
126
August 15, 1986
115, 126
August 16, 1986
126
August 17, 1986
126
August 19, 1986
126
August 20, 1986
126
August 21, 1986
126
August 27, 1986
126
August 29, 1986
126
August 30, 1986
126
August 31, 1986
126
September 1986
116
September 1, 1986
126
September 4, 1986
126
September 5, 1986
126
September 6, 1986
126
September 7, 1986
116, 126
September 8, 1986
126
September 9, 1986
126
September 10, 1986
126
September 11, 1986
126
September 12, 1986
126
September 13, 1986
126
September 14, 1986
126
September 15, 1986
126
September 17, 1986
126
September 18, 1986
116, 126
September 19, 1986
126
September 20, 1986
126
September 21, 1986
126
September 23, 1986
126
September 24, 1986
126
September 25, 1986
127
September 26, 1986
127
September 27, 1986
127
September 28, 1986
127
September 29, 1986
127
September 30, 1986
127
October 8, 1986
127
October 9, 1986
127
October 10, 1986
127
October 11, 1986
127
October 12, 1986
127
October 14, 1986
127
October 15, 1986
127
October 16, 1986
127
October 17, 1986
127
October 18, 1986
127
October 19, 1986
127
October 22, 1986
127
October 23, 1986
127
October 24, 1986
127
October 25, 1986
127
October 26, 1986
127
October 29, 1986
127
October 30, 1986
127
October 31, 1986
127
November 1, 1986
127
November 2, 1986
127
November 4, 1986
127
November 5, 1986
127
November 6, 1986
127
November 7, 1986
127
November 8, 1986
127
November 10, 1986
127
November 11, 1986
127
November 12, 1986
127
November 14, 1986
127
November 15, 1986
127
November 16, 1986
127
November 17, 1986
127
November 20, 1986
127
November 21, 1986
127
November 22, 1986
128
November 23, 1986
128
November 24, 1986
128
November 25, 1986
128
November 28, 1986
128
November 29, 1986
128
November 30, 1986
128
December 1, 1986
128
December 3, 1986